Adam Jones, aka 'Bomb', won 95 caps for Wales and is the most decorated prop in Welsh rugby history. He is one of a very select group of Welshmen who have won three Grand Slams, and was also selected for two tours with the British & Irish Lions. At club level, Jones has played for Neath, Ospreys and Cardiff Blues. He currently plays for Harlequins.

Adam Jones was assisted in the writing of his book by Ro̶̶̶̶̶̶̶̶̶̶̶ regularly seen presenting the BBC's international rugby cover̶̶̶̶̶̶ ̶̶̶̶̶̶̶̶g BBC Wales' *Scrum V* and *Scrum V Live* programmes.

D0863531

BOMB

ADAM JONES
with **ROSS HARRIES**

headline

Copyright © 2015 Big Red Management

The right of Adam Jones to be identified as the Author of
the Work has been asserted by him in accordance with the
Copyright, Designs and Patents Act 1988.

First published in 2015 by
HEADLINE PUBLISHING GROUP

First published in paperback in 2016 by
HEADLINE PUBLISHING GROUP

7

Apart from any use permitted under UK copyright law, this publication
may only be reproduced, stored, or transmitted, in any form, or by any means,
with prior permission in writing of the publishers or, in the case of
reprographic production, in accordance with the terms of licences issued
by the Copyright Licensing Agency.

Every effort has been made to fulfil requirements with regard to
reproducing copyright material. The author and publisher will be
glad to rectify any omissions at the earliest opportunity.

Cataloguing in Publication Data is available from the British Library

Hardback ISBN 978 1 4722 3105 5
Paperback ISBN 978 1 4722 3107 9

Typeset in Bliss by Avon DataSet Ltd, Bidford-on-Avon, Warwickshire

Printed and bound in Great Britain by Clays Ltd, St Ives plc

MIX
Paper from
responsible sources
FSC® C104740

Headline's policy is to use papers that are natural, renewable and recyclable
products and made from wood grown in well-managed forests and other
controlled sources. The logging and manufacturing processes are expected to
conform to the environmental regulations of the country of origin.

HEADLINE PUBLISHING GROUP
An Hachette UK Company
Carmelite House
50 Victoria Embankment
London EC4Y 0DZ

www.headline.co.uk
www.hachette.co.uk

To Mam, Dad, Nicole and Isla.

ACKNOWLEDGEMENTS

I want to dedicate this book to June and Alwyn, without whom I wouldn't be where I am today. They're the best mam and dad a boy could have asked for. Without their love, support, and encouragement, I'd still be laying paving slabs in Abercrave. They've been my most ardent fans from the very beginning, and have travelled the world to watch me play, and cheer from the stands.

I'd also like to dedicate it to the women in my life – my wonderful wife Nicole and my beautiful daughter Isla. I hope she'll grow up to realise her daddy wasn't too bad at playing rugby. Nicole's mother and father, Malcolm and Janet, have also been wonderfully supportive over the years, as have her brother Jonathan and his wife Kate.

I'd like to thank my grandmother, Meg, for being my training partner all those years ago back in Abercrave, tirelessly returning my balls as I kicked penalty after penalty until the sun dipped beneath Cribarth mountain. Thanks, too, to my brother Nathan and his wife Claire for their support, even if he's as skinny as a rake and a more committed sportsman than me!

To all the coaches who've pushed, encouraged and inspired me, I owe a huge debt of gratitude. To Lyn Jones for having faith in me in the first place, for seeing the potential beneath the admittedly unpromising exterior. To Rowland Phillips for raising my standards and making me laugh while doing it. To Jonathan Humphreys for transforming me as a scrummager. To Sean Holley for always having my back, and encouraging me to work on my pass during my Llanelli College days. To Mike Ruddock for letting me play for more than half an hour! To Warren Gatland (despite him calling time prematurely on my international career) for giving me a kick up the backside when I really needed it. And to Mark Hammett for offering me a shoulder when I was at my lowest ebb.

Thanks, too to Mike Cuddy for offering me my first professional contract, and for being such a supportive presence throughout my playing days.

To Caroline Morgan at the WRU, my 'other' mother for the eleven years I played international rugby.

To my agent, Mark Spoors, and everyone at esportif, for looking after me since my early days in Neath.

And thanks to my ghost writer, Ross Harries, for all his help and hard work with this book.

Rugby is all about brotherhood, and I've made countless lifelong friends in this game that's given me such a rich and rewarding career. To all my teammates at Abercrave, Neath, the Ospreys, Wales, and the Lions, who've made this journey such an incredible ride, I salute you!

CONTENTS

PROLOGUE

THE car windows were steaming up as I sobbed uncontrollably in the driver's seat. The phone was still in my hand. Ten minutes earlier, I'd hung up in a rage. Now, I was consumed with sorrow. The call had been from my old mate Robin McBryde. Its purpose was to drop me from the Wales squad. There was no small talk, no preamble, no acknowledgement of our long history together. Just a curt message explaining that my services were no longer required.

It lasted less than two minutes.

I was so shocked, I could barely muster a word. The only question I managed to ask was who had been picked ahead of me.

'Samson Lee, Rhodri Jones and Aaron Jarvis,' came the reply.

I hung up before McBryde explained his reasoning. I wandered in a daze past the training fields that the Cardiff Blues shared with Cardiff City Football Club, and made my way through the packed car park towards my

Nissan jeep. I clambered inside and pulled the door to.

My wife, Nicole, could sense the pain in my voice when I called. I felt light-headed and nauseous, like someone had punched me hard in the stomach. Once I'd told her the news, I hung up, unable to sustain a meaningful conversation. My brain was still catching up to what had happened.

Once I'd said it out loud, the tears arrived.

It was a beautiful autumn day. There were light traces of white cloud against a clear blue sky, and the sun was shining brightly. The playing fields ahead of me were a bright emerald green. The world outside was at odds with the torment inside.

The easy option would have been to start the engine, pull out of the car park and drive home. But my years of playing rugby had conditioned me never to take the easy option. In ten minutes' time, training was due to begin at my club, the Cardiff Blues. It was my first season with them, after my eleven-year career with the Ospreys had come to a bitter end. I'd been rejected by them, and now I'd been rejected by my country. Just over a year earlier, I'd taken part in a lap of honour at Sydney's Olympic Stadium, having beaten Australia with the Lions.

Then, I was one of the fifteen best players in the British Isles. Now, I wasn't good enough for Wales.

I stared at my reflection in the rear-view mirror. My eyes were bloodshot and my cheeks were red. My long hair and beard obscured the rest of my face. Today, they felt like a mask. I took a few deep breaths to gather myself, opened the door and retrieved my kitbag from the boot.

● ● ●

There was only one topic of conversation in the changing room. My teammates Josh Navidi and Josh Turnbull had been tipped to make the

Wales squad, but had also been overlooked. Their friends were acting aggrieved on their behalf. Nobody said a word to me. I had been first choice in my position for more than a decade, so my omission seemed more significant. No one seemed comfortable raising it with me. The media, though, would make it their headline. It wasn't about who was in the squad, it was about who wasn't. Specifically, me.

Training went by in a daze and my coach, Mark Hammett, could see my mind was elsewhere. When the rest of the squad trooped back to the changing rooms, he collared me for a chat. He'd been with the All Blacks for seven years before being dropped without warning, and could understand intimately what I was going through. He compared it to a death – New Zealanders take their rugby seriously. It sounded dramatic, but I understood his point. Something that had always been there had suddenly gone, leaving an immediate and gaping void.

We sat for twenty minutes on the tackle bags out on the field. For those twenty minutes, he wasn't my coach. He was my mate and confidant. My emotions were raw, and he respected that. When I began to well-up, he gave me a hug.

Once we'd talked it out, he told me to write a letter to Warren Gatland, the Wales head coach, and tell him exactly what I was thinking. 'Keep hold of it for twenty-four hours,' he said, 'and then decide whether to send it.'

The writing itself would be an act of catharsis.

Dear Warren,

What the hell are you thinking? I can't believe you've dropped me. It's an absolute joke.

I'm clearly some kind of scapegoat for the series defeat in South Africa. I admit I wasn't at my best in the first test, but was I really the only player to play badly? Was dropping me the best way to man-manage one of your most loyal and experienced players?

Talk about kicking a man when he's down. I was out of contract in the summer, and without a club to train with. You could have picked up the phone and offered me a little support. It was a tough time for me. I guess that's not your style. But did you have to belittle me in the press? Tell the world it was my problem, and that I needed to 'sort my situation out'.

You knew what my situation was. You knew I was being used as a pawn between the Ospreys and the Welsh Rugby Union.

I've sweated blood since joining the Blues, and have been first choice all season . . .

I wrote the letter. But I never sent it. In fact, I never finished it. I was sobbing long before I reached the end.

I'd spent more than ten years at the top and was one of the best in the world in my position. Rugby defined me. It was my whole life. Pulling on that shirt, wearing the three feathers on my chest and representing my country meant everything to me.

Not any more.

I felt somehow reduced, shrunken. Emasculated. In an instant, everything had changed.

There was no reward for my services. No gratitude for the blood I'd shed. For the ligaments I'd torn. For the bones I'd cracked. For the sacrifices I'd made. Just a phone call telling me I wasn't needed any more. If the Lions tour of 2013 had represented the pinnacle, then I'd tumbled to the foot of the mountain. Dropped during the Six Nations, released from my club and now discarded by my country.

My career had hurtled into the abyss.

CHAPTER 1

You'll Never Play for Ystradgynlais

I wish I was able to manufacture some kind of hard-luck story about growing up in the poverty-stricken Swansea Valley, with rugby as my saviour – the galvanising force that kept me on the straight and narrow. But the truth is, I had a pretty idyllic upbringing. I didn't want for anything, and was brought up in the bosom of a warm and loving family. So, no complaints there.

I arrived in the world a week late, which annoyed my mother. It meant she was in hospital when Wales were playing France in the 1981 Five Nations. She never missed an international, and was more than a little peeved when the nurses told her she wasn't allowed into the common room to watch the match. Bed rest was the order – and as little excitement as possible – while she waited for her baby to arrive. Her response was that she'd discharge herself if she didn't have her way. She won that argument, and as she sat there watching Graham Price scrummaging in a losing cause against the French, little did she know that the ten-pound baby in her tummy would be following in his footsteps in just over twenty years' time.

My mother will tell you it was destiny. She says I looked like a prop when I emerged from the womb the following day, on 8 March 1981. I was a big lump, my nose was squashed against my face, and she felt she had to warn visitors about how 'ugly' I was before she allowed them to see me. Lucky for her that I eventually blossomed into the handsome, charming man that I am today.

● ● ●

The first present I received was a miniature rugby ball, and I have early memories of scrummaging against my older brother, Nathan, in the living room of our home in the mining village of Abercrave. It was a rugby-mad village in a rugby-mad country. The chances of me avoiding the oval ball were slim. From the age of four, I'd organise rugby matches on the living-room floor between teams captained by Han Solo and Luke Skywalker. My brother was an avid collector of Star Wars figures, which I used to purloin from his bedroom. As far as I was aware, they didn't play rugby in Tatooine, so I had to fashion my own ball out of a piece of Blu-Tack. The carpets were relics from the seventies, with a gaudy rectangular pattern, which served as the pitch markings. I'd while away hours presiding over these fictitious games. It was obvious to my parents that the passion for rugby was within me.

My father – like every Welsh father who had lived through the seventies – wanted me to be a fly-half. As soon as I was able to walk, he took me across the road to the local rugby pitch, in the shadow of

Cribarth mountain, and tossed me a ball. He swears that I scooped it up one-handed before it touched the ground, and was convinced from that point onwards that I would play for Wales. He told my mother that night.

The kick-about in the field became a daily ritual. I'd insist that my dad took me there every night. I was a right pain in the arse. He was a mechanic at the bus station in Pontardawe, and he worked incredibly hard. He'd be there at 5.30 every morning, and wouldn't get back until half-five at night, so the last thing he'd want to do would be to come and kick a ball around with me. But he almost always did. He'd last about an hour, before returning to the comfort of his armchair and a bit of television. In the summer months, I'd refuse to go in. That was when my grandmother took over. Grandma Meg, my mother's mother. She was well into her sixties and used to jog down the path to meet me. I had two rugby balls. She'd stand behind the posts while I endlessly practised my place kicks and drop goals, patiently booting them back to me over and over again.

Meg was my biggest fan. When I started playing professionally, she'd watch every televised game and write down everything the commentators said about me. So if Eddie Butler had talked me up, or slagged me off, she'd write it down and present me with her notes the following day. Her handwriting was shocking. It was really spidery and barely legible, but it was the thought that counted.

●　●　●

Grandma Meg was a big influence in my life. Her husband, Wyndham, died in a road accident the night after my mother found out she was pregnant with Nathan. He was fifty-five. His grandsons never got to meet him. He'd been travelling to his shift at the quarry above the village, when the van he was in collided with a lorry going the other way. Meg was working nights as an auxiliary nurse at the nearby hospital in Craig-y-Nos, and she rushed to the scene. Initially, it looked as though he was fine. The driver was a younger man, and Wyndham encouraged the paramedics to attend to him first. No one realised he'd suffered serious internal injuries, and he died later that day.

It was the latest in a long line of tragedies in my family. Wyndham had been a miner all his life, until his knee gave way and he swapped his job underground for one at the quarry. He'd left school early when his father died in a mining accident. He was still a child but was forced to become a man overnight. And to earn the money on which his family would survive, he had to descend daily into the hellhole that had taken his father's life.

Grandma Meg's father used to look after the horses in the same mine. When Meg was six years old, he was walking to work in a blizzard, following the railway line, and a train appeared from the gloom and ran him over. He died instantly. Meg was one of seven children, and her mother had an eighth on the way. Because the accident had happened away from the mine, she received nothing in the way of compensation, and faced the prospect of raising eight children as a single parent. It proved too much for her, and half of Meg's siblings had to move up to Llandrindod Wells to be brought up by distant relatives. It must have been heart-breaking. She'd lost her father, and was then split apart from her brother and sisters.

I cannot imagine how hard life must have been for Meg – growing up in the same village as me, two generations earlier – but I will always remember her as a happy old soul, full of vim and vigour for life. On several occasions, she accompanied me to school sports days when my parents couldn't make it. And instead of sitting politely on the sidelines, she'd insist on entering the parents' race. More often than not she'd win, against mothers twenty years younger than her. Her passion for sport — and for rugby in particular – was fairly typical. My family was a big rugby family: Wyndham played tight-head prop for Abercrave for years during the fifties, and my old man played hooker for the firsts for around fifteen years. I suppose there's a trend there. The Jones family didn't produce much in the way of fleet-footed wingers, but we supplied more than our fair share of hard-nosed front rowers!

As well as being my de facto coach and training partner, Meg was also something of a disciplinarian. If I was ever late back from playing up the mountain, it would be Meg who'd give me the bollocking – and a clip, if I talked back. And she worked me hard too. She was quite the keen horticulturist, and enlisted me from an early age as her unpaid labourer. Often, she'd take me down to the river and supervise while I collected stones for her rockery. Then she'd skip back home while I trudged behind her, laden with a bulging rucksack. No sooner had I unloaded it than she'd order me to vault the fence, into the field behind her bungalow, and gather up a load of horse manure for the garden. So there I'd be, literally shovelling shit while she barked orders from her garden gate.

Tragedy also haunted my father's side of the family. My paternal grandfather, Selwyn Rees Jones, originally hailed from Corris in North Wales, where his family worked in the slate mines. His father contracted tuberculosis and died at the age of thirty-five, when Selwyn was just seven years old. He moved with his mother to Brecon, twenty miles north-east of Abercrave, where she eventually remarried. He joined the RAF at the outbreak of the Second World War, when he claims to have 'seen a lot'. He never elaborated beyond that, other than to dismiss war movies when they came on the telly as sanitised, sentimental nonsense. He suffered a bad stroke when he was forty-five, and died four years later. He was a heavy smoker, often with a cigarette and a pipe on the go at the same time. Unsurprisingly, my parents raised me to consider tobacco and nicotine to be twin evils.

● ● ●

Despite the family obsession with sport, I could easily have ended up as a choirboy instead of a rugby player. One of Selwyn's cousins, Dick Rees, was a singer of some note in the Mid Wales area. He once appeared on the front cover of the *Radio Times* as the 'Singing Ploughman', so it's in the genes. My mother was very religious and insisted I go to church every Sunday. It was embarrassing. There I was, dressed up in my purple cassock, trying to hit the high notes, while my mates were kicking a ball about and getting muddy outside.

I suspect it had something to do with the fact that my mates all played for Ystradgynlais. My mother would never have allowed me to do that, church or no church. She's an Abercrave girl, and Ystrad were the hated local rivals. If I was ever to play club rugby, it was to be Abercrave or no one. She once threatened to break my legs if I ever turned out in Ystrad colours. I don't think she was joking either. They didn't have a mini-rugby section in Abercrave, so it came down to a choice: soil the family name by playing for Ystrad, or be a good boy and go to church. It was an early insight into the extreme tribalism of Welsh rugby and village life.

I could hold a tune, mind. I even sang a few solos.

Abercrave is in the middle of nowhere. It's not a million miles from the bright lights of Swansea, but it felt much more rural as we were at the southern edge of the Brecon Beacons National Park. It sounds old-fashioned, but much of my childhood was spent outdoors. I was a really active kid, always out climbing mountains and swimming in the river.

I look back on those days with a misty-eyed nostalgia. Instead of relying on games consoles and technology, we made our own fun, wandering off for hours among the sandy rocks, and riding our bikes around the lake. During the summer, all the kids in the village used to go out at around ten in the morning, and rock up back at the house at six in the evening. We'd have five-hour-long football matches, and never seemed to tire. All of us had limitless amounts of energy.

And it always felt very Welsh. I was never in any doubt about where I came from, but I never learned to speak the language, despite being surrounded by it. Abercrave was at the centre of a strong Welsh-speaking heartland. You'd hear Welsh spoken in shops, at the park, on the terraces, and there were a number of Welsh language schools in the area. My dad spoke it, and my mother could get by, but I – like many of my generation – was never encouraged to speak it.

These days, there's a certain social cachet attached to speaking Welsh, and since devolution the number of Welsh speakers has risen steadily. But when I was growing up, despite it being a constant presence, it was never something I felt belonged to me.

● ● ●

I've always looked up to my dad, Alwyn. Not literally – he's only about five foot eight – but he's always commanded my respect. And he was well respected at Abercrave RFC as well. As a former captain, he had a certain standing at the club.

I'll always remember being down there one Saturday afternoon when a huge fight broke out outside the club, with fists flying everywhere. My old man rushed out to break it up, and everyone immediately backed down. It struck me then that he was held in pretty high regard, and it made me feel strangely proud – as though he was better than those blokes who couldn't control their tempers.

Having said that, I later found out he was a dirty little scoundrel on the pitch. I've lost count of the number of people who've told me he would kick anything above a blade of grass. He was a good player, though, and could've played for Neath. Abercrave were approached, to inquire about his availability, along with an uncle of mine. But the message was suspiciously never passed on. The officials at Abercrave were none too happy about their players being poached. Welsh tribalism again.

My dad found out much later, and was fuming when he did.

● ● ●

My brother, Nathan, and I couldn't be more different. Chalk and cheese. Growing up, he was the academic one. He breezed through his GCSEs and A levels, was head boy at school and went on to university. I was the total opposite – a dreamer, and never a big fan of the classroom. Given our different temperaments, and the four-year age gap, we never had much to do with one another outside the house. We didn't have that close buddy–buddy relationship that some brothers do, but I remember one incident when I was nine that left me under no illusions as to how much he cared about me.

I was in Ynyswen, hanging out with some kids at the youth club, and there was this older boy, around eleven, who was picking on me. Being the coward that I was, I ran back to Meg's and burst into tears. She rang my parents and told them what had happened. I think my mam and dad were a bit embarrassed, to be honest. But my brother had overheard the conversation and, without a word to anyone, he pulled on his coat, got on his bike and cycled up to the youth club. He found this boy, grabbed him by the throat and smacked him one. He then told him that if he ever picked on his little brother again, he'd knock his head off! Now, let me just clarify that my brother was not some hotheaded brute always spoiling for a fight. He was a swot – the most 'un-fighty' bloke you could ever meet – more of a Clark Kent than a Superman. But that day he was my hero.

Nathan dabbled with rugby, and was pretty good, but it was never the path he was going to choose. He played for our school side, for his halls in Loughborough University and for the London Welsh Occies. He was a hooker too – the Jones genes do lend themselves well to the front row – but if you were to meet him now, you wouldn't believe he's my brother. He's become obsessed with triathlons and Ironmans, and has become as skinny as a rake. He has a full-time job working for Deloitte in Switzerland, so he'll be on his bike at five in the morning, do two hours before work, go for a swim in his lunchtime, then have a run after work. All for the love of it. If I had even half the drive he's got, I'd be some sort of player. Personally, I couldn't think of anything worse, but I take my hat off to him. He's got a strong competitive streak, and this is his outlet. If he takes fourteen hours to complete an Ironman, the next time he'll want to do it in thirteen.

● ● ●

We'd always go on holiday every year as a family. We weren't wealthy by any means, but my mother and father worked extremely hard so my brother and I could have what we needed. Camping and caravanning were their passions, and we spent several weeks of the year in Northern France or at random British seaside resorts like Scarborough. We went to the Lake District once.

Typically, though, I didn't remotely appreciate it. My attitude was, 'This is shit. What the hell did we come here for? Why can't we go to Spain like my other mates? I could be sitting in a hotel, watching a band play and eating as much as I want from the all-day buffet!' I was an ungrateful little tyke.

At the age of ten I took the first of many trips to Canada to visit my mum's brother, Wayne. That was a real eye-opener for a wide-eyed valley boy from a tiny village in Wales. My uncle Wayne hired a Winnebago, and we went on a massive road trip through the Rockies — covering hundreds of miles in three weeks. The wide open spaces, the majesty of the scenery and the sense of freedom really appealed to my imagination and sense of adventure.

The sights were entirely alien to me. One day, we came across a dead bear cub on the road. Its mother was at the roadside, wailing and crying. It was a harrowing scene, but an utterly surreal one as well. Back home, the most you'd see would be a squirrel, or very occasionally a fox. But here I was, a ten-year-old boy, staring out of the window at a huge brown bear.

Uncle Wayne seemed like a cowboy to me, strutting around in his ten-gallon hat. A cowboy with the thickest, deepest Welsh accent imaginable. He looked like John Wayne but *sounded* like a dyed-in-the-wool Abercrave boy — apart from the times he'd say 'gas' instead of 'petrol', or 'sidewalk' instead of 'pavement', and 'pants' when he meant 'trousers'.

● ● ●

I never wanted to be a Welsh international. I wanted to be an All Black. They were my idols.

The Welsh team of the 1980s lurched from one disaster to another, and they didn't inspire a sense of hero worship in a young boy from the

Swansea Valley. I vaguely remember the Triple Crown in 1988, but I'd be lying if I said I'd fallen in love with any of the players. Apart from, maybe, Bleddyn Bowen. I named my goldfish after him. My lack of patriotism led to a few fallings-out with my mother – most notably in 1991, when Wales lost 36–3 to France. I stood up and declared that I was embarrassed to be Welsh. It didn't go down well. My mother is enormously proud of where she's from, and wasn't going to stand for this display of petulance. I was given an almighty row and sent to my room.

I suppose it illustrates how strongly Welsh identity is entwined with rugby. When Wales are poor, you take it personally. It was disheartening being a Welsh fan.

The game was still amateur while I was growing up, and we lost a generation of our most gifted players to the professional code of Rugby League in the North of England. 'He's gone north' was the phrase you most feared to hear. Rugby League was anathema to the purists at the WRU, and lifetime bans were issued to those who even considered switching codes. Jonathan Davies was the one who tipped the balance. He was our jewel in the crown, a player of genuine world class. When he went north, it felt as though Welsh rugby would never recover.

So I didn't have any Welsh heroes. My favourite players were all Kiwis: Sean Fitzpatrick, Olo Brown and Craig Dowd. I was fascinated by them. There was an aura and a mystique surrounding them in the eighties that has dissipated with the advent of satellite TV and annual tours. But back then, they were this brooding, mysterious group of warriors. There was something sinister and unsettling about them. They appeared to be a different breed – a different species, even.

My dad used to talk a lot about the 1971 Lions tour, which took place at the other end of the earth, and the distance fuelled the sense of mystery. Where exactly was this 'New Zealand'?

I had a library of well-worn video tapes: *101 Best Tries* and *Another 101 Best Tries* were on constant rotation. While other kids memorised and recited song lyrics, I did the same for Bill McLaren's commentaries. The one that really resonated with me was '100 years of All Black rugby'. When I was five, I declared that I'd be moving to New Zealand to pursue my ambition of becoming an All Black. My mother agreed on the grounds that, if I did ever represent them, I'd have to have a Welsh flag sewn into my collar. I was happy to do that, but I expressed my doubts about whether their captain at the time – the notorious hardman Wayne Shelford – would allow it. 'You just tell him your mother told you.' Not even Buck Shelford would argue with my mother.

The former Wales scrum-half and coach, Clive Rowlands, ran a sports shop near us, and it was there I went to get my first school rugby kit.

'Right then,' said Clive. 'Who's your favourite player?'

I told him I wanted to be an All Black.

'OK, then. You'll need shorts without pockets. The All Blacks don't have pockets on their shorts. And when you run out to play, you have to stand with your hands on your hips, like this.'

Clive is an enormously charismatic man, and I was hanging on his every word. I left with two pairs of pocketless shorts, and thought I was one step closer to becoming an All Black. Looking back, he probably just had a job lot of shorts with no pockets to get rid of, and spied an opportunity to offload a few pairs. But I was convinced that my new shorts would make me a better player.

Later on, I made a sportsman's bet with Clive that I'd win more caps than he had. Every time I played for Wales, I made a point of walking past his shop, with my fingers held up – one for every cap I'd won. He'd chuckle away to himself when he saw me. When I reached the magic number of fifteen, I went outside and gestured 'fifteen' using my hands.

Quick as a flash, he rushed outside and said, 'Ah yes, but I played more bloody minutes than you.'

I couldn't argue with that.

I got to see the All Blacks in person, in 1989, when they played Swansea. I stood entranced, as they disembarked from their bus at St Helen's. Among those superhumans I was gazing at in awe was a young forward from the Waikato called Warren Gatland. I didn't know it then, but that moody-looking hooker would come to play a pivotal role in my career.

There was a real buzz around those tour games. Everybody took the afternoon off school to go and see them. Swansea lost that day 37–22, and Wales lost the test a week later by a bigger margin. But I'd seen my heroes up close, and that was all I could have wished for.

● ● ●

My mother's refusal to let me play mini-rugby for Ystradgynlais meant I was first exposed to it at school. I was a prop from day one, and our PE teacher, Mike Harries, encouraged a few of us to go down to try out at Swansea Valley Under 11s, a representative side that pulled in players from all over the valley.

I didn't want to go. I was painfully shy, and used to hiding in my brother's shadow. My mother was driving me down to Pontardawe Leisure Centre, and I pretended I wasn't feeling well. I told her my stomach was hurting and that I wanted to go home, but she saw right through me. 'Let's keep on going so you can at least meet them and say hello,' she said. She tricked me into getting changed, and I watched from the touchline in my full kit. Hywel Williams, the schoolmaster from Cwmtwrch, saw me kicking my heels, and dragged me on to the pitch.

By the end of the session I was hooked.

There were boys from all over the valley there – from clubs like Ystrad and Glais and Vardre – and I realised that I had to join one. Glais was a further ten miles south than Ystradgynlais, but it met with my mother's approval, so it became my first club.

Those nerves I felt on the way to training that day would never fully desert me. I've learned to control them better over the years, but that sense of apprehension that accompanied me on the journey to Pontardawe has been a constant companion throughout my career.

My ambition reached no further than wanting to play for Abercrave RFC. As with many villages throughout Wales, the rugby club was the beating heart of the community, and local pride was inextricably linked to the performance of its team. Abercrave were good back then. We played St Peter's in the Welsh Cup the year after they'd beaten Cardiff – a giant-killing act of monumental proportions that's still talked about today – and we beat them. According to my warped logic, that meant that Abercrave were better than Cardiff. They were my team, more so than Neath, more so than Swansea or any of the big clubs. More so than Wales, even.

Our weekends were totally shaped around Abercrave RFC. The whole family would go down to the home games, and my father and I would hit the road on away weekends, travelling all over Wales, lending the boys our passionate support from the sidelines. There were no blurred lines, as there are now, with clubs, regions and the national side. It was simple – you supported your local team, unconditionally.

There was a reassuring familiarity to it, a match-day ritual that touched on all of life's simple pleasures. Down the club, watch the game, hang around, drink a glass of squash or two, and then wait for my mother to pick us up. And there was always Bernard's Chip Shop on the way home.

A heavenly old-fashioned chippy, with a coal fire to heat the fat. Even now, that pretty much amounts to the perfect day for me. Maybe I'd have a pint now, instead of a glass of squash.

I was once asked to write a poem at junior school beginning with the line: 'Happiness is...' I wrote: 'Happiness is Bernard's chips, and being a professional rugby player.' I was eight at the time. It was a good six years before rugby would turn professional.

During my early teens, my dad started coaching Abercrave Youth, so we started following them every weekend. That side attracted all the nutters and 'headers' in the valley. They were a team short on talent, but brimming with testosterone. Violence was always bubbling beneath the surface, and most matches soon erupted into ugly brawls. My dad spent as much time peacemaking as he did coaching. On one occasion, the players had formed a tunnel at the end of the game – traditionally the moment when differences are put aside and players shake hands in the spirit of rugby – but some fiery words were exchanged and it all kicked off in front of me. Fists flying, the sound of bone on flesh. And my old man trying to restore some order amid all the chaos. I was thirteen or fourteen at the time and remember thinking, 'Is this really for me?'

But overall I have fond memories of those times, following my dad around and immersing myself in the social side of rugby. After the youth games, he'd collect up the kitty money, go to Bernard's and come back to the club with forty packs of sausage and chips for everyone. That was what appealed to me more than anything, back then.

In 1997 we had a good run, with our school side, Maesydderwen, reaching the Welsh Cup final, where we played Dwr-y-Felin comprehensive school. It was the first time I propped against Paul James – an aggressive and angry loose-head prop, who went on to become one of my best friends and colleagues. It was his brother, Kevin, who made the difference that day, though. Their game plan was simple – get it to Kev on the wing, and watch him steamroller everyone, just like Jonah Lomu.

●　●　●

I was on the cusp of entering the world of youth rugby, and once you reach that fork in the road, there are only two options: take it seriously, or embrace the beer. I chose the latter, leaving Glais for my hometown team. For the next three years, it was all about drinking. And a very good drinker I was too. Not many of the boys could keep up with me. It was a case of play the game, get showered, then head straight to the bar. The amount I put away depended very much on how much pocket money my mother had given me, but it all went on booze. And I rarely left before I'd sunk at least ten pints. Not that I'd ever keep count. We bought it in jugs, and it was just a free-for-all. Once one was emptied, another was ordered.

Our coach was a big fan of the sing-song too, and before long I had an admirable repertoire of rugby songs at my disposal. Journeys home from away games would be the prelude to our drinking sessions – a raucous, tuneless cacophony on the team bus. It was a vital part of my rugby development; those social bonds forged on the bus, and at the bar, are of enormous importance. You're more likely to come to the aid of a teammate on the pitch if he's your bona fide buddy off it.

These days, half the youth boys don't drink, and they're more likely to travel to and from games with headphones on. Some of the bonhomie is disappearing from rugby, as the game becomes more professionalised, more scientific – and more serious. Don't get me wrong, we were a tidy side – and were always desperate to beat the likes of Ystradgynlais and Crynant – but largely, it was all about the drinking, and I'm not ashamed to admit that.

When we started drinking in the rugby club, we all wanted to impress the senior players. They'd be at the bar, swilling ale and singing hymns in their booming baritones, and we'd be sitting meekly in the corner desperate to join in. In a small village like that, they were our heroes. They'd often segue into more modern stuff as well. 'American Pie' and 'Sloop John B' were particular favourites and could be heard reverberating around the Swansea Valley after several gallons of ale on a Saturday night.

Every Friday night from the age of fourteen, I'd rush home after school, have a shower and meet my mates down at Ystradgynlais Cross. It'd be like, 'Right, who's getting the 'Bow?' And if no one could pluck up the courage to try their luck in the off-licence, we'd have to persuade an older boy to go in and get two flagons of cider on our behalf. Then it would be over to the youth club for the disco. Before that we'd all be sitting around in the field, playing drinking games and trying to avoid Masky and Hugo, the two blokes who ran the youth club. They used to patrol in their cars, shining their headlamps into the fields, trying to find the rebellious drinkers. It was like the American film *Dazed and Confused*, but with Welsh accents.

There were two pubs in Ystradgynlais. That was our world, our bubble, and I felt uncomfortable leaving it. I remember going to Swansea for a school Christmas party when I was about sixteen or seventeen, and it felt like another universe. I was so nervous I couldn't enjoy the night. It was around about the time when some of the guys were chasing girls, but a ladies' man I most definitely was not. I was too shy, too big, too sweaty – and too fat. It was during this period that my weight really started to balloon.

It won't surprise you to learn that I've always liked my food. If it's in front of me, I'll eat it. Nathan would get a bar of chocolate, nibble a bit, and then save the rest for later. I could never do that. He reminds me to this day of the time I ruined his Christmas by stealing his Terry's Chocolate Orange from the tree. It had been hanging there for most of December, taunting me, and one day I devoured it, leaving a couple of slices, before delicately rearranging the foil into what passed for a sphere.

His face on Christmas Day was a picture. I'm not sure he's ever forgiven me.

● ● ●

School was something of a disaster for me. I left with two GCSEs. It's not because I'm stupid, it's just that I couldn't be bothered. My approach to lessons was always: 'Get through this, then go and play rugby.'

My laziness was thrown into sharp relief by my swot of a brother. I lost count of the number of times I heard my teachers say, 'Nathan would never do this,' or, 'Nathan would have worked harder at this'. While he aced all of his exams, I did my level best to fail all of mine.

The morning of my mock catering GCSE was spent around my mate Rowan's house methodically making our way through his dad's drinks cabinet. There were four of us and we spent the morning downing shots of whisky while another mate, Owain, necked half a bottle of Bacardi. He was in the worst state as we stumbled into our exams later that afternoon, giggling and shoving each other around. My exam was in catering, so I just kept my head down and made a barely edible flan. But Owain's was in graphics, and he was all over the shop. I think he just wrote 'I am a fish' over and over again.

It's funny, looking back on it, but it sums up my attitude to education as a kid. I really didn't care.

The day of my GCSE results was when it finally dawned on me that I should have worked harder. I waited around for two hours to collect my results, afraid to go in, before bawling my eyes out when I opened the envelope. I'd passed two – one in English literature and one in catering. As a big lad who liked his food, the irony wasn't lost on me. Once I'd got over the heartbreak, I couldn't complain, because I hadn't put any effort in.

While I was contemplating a future with two paltry GCSEs to my name, my brother was excelling himself at university in Loughborough. I think my parents twigged fairly early on that Nathan and I weren't cut from the same cloth. But I can never remember them being dis-appointed in me. I used to dread every parents' evening, because every year I'd end up having an almighty bollocking. Not because I was naughty, but because I was lazy. They tried in vain to get me into reading, even going so far as to get me a subscription to *Rugby World* magazine, but I just wasn't interested.

I guess you could say I lost my way a bit around this period. I didn't know what to do with my life, my self-esteem started to suffer, and my weight began to balloon. I'd always been a bigger-than-average kid, but I began to expand outwards as my appetite for junk food and booze grew. I virtually lived off fish and chips, and cheese on toast. Some of the fitness coaches I've worked with since would be horrified at what I was putting into my body, but I wasn't thinking then about becoming a professional sportsman. It was the furthest thing from my mind.

I think my parents were getting a bit worried about me – not so much at the weight gain, but all the other factors. I was drifting along in life, with no goals and no ambition.

CHAPTER 2

Battling the Bulge

I was rescued from a life on the dole by a dinner lady who worked at my mother's school. She happened to mention that a former Aberavon player by the name of Sean Holley had set up a rugby course at Llanelli College. It was a combination of rugby and sports science, and sounded right up my street. As the new term dawned, I was heading west in my dad's battered Citroën BX.

It was a journey I would become very familiar with.

Over the two years, I played an awful lot of rugby. The college team was decent, and I was turning out for Abercrave Youth at the weekends. Add in my summer job dressing up as a bear in Dan-yr-Ogof Showcaves, and it was a busy period.

Sean was a big believer in every player having strong core skills, and playing for the college allowed me to develop my game significantly. I was encouraged to carry the ball and became renowned for my charging, bullocking runs. I was also encouraged to kick, and I became one of my side's regular place kickers. Strange, considering I hardly touch the ball now. My attempted drop goal for the Cardiff Blues last season is the only evidence in my professional career that I had a useful right peg on me. (I should point out that I missed on that occasion. Just.)

My performances were attracting a bit of attention, and I got selected to play for Dyfed off the back of a college trial. I was told to drive to Pont Abraham services off the M4, where the team bus would pick me up. An hour passed before I realised I was at Cross Hands services, several miles away. This was in the pre-mobile-phone era, so I was left stranded. The guy who played instead of me went on to get a Wales A cap that year.

I was furious with myself, and lapsed back into my comfort eating. Every day, as I made the journey from Abercrave to Llanelli, I'd stop en route for a McDonald's or a bacon butty. Lunch would be Scotch egg and chips, and a bottle of full-fat Coke. And I'd usually pull over for another bacon butty on the way home. By the time I was eighteen, I was comfortably twenty-three stone. My head was like a beach ball.

I knew by this stage I was a good player, and that if I knuckled down I could do well, but my attitude was letting me down. By 'do well', I meant nailing down a starting spot with Abercrave. I had no inkling that I could make a career out of playing rugby. Llanelli RFC's head coach, Gareth Jenkins, popped down from time to time as part of his scouting brief, but he dismissed me as being too fat and out of shape.

●　●　●

I did get invited to train as part of the Welsh Youth squad around that time, after having a few run-outs for Neath and District Under 18s. The squad met up at Carmarthen Leisure Centre around Christmastime, and I felt really out of place. There were no academies back then, and no one giving us advice about nutrition. 'Fitness' meant going for a run. I would occasionally do some weights, but that's only because my uncle ran a gym in Sennybridge. So when I rocked up at the Welsh Youth session, I wasn't exactly what you'd call a 'specimen'! I was pushing about 30% body fat, which is pretty high. It's roughly what Richard Hibbard is these days! (At the last check, I was about 16.5%.)

At that squad session, we had all manner of bleep tests, fitness tests and shuttle runs, and it culminated in a trial match. Although I'd made a conscious effort to lose weight before the camp, I was still far too heavy, and it would be kind to say I was average in those tests. I came nowhere near making the cut. But rather than going away and resolving to get fitter, I just descended back into my routine of binge eating, and the weight piled back on. That was Wales Under 18 level, and it pretty much counted me out of featuring at Under 19 level. Much like my GCSEs, I think I just expected to do no real work, put no real effort in, and have it come to me.

It wasn't as though it was a great ambition of mine to play for Wales Youth, but I was disappointed when it didn't come to pass. I was still playing for Abercrave Youth and, occasionally, the firsts. We were in Division Four Central, playing the likes of Blaengarw, Pontycymmer and Maesteg Quins.

There were a few of us there who thought perhaps we could play to a higher level. Jonathan Stevens was one of them – a big second row, with a similar physique to mine. He also loved his food and struggled to keep the weight off. One summer, Llandovery RFC invited the two of us to train with them. I've got to be honest, the big selling point was that you had free fish 'n' chips after training, but there was something about being asked to train with a Division One side that tickled my ego, and we went for it. That's when I realised I wasn't fit. I was strong

– I broke the club bench-press record – but I was severely lacking in other departments.

Suddenly, though, it felt like I was on the verge of something. I thought I had no chance of ever playing at the very top level for the likes of Swansea or Neath, but Llandovery seemed attainable.

● ● ●

As the summer of 2000 came to an end, and my fitness levels improved, I got wind of a new Under 21s club league, and was invited to represent Neath at U21 level. I was summoned to the Gnoll along with fourteen other boys from the district. We turned up like it was the first day at school – a ragged bunch of misfits with mixed kit and mixed reputations. Rowland Phillips, a famous Neath player and Wales international, had been put in charge of the team. He was immediately engaging, and won me over by saying they had no time to work on fitness and just had to work on the game plan. That suited me down to the ground.

We had a month or so to prepare, but I still wasn't taking it remotely seriously. It was definitely a step up from Abercrave Youth and the firsts. Steve Tandy, the current Ospreys head coach, was captain. He was already playing for Neath, as an understudy to the Welsh international Brett Sinkinson, and was at a different level in terms of skill and commitment. He was as dour and miserable as he is now, but his rugby brain was impressive. He knew all about lines of running, how to offload in the tackle, and how to steal the ball on the floor. All the kinds of things I'd later find out were hallmarks from the Lyn Jones coaching manual.

Our first game was against Cardiff, and we were a little concerned. Tandy and scrum-half Mark Davies aside, there weren't many known players in our side, and we were struggling for numbers. A guy called

Lyndon Bateman was roped in to play for us from UWIC in Cardiff. He didn't look remotely like a rugby player, with his ridiculous buzz cut and his two massive gold earrings, and there was a definite feeling that we were the dregs of the league.

But that first game was a big turning point. Rowland bigged us up and convinced us we were capable of beating this Cardiff side that was packed with youth internationals. And so we did. Our scrum dominated, and we were off to a flyer. Trooping off the field, I jogged past the near-mythical figure of Lyn Jones, Neath's first-team coach.

He approached me quite earnestly and said, 'You played well out there, young man,' before slapping me hard in the guts and saying, 'now go away and get rid of this, will you?'

● ● ●

A few weeks later, I was back to my day job, laying paving slabs. It was a hard way to earn a living – and a daily reminder to me that I'd screwed up my education. My day would start at seven and would be spent shovelling dirt and laying slabs. It was hard, repetitive, physical labour, but I took a perverse kind of enjoyment from it. Peter Evans was my only colleague, and the two of us were big into our music. The sixties was our decade of choice, and the long days would unfold to a soundtrack of The Beatles, Elvis Presley, and Procol Harum. They were my favourites. I'd asked my mother, quite seriously, as an eleven-year-old, if I could have 'A Whiter Shade Of Pale' as my funeral music when I died.

At some point during that period, I received a call from Rowland saying Lyn wanted to meet the two of us in his local pub, the Bryncoch. Lyn offered me the menu and told me to pick whatever I wanted. With hindsight, wanting to impress a top coach, who'd clearly invited me there for a reason, I should have opted for a glass of water and a salad. But being a valley boy with a penchant for junk food, I went for the Southern-fried chicken, with a side order of potato wedges covered with bacon and melted cheese. Despite this, he said that he liked the look of me and wanted me to come and train on an informal basis with the first team.

As I was wiping the last of the mayonnaise from my plate, he looked me in the eye and said, 'I'd also like you to come and meet our fitness coach, Steve Richards.'

Not for the last time, I was being invited to a personal session with a fitness coach.

The first thing 'Ritters' did, understandably, was weigh me. Now, because I'd been engaged in manual labour all summer, I'd dropped to a lean (in my eyes) twenty-one stone – a colossal two stones beneath my regular fighting weight of twenty-three.

Steve Richards looked at Phil Pugh, the team manager, with an expression that said, 'What on earth is this on my scales?' before asking me to return in a few days' time with a 'food diary' telling him what I ate during a typical week. Because I was working, it wasn't that bad. I'd have a big bowl of cereal in the morning, sandwiches for lunch, and then work it all off in the afternoon. But it was all the extra bits – the beer, the Coke, the crisps and the snacks – that were doing me harm.

My diet changed radically overnight. After Ritters entered my life, my standard evening meal became plain chicken with a plain jacket potato. No sauces, no garnishes, no butter, no vegetables. It sounds miserable, but I was so chuffed Neath were keen to take a look at me that I was willing to go through with it. They weren't offering me a wage, so I was still holding down a full-time job and living at home. But my parents – because they'd put my brother through university – were more than happy to support me.

In addition to the diet, Ritters put me through hell. He ran me ragged. Twice a week he'd have me running through the woods above Neath, followed by hellish, lung-burning sessions up and down the dunes at Merthyr Mawr – the biggest sand dunes in Europe, I hasten to add! It was bloody hard work, but the weight soon dropped off, and before long I was down to a svelte nineteen and a half stone.

● ● ●

I trained with Neath every day and played for them occasionally, when the opportunity arose. But most of my rugby was for the Under 21s side – we ended up coming fourth in that league – and for Abercrave firsts. We had a great team at the time, with a big gnarly pack of forwards. Our game plan was based around the scrum and the driving line-out, which suited me perfectly, and we had a couple of wingers who could run the 100m in less than eleven seconds. So whenever we had parity up front, we'd take the piss with the ball in hand. Bryncoch and Maesteg Quins were the only sides that could live with us.

I like to think I was more than just a monochrome bruiser, though. All those years practising with Grandma Meg in the field behind my house meant I was a tidy kicker, and my skills had been honed under Sean Holley's tutelage at Llanelli College. So whenever the opportunity arose, I took on kicking duties. During one match, against Ogmore Vale, I scored 27 points – three tries, and 12 points from the boot. That is a fact. I was a frustrated fly-half in a fat man's body.

Because I was also turning out for Neath, I'd get the occasional dig because people always want to have a pop at someone playing at the top level. But the Abercrave boys were chuffed to bits for me. It had been a long time since someone from the club had gone on to play at that level, and they were proud. They felt protective of me, because almost every opposition prop I came up against would be taking cheap shots – knees in the face, jabs on the floor and occasional eye gouges.

One prop I played against (I won't name him) was clearly irked that I was playing for Neath. He thought I was some sort of Billy Big Time and was determined to bring me down a peg or two. He collapsed a scrum deliberately, and as I was returning to my feet he kneed me square in the face. There was blood everywhere and it bloody hurt, but I was determined not to show it. As is the code with rugby, he bought me a pint in the clubhouse afterwards, and the incident was soon forgotten in a fug of alcohol and bonhomie.

Some people might find that hard to take. It might seem to you that I'm condoning violence. In polite society, that would be considered an assault. But there's something about being out in that arena that changes the rules of engagement. It's brutal and it's violent. But it's all part of the ritual, and while that's not the way I like to play, I'm not going to shirk from it. And I'm not going to pretend it doesn't happen.

CHAPTER 3

An All Black at Last

YOU don't have to be an angry man to play in the front row. It can be a dark place in there. All sweat, gristle and raw flesh. You can smell last night's beer on the breath of your opposite number, feel the sand-papery scrape of their stubble, and taste the blood from their cuts and bruises. God knows, some nasty stuff goes on that most backs wouldn't have the faintest idea about. But if you're good enough, you can rely on your skill and your technique. Playing dirty and throwing punches doesn't make you a better player. I've never been an enforcer. Never looked to intimidate or frighten my opposite number. Just to get the better of him. To beat him, not to beat him up. I've always been too laid-back for that. Any of my mates will tell you the same. When I was at the Ospreys, as part of a formidable front row with Paul James and Richard Hibbard – they were my bodyguards – I could always be relied upon to start a pushing contest. But if things got tasty, they'd be the ones piling in to finish it off.

That doesn't mean you can be soft. Anyone growing up in South Wales and expecting to make it as a prop has to go through one hell of an apprenticeship. There is no exam to sit, no theory to learn. You just have to be prepared to get smashed by older, gnarlier, bigger blokes for years. Eventually, you emerge on the other side with a rhino hide and a mental toughness honed on those muddy fields and wintry pitches, the length and breadth of the country.

Places like Banwen. Banwen is only five miles from Abercrave, but it feels like it's on another planet. Even on a nice day, it's grey and bleak up there. Being that close, there was a sense of mistrust and animosity between us that so characterises Welsh rugby. It's both a strength and a weakness that we despise our near neighbours so much. The bad blood between us and Banwen was particularly toxic. They had three brothers – the Thomases – who played for them, and they were an intimidating bunch.

There'd been an unsavoury incident on the pitch the previous year, and the Thomas brothers would often come down to Abercrave seeking revenge, spoiling for a fight. They seemed to fancy themselves as the Swansea Valley's answer to the Krays (though I'm not suggesting for a second they were involved in any criminal activity!). We played them down there in the winter of 2000, and there was a real sense of menace around the game; a genuine fear that things would kick off. The WRU got wind of it and assigned three of their most senior referees to the match – Derek Bevan, Clayton Thomas and Rob Davies – which was ridiculous, considering it was such a low-level game. It'd be like Nigel Owens and Craig Joubert reffing Abercrave now.

Going up there as a nineteen-year-old was intimidating. Back then, before the game, we'd all gather in a circle, stamp our feet and count to ten to get us going. On this occasion, our coach insisted that our loose-head, Gethin, lead us through a rendition of 'Who's that man with the big red nose?'. It really spun the Banwen boys out to see fifteen blokes singing a novelty song before such a big game. Several hundred people were there — probably the biggest crowd they'd ever had. All their supporters were on one side of the pitch, baying for blood, and all ours were on the other. I might have appreciated the atmosphere if I hadn't been so on edge.

Their hooker was a Thomas brother, and so was the loose-head, so I was stuck between those two psychos in every scrum. Every time we'd pack down, they'd glower at me, snorting like bulls, with hate in their eyes. All through the game, I was expecting a clenched fist to come flying through and splay my nose across my face. Typically, it never did. The presence of the top referees had worked, and everyone was on their best behaviour. But that didn't mean the *threat* of violence wasn't there — and sometimes that is more frightening than a bout of fisticuffs actually erupting.

● ● ●

I had to get through the same rites of passage as any young prop looking to establish himself in the most macho position in the most red-blooded of sports. I had more than my fair share of cheap shots, gouges and stray kicks. Some bloke kicked me in the back of the head once in Abercwmboi. Our coach, Wyn Rees, went ballistic with my teammates because nobody weighed in to help me out. He was more annoyed with them than he was with the guy who kicked me. Such is the strange unwritten code that governs rugby. Even though there is an ugly side to the game — particularly at lower levels, where there are no TV cameras to scrutinise every transgression — there is still an honour in standing up for your teammates;

the one-in, all-in attitude that led to the creation of the infamous '99' call during the 1974 Lions tour.

Nothing ever happened that made me want to give up. You accepted that this kind of thing came with the territory. If you were unfortunate enough to be caught at the bottom of a ruck, you knew you were having it. You'd just hope that your arms weren't trapped, so you could at least try to protect yourself. Otherwise, you knew you'd be having studs rained down on your ribs, your chest, your face and – most painfully of all – your nether regions.

It reached the point where I was getting more and more off-the-ball attention because – and I don't mean this to sound big-headed – nine times out of ten, I was better than my opposite number. If they couldn't beat me through legitimate means, they'd resort to dirty tricks. I'd started to lose a bit of weight, and I was getting fitter and stronger. It was having a real impact on my game, and I picked up a string of man-of-the-match awards in a team that was brimming with good players.

We should have walked the league that year, but we blew it. We lost up at Bryncoch, and at Maesteg Quins. They were hard, difficult teams to play against. Those two were the only sides in the league, apart from us, with a good blend; a half-tidy set of forwards and a decent set of backs. All the other teams were just about the forwards; big, heavy sides who'd try and strangle you up front, but with no panache behind.

● ● ●

During the summer of 2001, I had a phone call from Lyn Jones inviting me to his house. Since he'd told me to lose my gut, he'd barely spoken to me, so I wasn't sure what he wanted. He revelled in his eccentricity, and was possibly a little unhinged. I'd heard stories – probably entirely fictional – of him conducting coaching sessions in the nude, and urinating in the middle of TV interviews, so I felt a little on edge as I rang his doorbell. The door swung open, and Lyn was standing there with an expression I took to be a grin. Mercifully, he was fully clothed. I was beckoned in, and invited to take a seat in his study.

Once the formalities were out of the way, he asked, 'How would you like to become a professional rugby player?'

I could barely contain my excitement. I'd had a suspicion that this was the purpose of my visit, but I hadn't dared contemplate it.

He leaned over to the computer, opened up a blank Word document and began typing. He was writing out my contract from scratch. He typed out the word 'salary' and put a miserly figure next to it. Sensing my obvious disappointment, he deleted it and inserted a slightly higher number. This charade continued until the figure reached the astronomical figure of £650 a month.

I was going to be rich. It was more money than I'd ever dreamed of earning. Since school I'd been living with my parents and relying entirely on their charity. Now, all of a sudden, I was a man of means. Lyn clicked 'print', the document emerged from beneath his desk, and we signed it there and then. Simple as that. A two-year contract with Neath RFC – one of the biggest clubs in the land.

Standing there with the contract in my hand, I was suffused with a sudden rush of self-confidence. 'Any chance of a car as well?' I asked, my voice sounding a little higher pitched and less authoritative than I'd hoped.

'Good point!' said Lyn, and he scribbled a phone number down on a piece of paper. 'This fella owns a garage in Skewen. You can buy one off him with your first pay cheque, you cheeky bastard.'

As I drove out of Lyn's driveway in my dad's ageing banger, I realised that a line had been crossed. Rugby was my job now, and I owed it to myself, and to Neath, to knuckle down, train hard and keep the weight off. Although I also owed myself a little celebration first, so I gathered together some mates and headed down to Swansea for an all-you-can-eat Pizza Hut buffet. That was my equivalent of popping the cork from a champagne bottle.

When I signed that contract with Neath, it felt like I'd stepped through a portal into another world. Whereas my brother couldn't wait to leave the valley, to go to university and travel, I was content where I was. I might easily have been one of those people who never left the village they were born in. I never had big plans and dreams. But rugby put me on a path and allowed me to see the big, wide world.

I had a word with my old man to get an idea of the history and the culture around Neath. A lot of very good players had passed through that club. As a prop, Brian Williams set the benchmark. He was hard as nails. All these stories about him had passed into folklore, like the time he mangled his hand in a horrific farming accident, developed a massive infection, and then returned to play a fortnight later. Or the time he dislocated his shoulder and refused to leave the field. Or the time he refused to have stitches in a massive gash beneath his eye, because he thought he hadn't played well and didn't deserve it. Apparently, he just sat there in the bar drinking a pint while blood continued to trickle from the wound, dripping into his beer.

Signing for Neath as a prop brought with it certain expectations. You were supposed to be hard, mean, and willing to play through the pain barrier.

● ● ●

I soon discovered that you had to earn your respect at Neath. During my first ever session with the seniors, I put my bag down in the changing room. Moments later, big Gareth Llewellyn strode angrily in, scooped it up in his giant hands and slung it into the showers. The zip was open and my stuff flew everywhere, all over the wet, slimy floor. There were no words, or even a look. That was his way of saying, 'Never sit in my seat again.'

I realised quite quickly there was a hierarchy at Neath, and I was on the bottom rung of the ladder. Suitably chastened, I ended up getting changed in the shower while Rowland Phillips looked on, laughing uncontrollably. There was an order in the Gnoll changing room. The tight-head's seat was behind the door. But even when I became the established first choice, I never felt as though it was mine. I continued to defer to Andrew Millward, even when I was keeping him out of the team.

This hierarchy extended to the team bus as well. Years passed before I was allowed anywhere near the back. That was exclusively the domain of Llew, Brett Sinkinson and James Storey. The back of the bus is a sacred place, and you had to earn your right to sit there – through seniority, playing prowess, or being a kiss-ass. The Kiwi scrum-half Jason Spice told me he once offered to catch some balls for Sean Fitzpatrick during line-out practice at the Auckland Blues. The next week, Fitzy allowed him up the back of the bus with the likes of Craig Dowd and Zinzan Brooke. It was the proudest moment of his career.

I hate to disappoint you all, but I was never forced to go through an initiation at Neath. I'd heard the rumours, and was dreading the day, but mercifully, it never happened. I can't go into too much detail, because it's sacred, but many before me had been forced to 'kiss the turd'. It doesn't take much imagination to figure out what's involved there. But the one I feared the most was 'the gauntlet'. That involved you being stripped naked and crawling on your hands and knees from the front to the back of the bus, while the senior players kicked, punched and whipped you with belts. The last two boys to have done it were Kevin James and a guy called Dylan Pugh. Dylan went through as quiet as a mouse, and took the punishment. But Kev tried to fight back, and got an absolute beating. Richard Francis, the old back rower, was one of the worst. He was a farrier by trade and had big old hands with big knuckles. He used the belt buckle to good effect on Kev. Poor old 'Kipper' was battered and bruised for weeks afterwards.

His brother, Paul James, and I went to Bourgoin with the team once, when we weren't playing. We were thinking, 'Oh God! This is the day when it's going to be done.' The whole bus journey we were on edge – paranoid and twitching – but it never happened. We totally got away with it.

There were dressing-room rituals that had to be adhered to, though. No one was allowed to wear pants in the shower, you had to be butt naked at all times. And you also had to cover your arse, literally. If you didn't – and readers of a sensitive disposition may want to skip this bit – one of the boys would stick their finger up your backside. It all stemmed from an incident on the pitch during an Australian Rugby League game when a guy called John Hopoate was banned for twelve weeks for 'interfering' with an opponent. That was the polite way of saying he'd stuck his finger up his bum. So after that, if anyone at Neath neglected to cover their arse in the shower, they'd have the same treatment while the rest of the dressing room shouted 'HOPOATE!' in unison.

Paul and I joined at the same time, but he enjoyed a lot more respect than I did. He'd represented Wales at age grade, and his brother played for the club, whereas I was just a fat kid from Abercrave. Paul arrived with a reputation, whereas I had to develop one. The turning point for me came when we played Newport at a time when they had a gnarly old pack of forwards including Adrian Garvey, Simon Raiwalui and Rod Snow. I did well against Rod Snow – didn't take a backward step – and I think the old stagers like Llew started to look at me in a different light. They saw that I could hold my own against seasoned professionals.

Llew was the Godfather. He was very much in charge. During my first season I was put in a weights group with Allan Bateman, Barry Williams and Steve 'Jabba' Jones. I loved Allan Bateman, growing up, so it was like training with one of my idols. We'd do a session in the gym, then the fatties would go for a run in the Gnoll woods behind the ground. Afterwards, we'd all go for breakfast down Belly Busters in town. Ritters would keep a close eye on us, so I'd have to restrict myself to poached egg on toast. Bateman would have the works – full fry-up with extra chips – but he never put on so much as an ounce. It killed me. He and Andy Moore were, without question, the fittest blokes in the squad.

The second row, Andy Newman, was at the opposite end of the scale. We bonded immediately because he was another one who struggled with his weight. The year he signed, he was keen to make a good impression. The first day of training saw us doing brutal shuttle runs on Aberavon beach, and he decided to take a load of Pro Plus tablets to get him through. He had so much of it in his system, he was flying and was hardly panting after three lengths of the beach.

Steve Tandy was glaring at him and thinking, 'Who's this English prick, coming down here thinking he's hard, sprinting around, trying to impress the coaches?'

On his fourth length, Newman collapsed in an ungainly heap. He'd passed out.

Lyn and Rowland rushed over, panicked and started pouring Red Bull down his throat in a desperate attempt to rehydrate him. But the tablets had set his heart rate soaring, and the caffeine only made it worse. They called an ambulance, while Newman came to and started writhing around on the floor. The backs had been off doing their own thing but they sensed that something odd was going on, and started jogging over. Allan Bateman knew Andy well from Northampton, where they'd won a Heineken Cup together, so he was looking particularly concerned.

Sensing an opportunity for a prank, Rowland covered Newman's face before turning to Allan and saying, with a sombre expression, 'We've lost him, mate.'

Allan's face went white as a sheet.

Rowland kept it up. 'I'm really sorry, mate, but he's gone. His heart's stopped.'

Allan was frozen to the spot, on the verge of tears. An interminable amount of time seemed to pass before Rowland whipped the towel off to reveal Newman's beetroot face. He was very much alive, if a little the worse for wear.

'Only joking, butt!' shouted Rowland, before collapsing into fits of laughter.

He thought it was hilarious, but Allan wasn't particularly amused. And neither was Andy, who spent the next three days recovering in hospital.

Unlike today, when pretty much everyone has to be at a certain level, the differing levels of commitment at Neath were staggering. I'll resist naming names in the interests of preserving reputations, but the coaches would regularly have to drive to a certain player's house on a Monday, where they'd inevitably find him fast asleep, fully clothed, bathed in a pool of sick and on the threshold of a monumental hangover. They'd have to wake him up, drag him to training and prop him up on a bench in the gym. He'd be useless, but he'd always turn it on when match day arrived. Nobody would get away with it these days.

● ● ●

I'd like to dispel the notion that Neath was an insular club that didn't like outsiders. They welcomed everybody. James Storey was a prime example. He was a posh plummy-mouthed kid from Hertfordshire. The son of Stuart Storey, the BBC commentator. He was skinny as a toothpick, but hard as nails, and his background was no barrier. He was honorary Welsh, as far as we were concerned – part of the gang. As was everyone who wore the Welsh All Black jersey.

The older boys would go out of their way to look after you. Not in a sentimental way. But you knew out there on the pitch, they'd have your back. Many was the time that Gareth Llewellyn would send a punch through from the second row of the scrum if he thought the opposition loose-head was taking liberties with me. Those bonds were forged not just on the pitch and in the changing room, but in the clubs and bars of Neath, where we spent a lot of our spare time.

We'd always end up in the Duke of Wellington – a crazy rock venue in the centre of town. It was grimy and dirty, with blacked-out windows and peeling wallpaper. From the outside, you'd swear it was derelict. We had our Christmas parties there, all of which were hard-drinking, debauched occasions.

One year, Gareth Llewellyn and Andrew Millward came to blows after some pointless argument. Both were standing outside with their chests puffed out and their fists clenched, shouting blue murder at one another. But their appearance rather undermined their attempts at macho posturing. Llew was dressed as Rod Stewart, and 'Bully' was dressed as Paul Shane from *Hi-de-Hi!*. It didn't take long for them to cotton on to the absurdity of the situation, and within minutes normal drinking had resumed. Michael Jackson was the peacemaker, if I remember correctly.

My parents frowned upon my excessive drinking. My father's side of the family had a history of high blood pressure and high cholesterol, and he was big on healthy living as a result. They disapproved on two levels. Firstly, from a health point of view. And secondly, because they thought I was undermining my career as a rugby player by spending half my time blind drunk.

It came to a head one morning, the weekend before the Celtic League final. We'd beaten Ebbw Vale on the Saturday, and had embarked on an enormous session that ended with a lock-in at the Duke. I woke up under one of the tables, only to discover that the sun had already come up. Arriving sheepishly back at my parents' house, I was on the receiving end of an almighty ticking-off.

'What on earth are you doing out drinking until this time? You've got the Celtic League final next week. Have you got no sense of responsibility?'

They only calmed down when I told them Rowland had been there. They held him in such high regard that his presence persuaded them it couldn't have been as debauched and crazy as they'd imagined. It could have been, and it was. But I quit while I was behind.

Rowland, as you can probably tell, was at the heart of Neath RFC's social scene. As was James Storey. One of our pre-season training camps was down in St Davids, at the westernmost point of Wales. The first night began with us getting to know the locals at the rugby club, and ended at two in the morning with me spewing my guts up round the back of the clubhouse. Allan Bateman – my childhood hero – was rubbing my back and trying to comfort me. I crawled into my tent to try and sleep it off, only to be awoken in the early hours by one of my more 'exuberant' teammates revving up an Audi TT and doing handbrake turns and 'donuts' on the middle of St Davids rugby pitch. I don't think their groundsman was very happy.

When the sun came up, we all crawled out of our tents looking and feeling decidedly the worse for wear. Rowland decided the best way to blow off the cobwebs would be to organise a naked touch rugby tournament on the beach. It was quite a spectacle for all the early-morning ramblers, shuffling by on the coastal path with their Ordnance Survey maps and their packed lunches. Thirty-odd professional rugby players booting a ball around while stark bollock naked.

I certainly didn't feel like a 'professional'. I was living the dream. Most days, we'd be done training by around 11.30, and we'd just pile into one of the boys' houses and end up playing Tiger Woods golf on the PlayStation until around four in the afternoon. I was hanging out with Steve Tandy, Duncan Jones and Steve 'Jabba' Jones.

If it wasn't the games console, it was cards. Three-card brag was a favourite. If we got bored, we'd jump on the train down to Swansea and gorge ourselves at a restaurant called Paco's on the St Helen's Road. You could get a bowl of pasta, a portion of chips and a plate of lamb cutlets for under a tenner. Lyn once tried to bring in afternoon training sessions, which would have meant being back at the Gnoll for two in the afternoon. An internal revolt soon put paid to that.

● ● ●

During my first year at Neath, we nearly won the league. The final game was a massive derby against Swansea. If we'd won that, we'd have taken the title. But a Garin Jenkins-inspired All Whites beat us comfortably.

There were thousands of people there. The stand was full, and the entire bank was covered. Our fly-half, Lee Jarvis, scored within five minutes, but it started to unravel soon afterwards. Their front row was Garin Jenkins, Darren Morris and Ben Evans. All three internationals, and all three unrelenting with the banter.

Garin had everyone fired up and was right in my face: 'Come on, pup! Let's see what you got, pup!'

Their two second rows were huge as well – Tyrone Maullin and Lee Jones. It was a grizzly, nasty front five and we were outmuscled. Even their backs seemed tougher than our forwards that day. Llew got bumped off and knocked out by Scott Gibbs, while Rowland got dumped by Gavin Henson.

Despite losing, the match and the occasion gave me a real flavour of what playing professional rugby could be like. It remains one of my highlights in a Neath jersey.

CHAPTER 4

Regional Revolution

WHICHEVER way you look at it, I'm a walking contradiction. Most tight-head props are angry, aggressive alpha males. I'm laid-back and mellow, and have always preferred the shadows to the spotlight. My international colleague Gethin Jenkins is one of the most miserable blokes in rugby, and he channels that misery into his performances. His anger off the pitch translates into energy on it, and his opponents bear the brunt.

I may be less angry, but I'm no less committed. I'm not aggressive in everyday life, but I have endless reserves to call upon when I cross the whitewash. Woe betide anyone who thinks they're going to get an easy ride when they pack down against me. The scrummage is what defines me. And you can guarantee that when I'm squatting, bound on to my colleagues and staring down my opponent, I'm going to put every last ounce of fury and power into it. Don't be fooled by the cuddly image and the laid-back demeanour. When I need to be, I'm a machine. And if I drive your head into the turf, or smash you out of a ruck, you'll know about it.

That's my job. I don't play rugby to have an outlet for my inner rage – I don't have any inner rage – I play because I love to. And I play to win. If I hurt someone, it's collateral damage. An inevitable consequence of contact sport. It's not because I go out there wanting to inflict pain. You don't have to be a frothing-at-the-mouth, eyeballs-bulging psychopath to be a front rower.

Having said all this, my wife would prefer it if I did vent a little more. She sometimes calls me Trevor Jordache after the character from *Brookside* who buried bodies under the patio. Not because she thinks I'm a serial killer, but because I keep things bottled up. I hate confrontation, and I'm hopeless at arguing. Sometimes it's good to shout things out and clear the air, but my instinct is always to go quiet and retreat into my shell. It's a trait I've had since childhood, and not a very good one. I'm not one of those guys who'll ring my coach up in a rage after being dropped, demanding an explanation. Nicole has tried to goad me into it at times, because that's her nature. She's the feisty one in our relationship.

That aspect of my personality probably explains why I was largely indifferent to the regional rugby revolution that transformed the landscape in Wales overnight. A decision was made to reduce the number of professional sides from nine to five. The WRU, headed by its controversial chief executive, David Moffett, had decided that there was only enough money to support five sides. So either four would have to bite the dust, or the nine would have to merge into 'regions'. It caused untold heartbreak among fans, and huge fault lines appeared in the fabric of the game that remain to this day. As far as I was concerned, it was just a sign of progress and the ongoing evolution of the professional game. The English had stolen a march, and we needed to do something to catch up.

Much of what I knew about the regional revolution I read in the papers. Every week new mergers were being proposed, with the map of Wales constantly being drawn and redrawn along geographical and tribal lines. There were also murmurings of a 'development team' to be based in North Wales — a part of the country that's never really had much of a rugby identity — which the WRU was keen to exploit. As the weeks rolled by, I heard a few mutterings that I'd been shortlisted, along with Paul James and several others, to join that side in the North. I was playing for Wales Under 21s at the time, and was fairly chilled about the idea. I thought it'd be a good step for me.

But just as I was getting settled on that idea, I had a phone call from Lyn Jones saying that Swansea and Neath had agreed to merge to form the nascent 'Ospreys' and not only did they want me to be part of it, but they were offering me a substantial pay rise.

'Where do I sign?' was my eager response.

● ● ●

The official launch of the Ospreys was held — incongruously — at Revolution nightclub in Swansea. Scott Gibbs, the Swansea centre and celebrated Lion, was the poster boy. He and Shane Williams were paraded around in the new jerseys, but it all felt very low-key. The place was less than half full, and there was little in the way of razzmatazz. Roger Blyth, the Swansea chairman, spoke before opening up the floor to the public. There followed a deluge of angry inquiries about the shirt, almost all from dyed-in-the-wool Swansea fans. They probably had a point. It did look remarkably like the old Neath shirt. It was black, with a Maltese cross. There was an Osprey on the badge as well, which supposedly represented Swansea, but this wasn't appeasing the irate fans who thought they were being robbed of more than a century of history and tradition for the sake of some random, nebulous 'brand' that had precious little to do with the team they'd followed all their lives.

The presence of Scott Gibbs was the only thing that seemed to mollify them. He was worshipped by the St Helen's faithful, and his appearance gave the brand a credibility it may otherwise have lacked. As it happened, he retired a few months into the Ospreys' inaugural season. But his involvement with the launch was a shrewd move in getting the organisation off the ground. He was the natural choice as captain.

Swansea had gone through a tough old year, and a lot of their senior players had disappeared, so you could argue that the merger came at the right time for them. Two years earlier, when they'd beaten us in the final game of the season with that big horrible old pack, they'd taught us a lesson. But the following year they were a shadow of their former selves and we wiped the floor with them. From a playing perspective, they were the weaker partner, and the new club seemed to be made in the image of Neath rather than vice versa.

Jonathan Thomas and Huw Bennett were among those from Swansea to be offered contracts, but some of their more established players went elsewhere. Darren Morris, the burly Lions prop, went to Leicester, which gave me an easier route to the first team. That, coupled with the fact that Lyn was head coach, meant it was a much easier transition for the Neath boys. I didn't feel any sympathy towards the Swansea boys who missed out. With respect, they didn't have many players who would've got into the Neath team at the time. The decisions were rugby ones, not sentimental ones.

But it wasn't just a merger of the two teams. We signed from elsewhere as well. Three Bath players – Andy Williams, Elvis Seveali'i and Gavin Thomas – all came on board. They were good signings where we needed to strengthen. A few boys missed out, and that was difficult for them, but most of my mates who weren't selected picked up professional contracts elsewhere. Guys like Kevin James, Jabba and Lee Jarvis went to the Dragons. And the likes of Andy Moore, Allan Bateman and Brett Sinkinson were heading towards retirement anyway. So it didn't feel to me as though many had been left on the scrapheap.

The question I'm always asked is: how on earth could two clubs with such a historic rivalry suddenly merge and play under the same banner? Personally, I've never bought into that weird parochialism that can dominate Welsh rugby. Some of the older Neath boys had a much bigger issue with Llanelli than they did with Swansea. I was just excited about where the rugby was going. I didn't feel as though I was leaving Neath behind. On the contrary, I felt as though I was stepping up to the next level. Something needed to change. Welsh club rugby was struggling to keep pace with its European neighbours. The money from the Union was being spread too thinly. It needed to be concentrated in fewer teams so that more competitive squads could be assembled.

Neath had been humbled by Munster in the Celtic League final at the Millennium Stadium in 2003. Despite my spectacular consolation try, we went down 37–17, and the writing was on the wall. Our clubs just weren't good enough to compete with the Irish provinces.

The brave new dawn took a while to materialise. The first year of our existence was a massive uphill struggle, and at one point we endured a ten-game losing streak, including an embarrassing home defeat to Edinburgh in Europe. We were way off the pace, and certain players were made scapegoats. The likes of Gareth Llewellyn and Gavin Thomas were either 'released' or sacked, depending on your interpretation.

Then came easily the most poisonous and toxic episode in the regional saga – the demise of the Celtic Warriors, the merger that had been set up between Bridgend and Pontypridd. It was an uneasy marriage off the pitch, and money troubles led to it being wound up after one season. All these years on, it's still a festering wound in Welsh rugby. Fans throughout the South Wales Valleys feel utterly disenfranchised by what happened. One of the most fertile breeding grounds in Welsh rugby history – not to mention one of the country's most economically deprived areas – was robbed of a professional rugby team to support.

My sympathies went out to those fans. But from a purely selfish point of view, we were lucky that everything went tits-up with the Warriors. We snaffled some good-quality international players who made a massive difference to us. Nobody knew much about Ryan Jones at that point. He'd been in the shadow of Nathan Budgett at Bridgend, but his star was beginning to rise. He joined the Ospreys, along with Sonny Parker, Brent Cockbain and David Bishop.

The impact those guys gave us was enormous, and we were transformed from a ragtag bunch of failures to league champions the very next season.

● ● ●

As has become a theme in Ospreys' history, we flattered to deceive in Europe.

After a seven-game winning streak in 2004, which took us to the top of the league, we travelled to Castres with confidence. We didn't know much about them, but we were riding the crest of a wave. It didn't take much for us to be dumped unceremoniously back on shore.

They smashed us to pieces. They were too big, too powerful and too good. It was a sobering experience. Jonathan Thomas's punch on Mauricio

Reggiardo was about the only resistance we showed all night. It earned him a red card.

It was the start of an uneasy relationship with the Northern Hemisphere's top club rugby tournament. The Ospreys have never won the Heineken Cup. But, by God, we should have done. There were a number of seasons when we were right in the mix, none more so than in 2007/2008. Our squad was ridiculously good. Easily one of the best, if not the best in the competition. It was littered with internationals. Welsh, Irish, Scottish and – crucially – a number of All Blacks. And not just fringe All Blacks, who'd maybe won a cap or two, but genuine bona fide superstars like Marty Holah, Jerry Collins and Justin Marshall.

That year we faced Saracens in the quarter-finals. Two weeks earlier, we had absolutely wiped the floor with them in the Anglo-Welsh Cup semi-final in front of 40,000 spectators at the Millennium Stadium. Gavin Henson had had one of those games where everything he touched turned to gold. Andy Farrell – the high-profile Rugby League signing – was his opposite number, and Gav made him look like an amateur. Farrell came with a reputation as a hardman, but Gav floored him with a brutal hand-off on his way to the try line early in the second half. It was one of four tries we scored on the way to a 30–3 demolition.

So we travelled to Watford a fortnight later thinking we just had to turn up. It was the wrong attitude. Their flanker, Richard Hill, was hugely influential and dragged his team over the line. He seemed to be in every ruck and maul, chucking his arms in, slowing the ball down and making tackle after tackle. We never got into our stride, and they won 19–10.

We were dumped out of Europe prematurely again. It was unforgivable.

Wales had won the Grand Slam the previous month with a squad loaded with Ospreys. Thirteen of us had started the game against England, so you could argue that the Ospreys – bolstered as we were with our All Blacks – were stronger than the Welsh national side.

Lyn went berserk afterwards and gave us the mother of all bollockings. I'd never seen him so angry. But I struggled to take him seriously because he reminded me so much of Bryn Cartwright from the Welsh film *Twin Town*. (Lyn was mad for that film. Whenever we had a long bus journey with Neath or the Ospreys, he'd have it on repeat. And he could quote it word for word.) The Saracens players were walking past our dressing room, whooping and hollering.

Lyn stood by the door shouting, 'Fuuuuuuck you!' just like Bryn Cartwright. It was an unexpected bit of comic relief amid all the misery and hand wringing.

But in all seriousness, I thought he was going to rip a wall down. He'd put a lot into the Ospreys, and all his passion and frustration came gushing out in a torrent of rage.

I wasn't singled out for attention on that occasion. But another time, when we'd played Ulster, he pinned the blame for a poor first-half display squarely on me. He told me I was playing like a 'fucking c**t', took a run up at a stack of water bottles on the changing-room floor, and swung his leg violently towards them. Several bottles rained down on me.

It wasn't quite an Alex Ferguson hairdryer moment, but he got his point across.

● ● ●

I wouldn't say I was scared of Lyn. But because he was so unpredictable, you never knew quite where you stood with him. He was a master of playing with people's heads. And because he was the boss, you were never sure how to react.

After one particularly good victory over the Scarlets, all the boys were in the shower and Lyn came in to shake our hands and congratulate us on the victory. He went round us all individually, looking po-faced and saying, 'Good game, good game.' When he got to Brent Cockbain, instead of shaking his hand he just reached down for his private parts and gave his todger a vigorous shake!

It was Brent's first season, and he had no idea how to respond. I guess it's what all good managers do – maintain a line between themselves and their employees – but Lyn's methods were a little more maverick than most.

But for all his mind games and eccentricities, he was a tremendous coach. He thought so far outside the box, it's unreal. People talk now about how innovative the Ireland coach, Joe Schmidt, is. How he can conjure up a specific game plan to target every opponent Ireland faces. Lyn was doing that twenty years ago. He was such a creative thinker when it came to analysing weaknesses and exploiting them.

Neath invented the line-out move that won New Zealand the World Cup in 2011. You know the one I'm talking about – the ball's won at the back, and passed back down to the middle for an onrushing scrum-half, or prop, to score. Duncan Jones scored about ten tries through that move, and then the world saw New Zealand do it in the World Cup final. I'm telling you now, Lyn invented it. It's exactly the same move that we were doing at Neath, ten years earlier. It's all about precision with Lyn. A move like that, when executed well, looks incredibly simple, but it's not. There are so many elements that need to be synchronised. A dummy here, a block there. The scrum-half would run a hidden line before emerging through the gap, which had been created almost by illusion. There's so much attention to detail, and some of the detail can seem so small, so peripheral, that it doesn't really matter. But it really does.

Precision and repetition were the buzzwords. What looked spontaneous on the field would have been practised with military zeal over and over again. We had about five special moves like that. And we'd drill them, and drill them and drill them – until we could do them with our eyes closed.

One was called 'Malta Elvis'. It was incredibly complex and involved numerous dummies and decoy runners. But its main aim was simple: get the ball to Shane Williams so he could have a crack at the fatties. It required such precision that we had to do it over and over again. And don't get me wrong, it could be an absolute pain in the arse. But when you pulled it off in the game, it was immensely satisfying. Things have changed since those days, and there isn't as much emphasis on developing and honing skills any more. Nowadays, it's all about using brawn to bust through defences, rather than using your brain to unpick them. It's a real shame.

Lyn invented moves based on deception as well as skill. He'd seen some American football film where a fat blocker wanders aimlessly across the field to act as a distraction. He developed his own version of it, called 'milkman'. We'd have a scrum in the middle of the field, and our front row would deliberately hold the opposition's down after the ball had been released. James Bater would then just wander, seemingly aimlessly, towards the touchline. Our back row would fold hard around and suck their defence in tight, whereupon our scrum-half would launch the ball out to an unmarked Bater who could saunter unopposed over the try line. It was genius.

Now it's more just 'run hard down the middle'. If you've got the right personnel – like a Jamie Roberts-style crash-ball centre – then you expect it to work, and it is effective. But you pay less attention to the opposition. You'll employ the same tactics, regardless of who you're playing. With

Lyn, it was much more like a game of chess. He'd study the opposition and come up with specific plays to beat them.

He was like a matador – taunting the opposition until the opportunity arose to plunge the knife in. But it *was* all about winning. So while Lyn enjoyed the cerebral aspects of coaching, there were times when pragmatism would win out.

The year before the Ospreys were formed, Neath played Llanelli away. Lyn decided that in order to beat them, we'd have to play a really boring, territorial pattern. He instructed us to kick the ball away every third phase. Every time we were in possession and the ball went to ground for a third time, Shaun Connor or Lee Jarvis would be standing either side of the ruck and one of them would pummel it in the corner. We were lambasted for employing such a conservative style, but we won the game. In Lyn's eyes, that was all that mattered.

His rugby brain is incredible. But he's almost too much of a maverick to ever coach the national side. The WRU has always been fairly conservative in their appointments, and – like Carwyn James in the seventies – he's probably considered a square peg in a round hole.

● ● ●

Sean Holley was a big influence on me as well. I was chuffed when he joined the Ospreys because he'd taught me at college, and we'd got on well. Ryan Jones aside, he's comfortably the cheesiest man on TV. But he really knows his rugby, and studies it to a forensic level. He was the good cop to Lyn's bad cop. Some people criticised him for being too 'pally'. But believe me, if he had to give someone a bollocking (Gavin Henson more often than not), he would. And they'd take it, because he commanded a lot of respect.

His head is a directory of rugby moves and tactics. He was 'Mr Osprey', living and breathing club rugby, and he inspired a real sense of loyalty and brotherhood in his troops. He understood that success is based on a firm foundation of friendship and trust. It annoys me that some question his coaching credentials because he never played for Wales. José Mourhino and Graham Henry never played football or rugby to any level, yet they're arguably the best coaches in their respective sports. It is not a prerequisite to have played at the top level in order to coach at the top level.

Sean Holley knows far more about the modern game than most of the so-called pundits who are paid to critique it. When he does his media work, Sean is speaking from a position of intimate, relevant and – most importantly – contemporary knowledge. He's a scholar of the game, and people who genuinely know their rugby will understand that he's a class act.

● ● ●

The European defeat that rankles the most was the one in San Sebastián against Biarritz. They were a good side, but ours was way better on paper. Our back row contained the Welsh captain, Ryan Jones, and two All Blacks in Marty Holah and Jerry Collins. You'd struggle to get a better unit than that, and JC was on fire at the time. Alun Wyn Jones and Jonathan Thomas were in the second row, and it was Paul James, Huw Bennett and myself in the front row. We dominated that game for long periods, outscored them by four tries to three, and had a number of opportunities to win it. Dan Biggar missed the drop goal at the end. And there was a degree of controversy over whether we should have had a penalty because their scrum-half, Dimitri Yachvili, appeared to have knocked on deliberately. As in 2008, if we'd won we'd have had a home draw in the semi-final, and could well have gone further.

I cannot fathom why we didn't do better in Europe, but I strongly refute the suggestion that we were a bunch of superstars who didn't gel as a team. We were labelled the 'Galácticos' and the 'Chequebook Charlies' of Welsh rugby, the inference being that we were a bunch of mercenaries, and that the club had no soul. It was a load of rubbish. In the 2010 season we beat Leicester with a front five of me, Richard Hibbard, Paul James, Alun Wyn Jones and Jonathan Thomas, all of whom had come up through the Ospreys system and been there from the start. There was, and remains, an emphasis on developing players from within. And the signings we made from outside the region were all, without exception, positive ones.

The spirit in that squad was brilliant, and it was driven to a large extent by the foreigners. They were not journeymen coming over to top up their pensions; they were first-class performers capable of elevating the standard of the entire team. Filo Tiatia was a massive influence. He was almost forty when he came over, and was signed essentially as a big lump who could come on during the last twenty minutes of a game and act as a battering ram. He turned out to be so much more than that. He was a brilliant bloke, and everyone looked up to him. He was the only player I knew who never whinged about the coaches or about training. He took an interest in everyone, in their families and their well-being, and acted as a mentor to the youngsters coming through. I cannot speak highly enough of him.

Marty Holah was exactly the same. A bit quieter perhaps, but a legend of a bloke. He won thirty-six caps for the All Blacks – and would have had so many more, had a certain Richie McCaw not been born at the same time as him. Playing alongside him made me realise just how good Richie McCaw actually is.

And Jerry Collins was an absolute human wrecking ball. No one loved a drink more than him, and he was a bit loose after a few pints. But it never, ever affected his performance. Some players who love the booze will never reach the highest level because their drinking habits will always impinge on their performance. If you've had one too many on a night out, it's rare you'll be able to put 100% in on the training paddock. JC never had such problems. He'd put away a skinful and head for his bed as the sun was coming up, but he'd always be at training on time. And his performance levels never dipped below sensational. I honestly don't know how he did it.

Justin Marshall was a flash bastard whose aloof manner rubbed a lot of people up the wrong way, but I liked him. Beneath the facade, he was the ultimate team player. You'd struggle to find a more competitive animal. Mike Phillips would run him close, but Marshy's hatred of losing made him possessed at times.

The two of them clashed during the Anglo-Welsh semi-final at the Millennium Stadium when the Ospreys played the Blues. Phillsy had signed for us for the following season, and Marshy was keen to let him know who was boss. He got inside Mike's head and subjected him to eighty minutes of mental torture. It kicked off between them in the tunnel after the final whistle. Marshy kept his cool and offered to shake Mike's hand, but Mike just dropped his shoulder and slammed into him. I love Mike to bits, but he lost the mental battle with Marshy that day, big time.

It was rare that anyone got the better of Marshy. He was uber-confident, as you'd expect from someone who won more than eighty caps for New Zealand. When he first arrived at the Ospreys, we spent most of our pre-season working out how to play off him. He became the pivot for the entire side. He'd take the training sessions and would be confidently barking orders to the rest of the squad, most of whom he'd only known for five minutes. He'd say, 'Right, if there's a ruck here, I'll run here, and I want you to run here, and at this angle.' He always insisted on having four options around him, to keep the opposition guessing. He couldn't actually kick or pass that well, and he'd lost a yard of pace, but he was a class act who could read the game better than anybody I'd played with.

His innate understanding of the game now shines through in his commentary. His knowledge is exhaustive and bang up to date. I watch a lot of rugby, and cannot stand lazy commentators – people who played decades ago and have made no effort to study the way the game has changed, or how the laws have evolved. You can't accuse Marshy of that. What you can accuse him of is poor timekeeping. He used to drift around in his own world, oblivious to the rules and regulations governing everyone else at the club. He seemed beyond reproach at times, like a little emperor floating around among his fawning subjects.

He was often late for team meetings, but instead of sneaking in apologetically and taking his seat at the back, he'd burst in noisily with a tray of coffees for everyone, taking the sting out of any bollocking that may have been coming his way. He was truly on his own.

● ● ●

If the 'Galácticos' label always stuck in the craw, the other label that was pinned on the Ospreys was one that couldn't be denied. That of the glamour boys! There was a certain contingent among the backs that were partial to their fake tan, their grooming products and their coloured boots. As a fully paid-up member of the front-row union, I found this totally unpalatable. The so-called 'Fab Four' consisted of Shane Williams, James Hook, Lee Byrne and Gavin Henson. Henson was the worst offender and copped a lot of flak because he didn't look like a rugby player was supposed to.

He got away with it because he was the most professional bloke I'd ever worked with. He'd come in every day with his plastic containers full of food that he'd cooked and weighed the night before, and he'd have all the right drinks and protein shakes for his hydration and nutrition. But off the pitch he'd continually let himself down. He's just one of those blokes who's a right pain in the arse when he's drunk. He was 'Gav', so people would always want their photo taken with him on nights out, and occasionally he'd lose his rag and refuse to oblige. And then things would turn nasty. I lost count of the number of times that fans would be invited to a WRU official dinner as an apology for the way Gavin had behaved towards them in public. People would complain about him, and that was the Union's way of trying to appease them.

To me, he could have been one of the all-time greats. And not just a Welsh great, but one of the finest players the world's ever known. He was big and strong and awkward, and he had a massive boot. And his individual skills were dazzling. When he was 'on', he was untouchable. But his problem was that he only played in fits and starts. He was inspired by the big one-off occasion, but would get bored by the drudgery of a long season. When we played Harlequins in Europe one year, he'd made plans to go out in London after the game and was pumped about his night out in the Big Smoke. That excitement translated into the way he played. He was utterly sublime, and orchestrated a fine win for us. He was the best player on the field by a country mile, because he had his 'game head' on. That was the way his brain was wired. If he was excited and pumped up, he'd play a blinder. If he was down and distracted, he'd go missing.

He was seduced by the media, and when he was in the public eye Gav the personality began to eclipse Gav the rugby player. But he always kept himself in great shape. When he came back into the 2011 World Cup squad, he was still a quality player. But he left halfway through one of the Polish training camps to go and film the Channel 5 reality show *The Bachelor*. Warren Gatland had sanctioned his early departure because he'd arranged the filming before his Wales recall, but it did give you some indication of his priorities.

I'd known him since the Under 21s and, speaking to him out in Poland, it was obvious that he'd really matured. He'd become a dad by then, and I was about to have a little girl myself. He spoke so tenderly about fatherhood and was really generous with his advice. It was at times like that that I realised how different the real Gav was from his public persona.

His biggest mistake was writing an autobiography off the back of the 2005 Grand Slam. He was brutally honest about his feelings and upset a lot of his colleagues. He was summoned to a players' meeting at the Wales HQ, to explain himself. Gareth Thomas laid into him, accusing him of disrespecting his teammates and undermining their achievements. Gav just seemed bewildered at the fuss it had caused. He'd missed out on a World Cup spot in 2003 to Garan Evans, and had said some fairly unpleasant things about Garan in the book. If you miss out to another player, it's not really the done thing to direct your anger towards them, particularly in print. It was naivety rather than arrogance on his part. But whatever the motivation, it unleashed an undercurrent of resentment towards him that lingered for some time.

● ● ●

While Gav was the most conspicuous of the Fab Four, he was by no means the only offender. Shane Williams has had some shocking haircuts over the years, and his teeth got suspiciously whiter and straighter within a few days of him winning the IRB World Player of the Year award. There must have been a cash bonus involved, because when he returned he'd had these veneers fitted that made him look like a short Welsh Freddie Mercury.

James Hook was another. He arrived from Neath skinny as a rake – about seven stone soaking wet – but was an amazing player. He *is* an amazing player. The way he's been treated by Wales amounts to nothing less than a travesty. Most international teams would kill for a player of his quality, but Wales seem to have no faith in him. There are rumours that he's upset someone on the inside, but if he has I know nothing about it. And to be perfectly honest, I can't imagine that's the case. He's one of the nicest blokes you could hope to meet, and isn't remotely confrontational. For my money, Wales have missed out enormously and allowed his talent to be squandered. (The same happened with Dwayne Peel – he and Mike Phillips in the same squad would be the envy of most other teams in the world, yet he was mysteriously discarded when he moved to Sale.) Hooky's natural instinct is to play. Any coach worth his salt should harness that and exploit it. Instead, he's been ordered to curb it and forced to play in a more proscribed, conservative way. I wish I could reveal why his inter-national career has stalled so badly. But I'm as mystified and frustrated as the fan on the street.

Lee Byrne was a lover of the fake tan, but you could forgive him that indulgence because he was so bloody good. For a time, there was no other full-back that could touch him. But for all his ability and courage, he didn't half milk his injuries. He'd tackle anything that moved and launch himself skyward to claim high balls with no regard for his safety. But if he took a bang, he'd react as though he'd been shot. On one occasion, after an awkward landing, he convinced himself his head was stuck in the ground. Our physio, Brian O'Leary, had run on to the pitch to tend to his imaginary injury and was met by a hysterical Byrney screaming that he couldn't move his head. A bemused Brian tried to reassure him calmly that there was absolutely nothing wrong with him. Suffice to say, within five minutes Byrney was up and about, carving it up in his usual manner.

That was Byrney in a nutshell. Great player. Total drama queen. And without doubt the best full-back I've ever played with. He could kick the ball for miles, never dropped a catch, and could cut an angle better than anyone. What he lacked in out-and-out pace he made up for with his mesmeric running lines. For a magical period of about three years, he and Shane shared a telepathic understanding. They were an irresistible combination for the Ospreys and for Wales.

If those two weren't enough, we then signed Tommy Bowe who became an absolutely phenomenal player. That back three – with him, Shane and Byrney – was the best I've played with, by some distance. Bowie's an incredible footballer. People talk about George North now as being the archetypal modern winger, but he's got a way to go before he can be spoken about as being in Tommy's class.

If you need evidence of quite how valuable he is, think of the Lions tour in 2013. He missed the first test with a broken hand, and everybody assumed his tour was over. Most players with the same injury would have been sent home. But he was so valued by the management that they kept him on tour, and did everything within their power to help him recover. Despite his hand being heavily bandaged he replaced Alex Cuthbert in the team for the second test. An injured Tommy Bowe is better than most fully fit wingers in world rugby.

And in among all those amazing backs was Andrew Bishop – a ridiculously underrated player, and as important to that team as any of them. He may not be lightning quick, but even the most elusive runners would struggle to get past him. He was our defensive rock, and would act as a bodyguard to whoever was playing ten, whether it was Dan Biggar or

James Hook. If the guys around him were the glamour boys, he was the polar opposite. Pound for pound, he's the hardest bloke I know.

I'm running the risk of Alun Wyn Jones never speaking to me again by revealing what I'm about to reveal. But here we go.

Alun Wyn gets a bit 'playful' when he's drunk. He's a big man and enjoys a wrestle and a bear hug. It's almost always a show of affection but sometimes he gets overly tactile. During one of our infamous fancy-dress Christmas parties, he started picking on Bish, who was dressed as Zorro. Alun Wyn was Captain America, if I remember rightly. Zorro politely told Captain America to back off, wounding his pride in the process. Alun Wyn squared up to Bish in what turned out to be an unwise display of machismo. A few of us turned away, anticipating that things might get a bit spicy. Now, bear in mind that Bish is five eleven, and about fourteen stone. Alun Wyn is six foot seven, and more than eighteen stone. Most people would back down in a confrontation with a man of those dimensions.

Not Bish. With the speed and precision of a pugilist, he unleashed a single punch that landed squarely on Alun Wyn's jaw.

He dropped to the floor like a sack of spuds. It was a remarkable sight.

Within seconds, Al recovered his senses, and gingerly returned to his feet. Within ten minutes, they were at the bar together, hugging and buying each other drinks.

I learned a valuable lesson that night. Don't mess with the Bish.

● ● ●

So we had a team brimming with world-class talent, but we couldn't deliver on the highest stage. We had a big ugly pack and got used to bullying teams in the PRO12. Our scrum was a real weapon and could be relied upon as a points machine. We'd squeeze teams up front, forcing them to give away penalties. But when we came up against big teams in France that refused to be bullied, we often came up short. That Heineken Cup quarter-final in Biarritz was a prime example. We looked like we were playing touch rugby at times, carving it up through the three-quarters. But we allowed ourselves to be drawn back into a forward-oriented game, and we lost.

That really hurt, because our identity was very much based around our scrum and our forward power. Other PRO12 teams used to hate playing us because our pack was such a nasty unit. That was particularly the case around 2008, when the likes of Richard Hibbard emerged from the ranks. He'd always been a lazy bugger, but he started to take it a lot more seriously then. Him and me are cut from the same cloth. We've spent our entire careers battling the bulge, and he's always used me as his point of reference. Whenever a coach has been on his back about shifting a few pounds, his defence has always been that he's lighter than me (he rarely was, by the way). What he always fails to realise is that he's a hooker and I'm a prop – I'm allowed to be heavier! – although our forwards coach, Jonathan Humphreys, always referred to him as the 'middle prop', which is perhaps more accurate.

An awful lot of credit needs to go to Jonathan Humphreys, or 'Humph' as he's universally known. He changed everything when he arrived from Bath. My philosophy, my technique, my entire outlook was reshaped by Humph. I was always a decent scrummager, but he made me a world-class scrummager. When he took over as forwards coach, I had twenty-odd caps for Wales. But he identified a number of deficiencies in my game, the biggest of which was lack of confidence.

We started from the ground up. The so-called 'hit and chase', when the opposition front rows come together, is a massive psychological battle.

It's been de-powered now, with the changes in the law, but back then, it was a key way to establish dominance. I wasn't being anywhere near aggressive enough in Humph's eyes. He encouraged me to use my size and bulk to smash into my opposite number and destabilise their scrum from that first moment of contact. I used to go 'across' the hooker and scrummage at an angle. He wanted me to scrummage straight and square, like New Zealanders do. Humph worked tirelessly on it, poring over videos and picking out tiny little nuances here and there to help tweak and improve things over time.

There's a real science to correct scrummaging, and he's a professor of it. It's all about the process, about doing things precisely and in order. One: half crouch. Two: chest down. Three: head up, and so on. It's all about physics – about motion and resistance. But Humph realised that teaching a fatty from Abercrave with two GCSEs about biomechanics was probably a bit overambitious, so he simplified things. He translated everything into Adam-speak.

We weren't averse to dirty tricks, as well as being a technically efficient scrummaging side. Ian 'Ianto' Evans liked playing the role of enforcer but was often too blatant or clumsy to get away with it. Before a game against Leicester in 2005, Lyn Jones had identified their scrum-half, Harry Ellis, as a danger man and had given us specific instructions to 'block him' when he came round the scrum. It was clearly the job of a flanker or a Number 8. But Ianto, being Ianto, thought, 'Brilliant! I'll take care of that.'

A scrum was set, and Andy Newman was in the second row with Ianto. All of a sudden, Ianto's leg came snaking round Newman's and he unleashed a karate-style kick on Harry Ellis's leg. He caught him in the knee, and injured him quite badly. He was forced off, and the game descended into a predictably bad-tempered affair.

That illustrated Ianto's nasty streak – and he is prone to major lapses of judgement on the pitch – but if you can forgive him those, he's one of the sweetest, funniest blokes you'll meet. A genuine one-off.

For two guys who've played alongside each other for so long, he and Alun Wyn Jones could not be more different. On game day, Alun Wyn gets himself firmly in the zone. He barely speaks, sitting stock still in the changing room and staring into space. Ianto is a bundle of nervous, childish energy and loves winding Alun Wyn up. Before one game, his iPod was on shuffle in the changing room, and Queen's 'I Want To Break Free' came on. Ianto leapt up and started dancing in front of everyone, pretending to be Freddie Mercury in drag. He was camping it up big-style, doing everything he could to get a reaction out of Alun Wyn. But his second-row partner was having none of it, doing his level best to ignore him.

So Ianto upped the ante, picking up a water bottle and pretending it was a feather duster. He started dancing really closely to Alun Wyn, prodding him with the bottle, tickling him, taunting him. We were all tittering away, but Al wasn't remotely amused. Ianto was relentless, and determined to break him. He eventually got his reaction when Alun Wyn stood bolt upright and stormed out, shaking his head in derision.

On another occasion, I saw him knock himself out on a ceiling. We were walking out of the tunnel at the Liberty Stadium ahead of a game and he was his usual hyperactive self.

'I'm bouncing today, Bomb! Well up for it.' He was jogging on the spot and shadow boxing, unable to keep still.

Next thing I know, he does a tuck jump, smacks his head on the ceiling and collapses in a heap on the floor. His spindly legs just buckled underneath him. The whole team were howling with laughter as he returned to his senses and started scrabbling around on the floor. I'm not sure he should have played. He was all over the shop for the first ten minutes or so, and was clearly concussed. Had he been knocked out on the pitch, the medics would have insisted he came off. But the medics don't hang around in the tunnel on the off-chance that someone knocks himself out doing a tuck jump. Idiot.

During that same game against Leicester in 2005, Ben Kay was their line-out caller. He was a World Cup winner, and a second row of considerable repute. The kind of guy who commanded respect. Lyn Jones had identified him as a threat and tasked Ianto with the job of man-marking him. Lyn considered him a bit of a 'shithouse' – a coward, for want of a better word – a great technician, but not a hardman.

So throughout the game, whenever Ianto was standing next to Kay in a line-out, he'd declare loudly in his deep Aberdare accent, 'It's all right, boys. I've got the shithouse.'

Kay was clearly bewildered, but he didn't help his cause by wearing yellow gloves, which allowed Ianto to vary his banter.

During the second half it was, 'It's all right, boys. I've got the boy with the Marigolds on.' Vintage Ianto.

● ● ●

There was a bunch of us at the Ospreys who were really close. Myself, Ianto, Hibbard, Paul James aka 'Assey', and Alun Wyn Jones.

We'd all play hell with Alun Wyn. He's got this image as an intensely serious, moody bloke who gives little away. But if you get beneath that outer shell, you'll realise he's a big softie. Within that group, he's an easy target. But only us lot could get away with ribbing him the way we do. If anyone else said the things to him that we do, he'd get a massive cob on and either storm off or start a fight. But our relationship's so close, we can get away with anything.

To most rugby fans and journalists, he's a total enigma, but I'd defend him to the hilt. He's my best mate, and I was best man at his wedding. Anyone who thinks he's a psychopath and has no affectionate side just needs to see him with my daughter, Isla. He's the soppiest bloke on earth in the company of children. Isla's a massive *Toy Story* fan, and for her third birthday he turned up dressed as Buzz Lightyear. He hadn't told us he was going to do it – he just took it upon himself, because he knew how much she'd love it. And he was right. She was absolutely made up.

And contrary to his public image, he can take the piss out of himself.

We always joke that he was the real Lions captain in 2013, and that he's the real Wales captain. That's not to disrespect Sam Warburton in any way, but Alun Wyn is such a towering influence that he's seen by many to be the unofficial captain. So on his stag do in London, we dressed him up as Sam Warburton, with a headband and a Number 7 jersey. He was clearly uncomfortable with it, because he didn't want it to be seen as disrespectful, but Ianto and I thought it was the funniest thing ever.

Hibs and Assey have got an extreme love-hate relationship, like an old married couple. They argue all the time about anything and everything. Especially if it's to do with something manual, like renovating the house or fixing the car. They're both alpha males in that respect. They'll curse and swear, and push and shove, and it usually ends with Assey storming off and calling Hibs a fat prick.

I'm the arch manipulator, sitting there quietly, pushing their buttons and laughing inwardly when their anger escalates. But they love each other. They'll never admit it because they're too macho for that, but they bloody love each other.

● ● ●

While we always flattered to deceive in Europe, we pretty much dominated the PRO12, certainly from a Welsh perspective. Until Leinster won the title in 2014, we were the most successful side in the history of the competition, with four titles.

The one I remember most fondly was the first one, in 2005. Wales had won the Grand Slam a few weeks earlier, and we played Edinburgh at the Gnoll. It was packed to the rafters, in a way it hadn't been since the halcyon days with Neath, and the atmosphere was raucous and hostile. At the final whistle, the entire crowd spilled on to the field, and Barry Williams was hoisted high by the fans as he held the trophy aloft. We'd technically won the title with two weeks to spare, but that last match still had the feel of a cup final.

We did it again two years later, by beating Borders up there on the final day, but it was a strangely muted occasion. Borders were being wound up as a professional entity, so it was their last ever game. Their hearts weren't in it, and the crowd was fairly lacklustre. We had to catch a flight home within hours of the final whistle. By the time we got home, we were too knackered to celebrate. The highlight of that particular season was beating Australia under Paul James's captaincy.

The other two titles were in the era of the play-offs, when you had to win a 'cup final' tie played at the home of the top seeds. On both occasions we had to go to Leinster, in Dublin, who were a real force during that period. The first one, in 2010, was Filo Tiatia's last game, and we desperately wanted to send him off with some silverware. That was also the year we'd been knocked out of Europe by Biarritz, so it was important that we redeemed ourselves domestically. We were up against it, because Leinster hadn't lost at home for nearly two years, and they'd won their last six matches against us. But we were confident and scored two tries in the first half through Lee Byrne and Tommy Bowe. The second half was a little more tense, as Leinster came at us. But our defence held firm and we kept our try line intact to win 17–12.

The fourth title, in 2012, was really special. Leinster had won the European Cup two years running and were overwhelming favourites. We put ourselves under pressure in the first half by conceding a silly try from a kick-off. And as the half progressed, tempers began to flare. We tried to attack them through our scrum, and for long periods it was working. We were camped on their line at one point, and had five attempts at a pushover try. Each time, the scrum was reset. Ryan Jones was making increasingly desperate pleas to the referee to award a penalty try, but they were falling on deaf ears. As far as we were concerned, Leinster were deliberately collapsing the scrum. On the sixth attempt, I slipped and ended up with my face in the turf. Penalty Leinster. Ryan was fuming, and his flurry of expletives as we jogged off for half-time led to a bit of a scuffle in the tunnel with Leinster's captain, Leo Cullen.

In the second half our centre, Ashley Beck, took the game by the scruff of the neck. His career has been cruelly interrupted by injuries, and he's spent long spells on the sidelines having painful operations on his hips, which means he can't always train at 100%. But he's a special talent and he was on fire that day. His try put us back in the game. And then the little man, Shane Williams, bust open his box of tricks. His first try gave us hope but his second, three minutes from time, was unbelievable. He'd scored the last international try of his career that December against Australia in the last play of the game, and here he was, doing it again in his last ever game for the Ospreys. It was an outstanding bit of play and got us to within a point of Leinster at 29–30.

But because Shane had appeared on his opposite wing, the score was wide out on the right, and it left Dan Biggar with a devilishly difficult conversion. It was one of the best pressure kicks I've ever witnessed.

Right up there with Gavin Henson's against England in 2005. It couldn't have been closer to the touchline, but he just slotted it, cool as you like.

It was Steve Tandy's first title after he'd taken over as head coach, and he deserves an enormous amount of credit for that.

● ● ●

It's the no-nonsense attitude at the Ospreys that's made them the best Welsh side in the regional era. The environment there does not have any patience for whingers and moaners – or 'energy sappers', as we call them. If anybody starts to play up, Steve Tandy or Alun Wyn Jones will give them a boot up the arse.

There needs to be a hierarchy in rugby squads. Players have to respect the coach and abide by his rules, otherwise mutiny is never far away. The Ospreys have always had a strong creed and sense of brotherhood that the other regions have lacked. Selfish or egotistical behaviour has never been tolerated. The philosophy has always been to develop from within, and to pay as much attention to a man's character as to his talent. The next generation of forwards like Lloyd Ashley and James King may not be the world's best rugby players, but they're workhorses and athletes who'll give 100% every time they pull on the jersey.

In addition to the talent coming through the academy, they've made some increasingly shrewd signings. Purse strings have been tightened considerably in recent years in a bid to balance the books. Instead of blowing the budget on marquee players like your Marty Holahs or your Justin Marshalls, they've bought in hard-grafting Canadians like Tyler Ardron and Jeff Hassler. Guys who no one had heard of two years ago, and who won't be breaking the bank, but who have come in and done a fantastic job.

No one can deny the level of success we enjoyed. Yes, we under-achieved in Europe, but to win four PRO12 titles is no mean feat. The notion propounded in some sections of the press that it's a weak league that has been treated with derision by the Irish is a total nonsense. Yes, those sides may have rotated their squads over the years, and saved their big names for the plum fixtures in Europe, but they had such strength in depth that even their so-called 'second string' sides were tough to beat.

I'd back the Irish provinces against English clubs most of the time. There's been a snobbish dismissal of the league from the English press, because it doesn't have the same amount of TV money as the Aviva Premiership, and it doesn't get the same amount of coverage. It's led to a lazy assumption that it's an inferior league. It's not. The rugby is of equal quality to the English Premiership, and Ireland's domination of the Heineken Cup for several years is testament to that.

So while I have a lingering, grudging respect for what the Ospreys have achieved, there's no doubt that my decade-long association with them ended on a sour note. I was coming out of contract at the end of the 2013/2014 season, and I was keen to resign. But this period coincided with one of the ugliest 'civil wars' in Welsh rugby history.

The Welsh Rugby Union and the four regions were at loggerheads over issues like funding and player release, and the regions were refusing to sign a new participation agreement with the Union. It dragged on and on, and became increasingly ugly and bad-tempered. The whole thing was being played out in the media, and neither side was doing much to preserve its dignity.

My time here was not to end the way I wanted it to.

CHAPTER 5

Wales

'WHAT would you do if the ball was at the back of the ruck, and you were the first player to arrive?'

'Um, I'd protect it. Seal it off.'

'Why wouldn't you pass it?'

It was a simple question. And I'd got it wrong. That was the first conversation I had with Steve Hansen. He was the Wales head coach, a man known for his gruff demeanour and brusque manner. I was at a Wales squad session just before Christmas 2002, looking to make an impression, and I'd made the wrong one. It was only a minor thing but it annoyed me.

When I was playing all those years for Abercrave, I never thought I'd play for Wales. I was nowhere near good enough. But during that 2002/2003 season, I'd become the established first choice tight-head for Neath. Just before Christmas, I had a phone call asking me to attend an extended Wales squad session. It was beyond my wildest dreams. I – a fat prop from the Swansea Valley – had somehow risen far enough through the ranks to be considered one of the best players in the country. There were about sixty players at the session, so I wasn't getting too far ahead of myself. I imagined I'd snuck in by the back door. But I was on their radar, and it felt good.

That question Hansen asked me was part of a wider quiz. A test designed to assess our rugby instincts. He put people on the spot with individual questions. It was unnerving. A good deal of them weren't yes or no questions, but you sensed there was a right and a wrong answer in his mind. There was no training as such, just a few skills sessions. And no fitness testing, thank God. I enjoyed myself, but I felt very much on the periphery.

Then, over the Christmas period, I had another phone call saying they'd been sufficiently impressed to invite me into the actual Wales squad. I took myself off to the Wales team HQ at the Vale Hotel near Cardiff, thinking, 'This is it – I'm in the inner sanctum now.'

But it was a strangely unsatisfactory experience, and I felt very much as though I was still on trial. I'd been a late addition, so I didn't have my own room. The rest of the squad would disappear to their rooms during the training break between midday and three o'clock, and I'd be left on my own like the new kid at school. They'd be chilling out and having a nap while I was wandering around aimlessly, willing the clock to tick down. The only guy I knew well was Gareth Llewellyn, and he's about forty years older than me, so I didn't just want to go and sit in the corner of his room like an annoying younger brother. I was left under no illusions that I was the new kid and I had to earn respect. I was cannon fodder for most of those training sessions. Much of my time was spent holding tackle bags for the more experienced players to smash into.

I must have done OK, because I was invited back to train with them down in Saundersfoot in Pembrokeshire, ahead of the 2003 Six Nations.

I shared a room with Huw Bennett, who was nineteen at the time to my twenty-one, so I didn't feel quite as young and fresh-faced any more. It was also the first time I encountered Jonathan Humphreys – a man who would come to have such an influence on my career, and who I'd come to respect enormously. My opinion of him back then couldn't have been more different. I thought he was a knobhead. As a player, he was always giving away penalties and killing the ball. Meeting him in the flesh did nothing to change that perception.

He'd been recalled to the squad after five years in the international wilderness, and he was being hailed as a knight in shining armour, returning to restore some pride to a beleaguered team. Huw Bennett and I were sitting sheepishly at breakfast one morning when he strode in, looking mean and moody – his standard look. We both said hello. He blanked us, helped himself to the buffet, and sloped off without saying a word. What a charmer.

I later discovered that he was a big fan of mine and had been lobbying Steve Hansen for me to be picked at tight-head. Gethin Jenkins was playing out of position there at the time, and Humph felt he was a weaker scrummager than me. But for reasons we'll come to later, Steve Hansen didn't agree with him.

There were plenty of characters in that Welsh squad. None more so than the enigmatic captain, Colin Charvis. A Welshman by residency, he spoke with a laconic Brummie drawl and was one of the most laid-back blokes I'd ever met. My first encounter with him was in the weights room at the gym. He was fast asleep on a Swiss ball. Wrapped awkwardly around it, limbs trailing in all directions, dead to the world. Everyone else was pumping iron, sweating and grunting, in a desperate effort to impress. The captain was taking a nap. He hated training. Couldn't be arsed with it. He never looked like an athlete – he was always stiff and ungainly-looking

– but he was an outstanding player. He may have been useless in training, but he could pull things out of his arse on the pitch.

His magic alone couldn't drag Wales out of their trough that year, though, and we ended up with the wooden spoon. In an indication of how much rugby influenced the mood of the nation, Charv was subsequently voted the second most hated man in Wales in a newspaper poll, narrowly behind Saddam Hussein.

I'd been on the periphery for the entire campaign and hadn't been picked for any match-day squads, but I had my foot in the door. I was paid about £600 for the eight weeks I was with Wales. £600 for sitting on the bike, carrying a few tackle bags and doing a few scrums.

Not a bad way to earn a living. Better than laying paving slabs, that's for sure.

● ● ●

It was a similar story on the summer tour that year to Australia and New Zealand: I was in the squad, but I didn't play. Gethin Jenkins and Ben Evans were ahead of me in the pecking order, although 'Melon' – as Gethin is better known – was a reluctant tight-head.

The night before the Hamilton test a few of us 'dirt-trackers' – me, Alix Popham, Huw Bennett and Matthew J. Watkins – went out drinking. Our fitness coach, Andrew Hore, found out and came looking for us. We spent three hours flitting from pub to pub, hiding in dark corners while Horey wasted his night trying to find us and give us a bollocking. In the early hours of the morning, we stumbled into a burger bar and there in the corner was a certain Warren Gatland, the All Black reserve hooker I'd seen coming off the bus in Swansea all those years ago. He was now in charge of London Wasps, one of the best teams in Europe.

Imbued with the confidence that comes from drinking ten pints of lager, I introduced myself, swapped my triple-bacon cheeseburger to the other hand in order to shake his, and spent ten minutes explaining to him – quite persuasively, I thought – why he should sign me for Wasps.

He'd had a few himself, so I think he saw the funny side, but the offer of a contract was – unsurprisingly – withheld.

I didn't see any action on tour, but it was an honour to travel, and it made me realise how wide the gulf was between playing for Neath and playing for Wales. The level of detail under Steve Hansen was incredible. He may not look like the most intelligent bloke, but that gruff demeanour hides a sophisticated rugby mind. Nothing was left to chance; everything was analysed with a level of precision that was alien to me.

His attitude to angles of running in attack was almost scientific. I always used to take the 'fat man' angle. In other words, running from A to B in a straight line. But he would insist that I run between A and B in an arc, because it would make the opposition defence work that bit harder. There was a lot of 'micro-detail' in the scrum, and a strong emphasis on core skills – on being able to handle and pass the ball, regardless of what number you had on your back. Forwards were often told to stand in the fly-half position during training so we'd be forced to make decisions. It was in stark contrast to my early club days, when forwards were told never to touch the ball.

He was quite innovative when it came to the tackle area, always coming up with new ways to clear people out of the ruck. His background as a policeman meant he knew all the methods of disarming people and targeting their weak points. So instead of just piling into rucks to smash the opposition off the ball, he'd teach us to twist and grapple them, to target pressure points, using martial arts and wrestling techniques instead of just relying on brute force.

Once, when we were practising 'jackling' – trying to strip the ball away from a prone ball carrier – he leaned in and pulled my hair. I shot out of the ruck, outraged.

He just raised his eyebrows, saying, 'It's a weakness, and people will target that.'

He was indisputably in charge, but he wasn't the dictator he's often portrayed as. He was more than willing to let senior players have their say, and encouraged people to question him. He delegated a lot to Scott Johnson, the backs coach, although he was a little less generous to our defence coach, Clive Griffiths. I loved Clive and respected his expertise, but he was marginalised on that tour. He and Hansen didn't get on well. There was a personality clash, as well as a clash in rugby philosophies. In the Southern Hemisphere, teams tend to defend from the outside in – in other words, you'd start with the winger at the edge of the field, and count inwards – whereas in the Northern Hemisphere, it tends to be inside out. They argued about that many times, often shouting at each other on the training pitch. As a green twenty-two-year-old, I assumed that's what coaches did. I didn't realise the problems ran deeper.

Like the Six Nations that preceded it, the tour was one to forget. The Hamilton test ended in a humiliating 55–3 defeat, and will be remembered for a sickening collision between Jerry Collins and Colin Charvis, which saw Charv knocked clean out. Tana Umaga received a lot of praise that day for rushing to Charv's aid and making sure he didn't swallow his own tongue. (Ironic, considering he was pilloried two years later for his part in a tip tackle that put Brian O'Driscoll out of the 2005 Lions tour.)

● ● ●

The trip was poor preparation for the World Cup later that year. It was the first season of regional rugby in Wales, but instead of doing my pre-season training with the newly formed Ospreys, I took part in Wales' brutal pre-World Cup regime.

One session that sticks in my memory took place up in Pyle, near Bridgend. We were doing these horrendous 'hill repeats', which involves running up a hill, running back down, running up a bit further, running back down, and so on. There were some fit boys in that squad, but the whole mountainside was covered in vomit that afternoon. It was brutal.

Another of Horey's favourites was boxing in the sand dunes at Merthyr Mawr. He'd make you spar with someone until all the energy was drained from your body, and then order you to run to the top of the sand dune and back. On several occasions, I thought I was going to have a heart attack. My chest would get tight, my vision would start to blur and my legs would turn to jelly. It was punishment of the highest order.

But I was beginning to feel good. The weight was dropping off, and I was a different shape altogether to the wobbly teenager from Abercrave. The weights were helping in that department. Prior to joining up with Wales, all I'd ever done were bench presses, squats and bicep curls. Under Horey's tutelage that expanded tenfold, and he also made sure that I exercised between sets. So instead of doing ten reps, then sitting around getting my breath back, I'd do ten reps, then sprint or push a sledge.

There was no hiding place. It was an entirely new world.

Melon was infuriatingly fit. Especially considering how he looked, with his big old drum of a torso and skinny legs. All the front row forwards were in the same training group: Iestyn Thomas, Duncan Jones, Robin McBryde, Mefin Davies, Melon and me. But some things we did as a full squad, like the 3k runs at the National Indoor Athletic Centre.

The first time we did it, Melon lapped me, tapping me on the arse as he accelerated past, shouting, 'Dig in, Bomb!'

Mark Taylor, the fittest in the squad, was way out ahead. Gareth 'Alfie' Thomas and Melon were neck and neck coming into the straight. Alfie was ripped and lean – as fit as they come – and he had a hell of a shape on him. But when he accelerated for the line, Melon out-kicked him and sprinted past. It was a bizarre and inexplicable sight.

Of course, we can now look back on a long and successful period in the Welsh side together – he as loose-head, me as tight-head. We became an enduring partnership. But back then, he was playing out of position at tight-head, and was thus my main obstacle when it came to winning the jersey. I knew I was a better scrummager than him. But he was a better rugby player. And the fact that he was being forced to play out of position meant he had a ready-made excuse if the scrum started going backwards. He couldn't be made the fall guy, because he didn't want to play tight-head anyway.

If the training regime wasn't already brutal enough, they made it worse by ramping up the heating at the Vale Hotel's indoor barn. It was to help us acclimatise to the warmer Australian weather. We'd have agility sessions where we'd emerge dripping wet and sweating buckets. We also went for a warm-weather training camp in Lanzarote – holiday destination of choice for thousands of Brits every year. Not us. It was another uncompromising boot camp. We'd have skills sessions at six-thirty in the morning before the sun had come up. Johnno and Hansen would be these shadowy figures in the gloom berating us for dropping balls left, right and centre, insisting that the poor light was no excuse. I spent the sessions getting hit in the face by the ball over and over again.

It was all part of a plan to make us more agile. I was forced to spend the last fifteen minutes of every session defending against Shane Williams and Iestyn Harris, and they'd just take the piss. Shane was lightning quick, and Iestyn could turn on a sixpence. I never got anywhere near either of them.

Steve Hansen once stepped in, claiming he'd show me how to do it, and telling Iestyn to run at him. I wondered whether Iestyn might make it easier for him, to curry favour. But he showed no mercy, and skinned him.

Steve turned, chased him down and launched himself at Iestyn, flailing and swiping at thin air. 'Got him!' he said to me, as he walked past with grass stains on his knees.

He hadn't got anywhere near him. But who was I to argue with the guy who stood between me and my Wales debut?

We were allowed one night out, in the middle of the week, and we all bundled into a bus to take us into the nearest town. It was deathly quiet but there were a few bars open, and we all scuttled excitedly off into the night, eager to let off steam. Hansen and Johnno had no idea how Welsh boys behave on a night out on tour. We had three hours. Midnight was a strict curfew, but that was enough. Within seconds of arriving at the first pub, Iestyn Thomas was up on the bar, having spirits poured directly down his throat à la Paul Gascoigne in the 'dentist's chair'.

We were like animals released from the zoo. That bar probably made as much in the one night as it usually would during the entire season. Within three hours we'd drunk the place dry.

Miraculously, we all made it back on the bus, but I've never seen a more bacchanalian scene of wanton debauchery than the ride back to the hotel. It was total carnage. Mark Jones, Sonny Parker and Mefin Davies were the only boys who hadn't had a drink. They looked like horrified victims trapped in a nightmare. Headrests were being hurled around, and people were puking everywhere. Some of the lads were trying to piss into bottles, and missing. It was disgraceful. Not a good advert for the Welsh abroad. The driver was utterly disgusted.

We bundled back into the hotel, and Melon announced his arrival by theatrically spewing all over the foyer. Steve Hansen was not impressed. He angrily ordered us to bed before sourcing a mop and cleaning it up himself. The head coach of Wales, mopping up Melon's sick. It was quite a sight.

We all woke up the next day, feeling like death, and assembled guiltily on the training field.

Hansen strode out and barked, 'Right. Who drank last night?'

Most of us raised our hands.

'Who didn't?'

Mark Jones, Mefin and Sonny raised theirs.

'OK. You three. You're doing tackling drills.'

The coaches proceeded to put the three non-drinkers through a brutal session of tackling, forcing them to smash into one another over and over again. They were shown no mercy, while the rest of us watched, wincing.

Hansen considered it some sort of masterful psychological ploy. He thought it would make us feel guilty that we'd gone out and behaved so shamefully and had inadvertently inflicted punishment on the innocent. But for the second time that week, they failed to understand the Welsh mentality.

We drinkers just thought, 'Brilliant. We've got away with it. You crack on, boys!'

The non-drinkers didn't see the funny side.

CHAPTER 6

Thirty-Minute Man

NO game against England is ever a friendly. The pre-World Cup warm-up against them in Cardiff may not have had anything riding on it, but we wanted to lay a marker down. We wanted to smash them. And when they picked a second-string side, we genuinely thought we would. I was yet to break into our first fifteen, so had to settle for a place on the bench.

Andrew Hore was skulking around our changing room, trying to fire the boys up before kick-off. Rob Sidoli had recently joined the squad, and Andrew had worked hard with him on his physique, helping him stack on the muscle. He transformed him from a lanky string bean into a musclebound warrior. Horey was getting inside his head, telling him how much bigger he was than his opposite number, Danny Grewcock. It was a tactic that would work on some players – feeding them positive lines, as they worked themselves into a pre-match frenzy of adrenaline and nerves – but 'Sid' is the most laid-back bloke I've ever met. All he could muster in response was a casual, 'Cheers, brother.'

It worked on everyone else, because we ran out at the Millennium Stadium convinced we were going to win. A fully loaded Wales, playing against a second-string England in Cardiff. How could there be any other outcome? I was beside myself with nerves and excitement. This could be it, this could be my first cap. All the times I'd been told I was too fat ever to make it, and here I was on the verge of becoming an international player. I was about to represent my country at the sport I loved. And if the script unfolded as it should, I'd play my part in a victory over the team we loved to beat more than any other.

But it didn't unfold like that at all. England were far too good for us.

Even their fringe players were better than our first choicers, and they tore us to pieces. I watched from the bench as players like Stuart Abbott – a decent enough club player who was making his debut – carved our defence up with alarming ease.

Then the moment arrived. Sixty-five minutes on the clock. Thirty points down on the scoreboard. And with a scrum on our own line.

'Adam, you're on!'

Hands down, the worst scenario in which to make your international debut as a tight-head prop. Instead of a nice run-on cameo at the end, I was chucked in to hold up a scrum in the worst area of the field. Just in front of our own try line.

Jonathan Thomas came on at the same time. He'd already been capped but was still raw, lightweight and skinny. Probably about ten stone soaking wet. He was told to pack down out of position in the second row, behind me. Cheers for that. All I could think of as I jogged on for my first cap was, 'For Christ's sake! Really?'

So there we were, packing down respectively against Jason Leonard and Simon Shaw, two absolute monsters with a frightening amount of international experience. Jason Leonard was probably older than JT and I put together. They were both Lions, and we were easy meat. I feared we'd be driven backwards, concede another try, and that my international reputation would be destroyed in an instant. But we held them out. We locked the scrum, and didn't take a backward step.

It was a tiny consolation in the scheme of things. But for me, individually, it was a moral victory. I remember standing up after that scrum, looking Jason Leonard in the eye, and thinking, 'I must ask him for his autograph after the game.' I guess it would take me a while to realise I was among these people now.

I, too, was an international rugby player.

That scrum was the abiding memory of my international debut. That, and the realisation that this was a huge step up. It wasn't just that the crowds and the sense of occasion were bigger. The players were too. They were fitter, faster and stronger than anything I'd been used to, and they ran much harder.

My first tackle was on Martin Corry. I hadn't ever considered him to be a strong runner, but he clattered into me and left me reeling. It was a sobering start to my test career. I wish the result had been different, obviously. But your first cap is your first cap, and I'll always treasure the memory.

After the game I went to a mate's wedding down the Gower, and all my Abercrave buddies were there, patting me on the back and buying me drinks. If I'd gone out with the Welsh squad, we'd probably have got depressed about the result. But being with all my old pals allowed me to celebrate my cap, rather than agonise over the defeat. Two years earlier, I'd been playing with my mates in Abercrave so, for them, it was all about the fact one of their boys had become an international. It made the bitter pill of defeat easier to swallow – that and the ten pints I drank, which rendered me paralytic from about ten o'clock onwards.

It was crisis time for Wales, though. After all that hard work in the summer, we'd been badly exposed when it came to the business of actually playing rugby. It was a record defeat against England in Cardiff, and our eleventh loss in a row.

Steve Hansen was summoned to a meeting with David Moffett, who told him that unless he won the next game against Scotland, he'd be gone. Sacked, just six weeks before the start of the World Cup. When he'd first arrived, Steve had recognised that Wales were light years behind the likes of England when it came to professionalism and standards, and had striven to improve our fitness and preparation off the field. But his mantra of 'performance over results' was beginning to wear thin – and not just with the fans and the press, but with the WRU board.

Scotland was shit or bust time.

I was picked to start along with Duncan Jones and Robin McBryde, and we won comfortably, 23–9. The scrum went well, which obviously reflected well on us, and we got Hansen the win that saved his job. Charv was on fire that day. As I've mentioned, at training he often couldn't be bothered and sometimes looked as though he couldn't even catch a ball. But he was a big-game player, and this match required just that. On one occasion, he was running at full tilt, scooped up a pass from around his ankles, drove into a tackler, and then deftly flicked the ball out of the back of his hand for a try-scoring pass.

The victory meant we travelled to the World Cup in Australia off the back of a win, rather than twelve straight defeats. Sometimes that's all you need in sport for your fortunes to change.

● ● ●

We flew down under more in hope than expectation, but it was exciting. They love their sport out there, and to take part in a World Cup in such a sports-obsessed country was something I was relishing. It was quite the start to my test career.

Scott Johnson is as Australian as they come, and wanted us to embrace the culture and history of the place. He'd arranged for a famous Australian to speak to us prior to every game. First up was Andrew Johns, the Rugby League player regarded by many as the best ever. People of a certain generation in Wales consider Rugby League to be the sport of the devil, as we lost a golden generation of players to the code during Rugby Union's amateur era. But it's always been a guilty pleasure of mine, and I was one of the few who knew who Johns was. Our analyst, Alun Carter, had put together a video montage of him which was played before his talk, and that left our boys in no doubt as to the scope of his talent.

He was a little dwt of a bloke, but didn't take any prisoners on the field. Johnno's idea was that we'd get a sense of the level of professionalism adopted by the League boys, and that some of it would rub off. But Andrew wasn't exactly on message. He'd played in a few State of Origin series – where Queensland and New South Wales play each other. It's a massive deal in Australia. The stadiums are always packed, and the TV viewing figures are off the scale. Gareth Llewellyn asked a question about preparation, because they're effectively scratch sides pulled together according to their 'state of origin'. Andrew explained that they basically get together and go on the piss. They'll meet on a Sunday night and go out drinking. Then they meet up on Monday morning and go on an all-day drinking session. On the Tuesday, they'll be too hungover to do anything other than run through a few moves. And then on Wednesday they play the game.

We could see Hansen and Horey sinking into their seats. They'd spent so long instilling a sense of discipline into us, and trying to transform the culture of the Welsh changing room. And here was this uber-professional Rugby League guy telling us they prepared for the biggest matches of their season by going on a two-day bender! Probably not the kind of inspirational message the Welsh management were hoping for.

We played Canada first, in Melbourne. As much as a loose-head prop can be called a talisman, Rod Snow was theirs. We knew him well from his days at Newport, and we knew if we put a few big hits on him early, it would dent the morale of the team as a whole. We'd noticed during our analysis that he stood out in the wide channels a lot as ball carrier, which is very unusual for a big prop. Steve Hansen challenged the boys to see who could make the biggest hit on him. Robin McBryde accepted the gauntlet and absolutely smoked him early on.

It set the tone for a comfortable victory, and we were up and running.

● ● ●

After Canada, we flew to Canberra, where we were booked into shared apartments as part of the management's grand plan. Instead of staying in a hotel and developing cabin fever we were granted a sense of independence and encouraged to hang out together, bond and cook all our own meals. I was staying in a unit with Gareth Thomas. As we were both shocking cooks, we ended up subsisting almost entirely on breakfast cereal. I was in awe of him, because he was a rugby legend, and while we got on, there was a bit of an age gap. Martyn Williams, the man they call 'Nugget', was in the room next door, and those two were good mates. So they'd often go out together, leaving me indoors twiddling my thumbs. But as roommates go, he was decent. And he looked after me.

My mate Huw Bennett was paired with the famously eccentric Chris Wyatt, who spent the entire trip taunting him. The first night they were there, Huw woke up at about three in the morning to go to the toilet. He was tip-toeing across the room, when he heard, 'HEY-ooo!' He turned round to see Wyatt out on the balcony sipping a black coffee and smoking a fag. He soon came to realise that this was totally standard behaviour. Wyatt barely ever slept – which was hardly surprising, when you consider the amount of coffee he drank. Benny would often wake in the middle of the night to see him wide awake playing computer games.

Wyatt was a social animal and loved a night out, whereas Huw was a wide-eyed youngster, eager to impress. One week, neither of them were playing, and Chris had gone out. He called Huw and told him to meet him for a drink. Huw refused, so Wyatt just kept calling his room phone and haranguing him. Eventually, Huw stopped answering it, so Chris rang it solidly for twenty minutes. When that didn't work, he returned to the apartment and sat outside Huw's door, knocking constantly, like Chinese water torture.

Huw would be shouting, 'I'm not coming out! I've got training in the morning.'

And Chris'd be like, 'Come on, Huw. Just a few cheeky drinks.'

Inevitably, Huw would buckle and be coerced into going out drinking. You need guys like that on tour.

The first match in Canberra was against Tonga, and we laboured to a narrow 27–20 victory, the highlight of which was a Martyn Williams drop goal. As with the Canada game, I'd come on as a sub.

But for the third pool game, against Italy, I was picked to start. As always, they had a strong pack, and I was picked specifically for my scrummaging. Mike Cron, the New Zealand scrummaging guru, was with us for the World Cup as a consultant, and he worked hard with me in the run-up to that game. Their front row was Castrogiovanni, Lo Cicero and Ongaro – a really gnarly unit who I'd go on to play against dozens of times. That week, Mike Cron and I went through endless slow-motion footage of those three in action.

I was concerned going into the game, because I'd been having issues with back pain – never a good sign for a prop – and I'd been on anti-inflammatories for a while. We lost Duncan early on to a bad injury, and not long after, we were packing down for a scrum when I heard a loud pop coming from the small of my back. I feared the worst, thinking something awful had happened. But when I stood up, I felt better than I had in ages. The pain and the ache I'd been suffering with had gone. I'd taken large quantities of painkillers, and spent countless hours on the physio's bench, but one scrum eventually provided the remedy I needed.

Mark Jones, Sonny Parker and Daf Jones will remember that game for the tries they scored. But for me, as you'd expect, the pivotal moment was a scrum. It was on their line, and on their ball. Italy would always scrummage very square. All three front rowers would be in line, and push through the chest. In Wales, we'd always scrummage at angles, boring in all over the place. But on this occasion, we got it absolutely right. Their front row popped up under the pressure, and we drove right over the top of them. It led indirectly to Daf Jones's try, and that scrum alone won me Man of the Match. My second start in a Wales jersey – in a World Cup – and I'd been judged the best player on the park. Instead of a bottle of champagne or a medal, I was given a custom-made didgeridoo, with my name engraved on it. It still stands proudly in my memorabilia room at home.

As I jogged off the field, Mike Cron was wearing the biggest grin imaginable. I'd become his project on that tour, and everything we'd talked about and planned for had just paid off. For those of us who are fully paid-up members of the front row union, it was far more satisfying than a length-of-the-field try would ever be.

• • •

The victory against Italy meant we'd qualified for the World Cup quarter-finals with a game to spare. Our final pool match was against the mighty All Blacks. We didn't know it then, but that match was to prove a watershed for Welsh rugby in the professional era. People still debate now whether Hansen's team selection was an exercise in lunacy or a maverick stroke of genius. The consensus at the time was that he'd picked a second-string side to play the All Blacks. He knew that a win was highly unlikely, and would rather preserve his first-choice team for the quarter-final against England. Depending on which bookie you went to, England or New Zealand were the tournament favourites.

It certainly had the look of a second-string side. Garan Evans, who hadn't yet started a game, was picked at full-back. Jonathan Thomas and Alix Popham, who'd barely played, were selected in the back row. And a diminutive little fella called Shane Williams, who'd only been added to the touring party at the last minute as a reserve scrum-half, was picked on the wing. I was selected at tight-head, although I didn't see it as a demotion following my man-of-the-match performance against Italy. I was just happy to get another start.

If the press was to be believed, we were lambs to the slaughter. But we felt differently. Steve Hansen and Scott Johnson reminded us how hard we'd all worked, how fit we'd become, and told us to go out and express ourselves.

It started badly. Their lightning-fast winger, Joe Rokocoko, scythed through our defence to score a brilliant try after two minutes. It was the trigger for the game to erupt into a free-flowing Barbarians-style exhibition, with wild passes being thrown everywhere, and both teams attacking with almost careless abandon. They built an eighteen-point lead, but we hit back with two tries in the last six minutes of the first half.

Within five minutes of the second, we'd taken the lead. It was incredible. The All Blacks were clearly stunned, and we'd seemingly ascended to a higher plane. A historic upset was on the cards. But for me personally, while the fans and the team were approaching a state of euphoria, I was experiencing the biggest low of my career.

The Welsh turnaround coincided almost exactly with me leaving the field. I was hauled off after half an hour – given the old 'shepherd's crook'. I had no idea why. I wasn't injured. I didn't feel tired. But I saw my number come up, and was forced to suffer the indignity of leaving the field before the first half had even ended. It was unheard of. What the fuck was going on? The team masseur handed me a coat and a blanket. I sat down on the bench, threw the coat over my head and cried my eyes out. I felt humiliated, belittled and undermined. This was the biggest game of my life, being played in front of millions of people, and my coach had hauled me off for no apparent reason. Despite being in a packed stadium of thousands, I felt utterly alone.

How dare he? How fucking dare he?

I was an emotional wreck, and I didn't care who knew. My shoulders were heaving, and I was sobbing uncontrollably. Mike Cron could see what was going on. To his credit he came over and started rubbing my back, telling me to stay warm, in case I had to go back on. Mefin Davies was my saviour. He could see how cut up I was and did his best to comfort me. I didn't confront the coaches after the game. It didn't seem right after a performance like that, and I've always been one to bottle things up rather than to seek confrontation. The only person I asked about it was Gethin Jenkins, who came on to replace me. I asked him if he'd known about it beforehand. He claimed to have had no knowledge either. I later found out

Hansen had had plans to do the same during the Italy game, but had to reconsider when Duncan Jones went off injured.

While I was wallowing in a state of depression and confusion on the bench, Wales were transforming themselves on the pitch. There were all kinds of conspiracy theories circulating afterwards, suggesting that the team had lost faith in Hansen, had abandoned the game plan and thrown off the shackles. It certainly looked that way, and we had two free spirits in Shane Williams and Jonathan Thomas who were able to exploit space better than most. But what you have to remember is that Hansen and Johnno were always big on skills and creativity. Their philosophy from day one was based around playing a fast-paced game and keeping the ball alive. It just clicked into place that day – probably helped by the fact it wasn't a must-win game. The knowledge that we'd already qualified removed a layer of tension, and an even bigger layer of inhibition.

Wales became the darlings of the media overnight, and misty-eyed columns were written about the return of the 'Welsh way'. Romance had returned to rugby. I wasn't buying it. My view may have been coloured by my personal experience, but I refused to see it as some pivotal moment in Welsh rugby. Yes, we played our part in an entertaining game. But ultimately, we got pumped. The All Blacks pulled away in the end and won comfortably. That shouldn't have been a cause for celebration, and I think that's always been a fundamental flaw in the Welsh psyche. For too long we'd been happy with honourable defeats.

I struggled psychologically with what had happened, and retreated into my shell. I stayed in my room, moping about, torturing myself mentally and questioning whether I was good enough. I was worried I might self-destruct because I couldn't let it go. It consumed my every thought. I was young and I didn't know how to deal with it. My parents were out there, and were gutted on my behalf. But I didn't want to speak to them, because I knew they'd be biased. I wanted to hear the truth. I wanted to know why. I didn't want to be told, 'You're the best, you've been treated badly, it's an injustice.'

The sad thing was, it meant I didn't embrace the experience. A World Cup in Australia is a special thing. The travelling support was superb, and it felt like a major event. But I barely left my room. And the social, cultural aspect passed me by.

The day after the New Zealand game, I walked into the hotel lift and Steve Hansen and Jackie Maitland, our media officer, were there. This was my opportunity to confront him. In the confines of the lift, I could have vented my frustrations. Unleashed my anger. But I bottled it.

He asked me how it felt out on the pitch. I said it was hard. He told me I needed to get fitter.

What really bugged me was the fact he hadn't told me of his plans in advance. If he'd have done me that courtesy, I'd have been gutted, but at least I would have been prepared for it. Instead, I felt insulted. I took it personally, and I hated him for it.

It was a terrible bit of man-management, and it wouldn't be the last time a Kiwi coach would treat me with such disrespect.

● ● ●

My mood lifted slightly when I was told I'd been selected for the quarter-final against England, but I knew it was going to happen again – that I'd be subjected to the same humiliation. It preyed on my mind in the build-up. I should have been psyching myself up for the biggest game of my career. Instead, I was consumed by bitterness and self-doubt.

But I needed to focus, because this was the greatest England team ever. It was packed with players that I'd grown up idolising – the likes of

Lawrence Dallaglio, Martin Johnson and Jason Leonard. I had to get over this weird hero-worship thing and start thinking of them as opponents. As the enemy.

They'd been on an amazing run prior to the World Cup, which included a backs-to-the-wall victory over New Zealand in New Zealand. As well as those forwards, they had the world's best goal kicker in Jonny Wilkinson, and one of the world's best counter-attackers in Jason Robinson. It was, without doubt, the greatest England team ever. They'd gone through their group unbeaten, and were being talked up by most pundits as champions elect.

Our performance against New Zealand had people purring. Some were suggesting we could knock England off their stride. We knew we wouldn't win an arm wrestle with them. They were too big, too wily and too strong. We had to play to our strengths, and Steve Hansen would always talk about the width of the field. One of his catchphrases was 'use the facilities'. He'd bark it from the touchline constantly. It meant exploit the space, use the whole field, don't play too narrowly. Because the English were so big, they were by definition less agile. If we forced them to defend as wide as possible, their big lads like Vickery, Thompson and Leonard would have to cover more ground. In theory, they'd tire themselves out more quickly.

When you have guys on your side like Iestyn Harris and Shane Williams, who can exploit the smallest of gaps, it gives you confidence. We knew if we played a bit, we could win.

My excitement levels were dimmed by the knowledge I'd be taken off again after half an hour. But I decided to be positive, to go out and 'empty the tank'. It was inevitable I'd be taken off, so I thought I'd expend every last ounce of energy for my country while I was on the pitch. Things started brilliantly. With less than five minutes gone, I found myself moonlighting in the three-quarter line, and delivered what I thought was a beautiful scoring pass to Rob Sidoli, only to see him drop it over the line.

Then, as predicted, it happened. The clock rolled around to thirty minutes and my name was called.

I trooped back to the bench, and the other subs shuffled along nervously, not knowing what to say. They were as embarrassed as I was. I'd been through the 'crying under the towel' phase, so I didn't go through that again. And to be fair, I was as enthralled by the game as the fans were. We were pushing England as hard as we could and I desperately wanted the boys to win. Within a minute of me leaving the field, we scored a sensational try – probably the try of the tournament. Shane fielded a loose cross kick from Mike Tindall, skinned Ben Kay and offloaded to Gareth Cooper, who carved through the middle. Alfie took it on, before Shane reappeared on the left wing with an outrageous bit of skill, juggling the ball and whipping it back inside to Stephen Jones, who crossed for the score.

Just before half-time, Colin Charvis turned down three points to kick to the corner, and backed our driving line-out. Sure enough, it worked. Charv himself was the beneficiary as he dived, American football-style, over the try line. We were 10–3 up against the best side in the world.

The half-time team talk was essentially along the lines of, 'Keep doing what we're doing. And tighten up on defence.' Jason Robinson had skipped through us a few times, and we were warned to keep tabs on him.

Hansen and Johnno didn't talk to me. I felt surplus to requirements. But Horey told me to keep warm, in case I was needed to go back on. It was a weird feeling. We were on the verge of something massive, but I felt strangely peripheral. I was determined not to show it, because we needed to be united. It was the biggest forty minutes of any of our careers. We knew if our discipline was poor, Jonny Wilkinson could kick three points from anywhere. We knew if we kicked loosely, and left any gaps in our defensive line, Jason Robinson would run through them.

And that's exactly what he did, with just a few minutes of the second half gone. There was probably no better player in world rugby at exploiting gaps, and his acceleration from a standing start was frightening. He ripped our defence to shreds on the counter-attack, and flicked a lovely scoring pass to Will Greenwood. Just like that, England were right back in it.

Robinson was class, but the one man who really made a difference in that second half was the man Clive Woodward hadn't chosen to start with. Mike Catt came on at inside-centre, and it proved an inspired substitution. He took a bit of pressure off Jonny, and started putting England in the right areas. The forwards are like donkeys – put the carrot out in front of them, and they'll go after it all day. That's what Catt did. Every time those English forwards looked up from a scrum or a ruck, the ball was sailing forty or fifty metres in front of them. Manna from heaven for a forward.

I turned into a fan on the bench. I was far more nervous than I'd been on the pitch. It was impossible to watch at times, but as that second half wore on, it became apparent that England were edging away. They were marginally fitter and stronger than we were. And ultimately, they had too much for us.

I was obviously gutted by the result, but I was more gutted about being subbed off. That may sound self-centred but I couldn't help it. Everything was viewed through my bitter filter of self-pity. Comfort arrived from the strangest of places. As we were walking off the field, Jason Leonard jogged over to ask what had happened. I explained that it was Hansen's preordained plan.

He grinned and said, 'Chin up, mate, I was taken off after forty-one! Go and get changed, and let me buy you a pint.'

I can't tell you how much that cheered me up. I was still an impressionable twenty-two-year-old, taking my first tentative steps into the arena of international rugby. He was an old warhorse who I'd looked up to for years. I'd gone from my highest moment to my lowest ebb in the space of a fortnight, and it was an Englishman who dragged me out of the trough.

That pint tasted pretty sweet, and I'll be for ever grateful to him for it.

● ● ●

After the World Cup, I went back to the Ospreys for the 2003/2004 season and rolled my ankle against Munster. I was glad to be injured and miss the final three rounds of the 2004 Six Nations. It was hurting me so much to play and be subbed off after thirty minutes that I'd rather not play at all.

I know that might sound petulant – and there will be some people reading this who'd do anything for a Welsh cap – but I can't help the way I felt. I was just glad I didn't have to go through it all again.

The first game of that campaign, we played against Scotland and I scored. Nugget fed me in the corner, and I went over. It was a shit dive, but it was an amazing feeling. Ten minutes later, I was taken off. The same happened the following week in Dublin, although we were 19–3 down at the time, so some would say it was a good time to take my leave.

I was nineteen stone, which was exactly where they wanted me to be, and I was posting the same fitness results as Duncan Jones and Iestyn Thomas. I wasn't as powerful as Duncan, but because I was bigger there seemed to be this assumption that I was fat, although nineteen stone was a good weight – probably the lightest I'd ever been as an adult. But I'd been saddled with this tag of the fat guy, and it seemed as though nobody could see beyond it.

My supposed weight problems became public property – the subject of discussions in the media, and among fans. I was dismissed by a succession of armchair pundits as too fat to play international rugby. What the hell did they know? People see me as an amiable bloke, and assume these things don't bother me, but they do. It's deeply personal, and deeply upsetting. (I would actually be more than a stone heavier two years later, when we won a Grand Slam. Nobody complained about it then.)

I found myself secretly hoping that Steve Hansen would get sacked. I knew that as long as he was there, this would continue to happen. I wish I'd had the balls to confront him rather than let it fester. But I was a shy lad who didn't have the gumption to stride up to the head coach and have it out with him. Coaches always say they like to be challenged, but I think Steve would have held it against me if I'd done that.

The fact is I'm one of the least confrontational people you're likely to meet. I understand that may seem strange for someone who earns a living packing down in the front row of a scrum, but I've always been that way. When I was a kid and my parents used to argue about mundane stuff, I'd be up in my room crying. My brother always used to say, 'Don't worry about it, mun, they're just talking things out.' But I'd think it was the end of the world.

I internalise things and bottle things up. My anger over this never boiled over. I never punched a wall or went on the rampage. I just did what I usually do – I ate and drank more. That's my number one coping mechanism. Chocolate, junk food and booze. Ironic, really, considering it was my fitness – or lack of it – that was the supposed issue.

After that injury midway through the 2004 Six Nations, I pulled the ripcord. My motivation was gone, my morale plummeted and I piled on the pounds. I ballooned to twenty and a half stone. When I recovered from my injury, I struggled to get into the Ospreys starting XV. One minute I'd been running out for my country at the World Cup, the next I was battling the bulge and knocking around among the replacements for my club. It was a dramatic fall from grace. These days, you can theoretically get in better shape when you're injured. But then, you were left to your own devices with nobody breathing down your neck or barking orders.

Mefin Davies was one of my most supportive teammates during that period. The scrum was the be-all and end-all to him, so he was always on my side. Always better to have a scrummaging prop than a mobile one who can carry the ball. That was his philosophy.

But ultimately, no amount of advice or reassurance could help me through it. There was no precedent for it. No other player had been routinely subbed off after thirty minutes, so no one could truly relate to how I was feeling. I just had to 'take it on the chins', as I once glibly said in a TV interview.

The only time I ever raised it with Hansen was years later when he became the All Blacks coach. Wales had played New Zealand and I was having a drink in the Kiwi dressing room with Ali Williams. Ever the mischief maker, he dared me to go and ask Hansen there and then. I'd had about three cans of Carling so my confidence was high.

Taking a deep breath, I strode up to him and asked him straight out. 'Why did you put me through that, butt?'

He looked at me with a puzzled expression and said, dismissively, 'Cos you weren't fit enough, mate.'

That was it. I guess you can't accuse him of being dishonest. He may have since proven himself to be the best coach in the world, but man-management wasn't his strongest point. I don't resent him as a bloke, but I resent the way he treated me.

I was obviously delighted when he announced his departure at the end of the 2004 Six Nations. The players shoved him on to the pitch so that the fans could give him a standing ovation. Being the bitter kid that I was, I remember thinking, 'Who does he think he is? Milking the applause like that. What exactly has he won?'

But looking back I accept that he contributed enormously to Welsh rugby. Together with Andrew Hore, he instilled a thoroughly professional mindset, and laid the platform for the success that followed.

CHAPTER 7

Ruddock Arrives

AS the season with the Ospreys was limping to an end, I got wind of the fact that the new Welsh coach, Mike Ruddock, wanted to take me on the 2004 summer tour to Argentina. I'd not given up hope on my Wales career because, truth be told, I still thought I was technically the best tight-head in the country. But they also picked Darren Morris, who was probably ahead of me in the hierarchy. It's been a theme of my career that the international coach never quite seems satisfied with me. Perhaps it's my innate insecurity, but for a long time I always felt like I was keeping the jersey warm until someone better came along.

But it was a lifeline. Hansen was gone. Ruddock was in, and I was back in favour.

I didn't know Mike, but his reputation was solid. He'd done well everywhere he'd been – at Swansea, Leinster, Ebbw Vale and the Dragons. He was a surprise appointment, because Gareth Jenkins had been the overwhelming favourite, but he was a welcome one from my point of view. It was a chance for me to emerge from the doldrums and resurrect my international career.

Mike was much more 'old school' than Hansen. He explained to me that anchoring the scrum was my main and overriding focus. After that it was a case of making tackles, hitting rucks and lifting in the line-out. The basics. In training there were no 'hits', as such, in the scrum. He'd make us bind early and hold the bind for twenty seconds to test our strength and technique. It was all about staying in the fight, and not giving up. (Ironically, a bit more how it's gone now since the recent law changes.) And he loved an old-fashioned driving line-out, which was not something Wales had been traditionally associated with. Given that our first tour under Mike was to Argentina, followed by a one-off test in South Africa, it was perhaps no surprise that he focused so much attention on the scrum.

The first test was in Tucumán. I've never been to a rougher place. It was a real hellhole. Dirty, grimy, edgy and racked with poverty. Crime was rife, and we were told not to leave the hotel unless we were in groups of at least six.

The night before the first test, I was rooming with Duncan Jones, and the room phone rang. Duncan picked it up.

'Pipi? Can I see you, Pipi?'

Duncan thought it was one of the boys taking the piss, so he hung up.

It rang again. 'Pipi. I want to see you, Pipi. Can you give me the money?'

Again, Dunc hangs up.

I went off to the team room to get a drink. When I came back, Dunc was in the doorway of our room, wrestling this skinny Argentinian kid out into the corridor. He was claiming to be a rent boy responding to a summons. We managed to get rid of him, but Dunc was understandably shaken up and called our team manager, Alan Phillips. Within ten minutes, the hotel management had called the authorities and four armed guards with automatic rifles arrived to patrol our corridor.

To this day I have no idea what went on, but there were rumours of Argentinian subterfuge – that the Pumas had staged the whole episode to disrupt our preparation for the first test. If that was the intention, it backfired, because we slept far more soundly than we otherwise would have, with four armed guards outside our rooms.

The ground wasn't much of an improvement on the town. Barbed-wire fencing ringed the stadium. Litter was strewn everywhere, and a dead dog was rotting in the stand with a swarm of angry flies buzzing around its corpse. A stench of stale urine and decay hung in the air. We lost the match 50–44, but played our part in an entertaining spectacle. Conceding fifty points was embarrassing, and our defence came in for some deserved criticism. It was the first time we'd employed the 'blitz defence'. And believe me, it takes a bit of getting used to.

Clive Griffiths was given far more influence under Ruddock, and he insisted on the change. The blitz involves the defensive line rushing up as one, getting in the face of the opposition, closing down their space and forcing errors. It needs to be so precise and coordinated. Everyone needs to be in sync, and communication is vital. Done badly, it can be shambolic, as it proved to be that night. Before the tour, we'd beaten the Barbarians handsomely and hadn't had our defence tested, so we didn't realise quite how much it needed tightening up. It's all very well rushing up to smash your opposite number, but you have to be aware of the space you're leaving behind.

We improved as the match wore on. Jason Forster was making his debut on the flank at the ripe old age of thirty-three, and was having a stormer. He made twenty tackles, and scored a try. But the partisan crowd weren't about to acclaim his performance. They were frighteningly aggressive and hostile, and there was a real air of menace in the stands. Luckily, the abuse being rained down on us was all in Spanish, so we couldn't understand a word they were saying. At one point, Gavin Henson was lining up a kick from the touchline, and a toilet roll bounced off his head.

The crowd were most vocal during the scrums. They love a scrum and see that battleground as the ultimate expression of their manhood. Along with South Africa, Argentina is the hardest place to tour as a prop. You always feel as though you're packing down against the entire crowd, as well as the opposition eight. But we held them well in that first test. I played for sixty minutes, and felt as though I'd done a good job.

With another week to work on the blitz defence, we knew we'd be significantly better. But not everybody was buying into it. There was a small cabal of players with lingering loyalties to Steve Hansen who were expressing their doubts behind the coaches' backs. Steve had preferred to defend 'out to in', which is more the Southern Hemisphere way, and the cabal was questioning the wisdom of switching systems.

The debrief the following day got a little bit heated. Everyone was hungover. Some were still drunk, and a lot of the old guard were piping up with their opinions. The quieter guys, emboldened by the alcohol sloshing around in their systems, were chipping in too. It got a bit lively and argumentative, and was perhaps a harbinger of things to come. That kind of dissent didn't happen so much under the old regime.

Mike focused heavily on scrummaging that week, mindful that we'd be playing South Africa on the way home, and seeing it as the platform from which everything else could flourish. He worked us hard, and kept the game plan simple. We won the second test in Buenos Aires comfortably. Shane Williams was on fire, making their full-back look ridiculous on a couple of occasions, and scoring a hat-trick before half-time.

• • •

There was a feeling of creeping dread about heading to South Africa, despite the victory in Buenos Aires. The flight was about fourteen hours from Argentina, and was the worst I'd ever been on. The turbulence was off the scale. For about three terrifying hours, the plane didn't stop bouncing up and down. Everyone was deathly pale, gripping their armrests and trying to appear calm, but we were all crapping ourselves on the inside. Sonny Parker kept repeating a story about how he'd once been on a plane when an engine had cut out, and how that was far worse than a 'bit of turbulence'. He was trying to make everyone feel better, but it wasn't working. You know it's bad when even the stewardesses look worried.

So it was a bad journey to a place none of us particularly wanted to go to. I'm assuming the WRU were getting a handsome pay cheque from the South African Rugby Union, because there didn't seem any sense in following a tough tour of Argentina with a test in one of the most brutal rugby countries on earth.

A few days in the five-star surroundings of the Vineyard Hotel in Cape Town helped soften our mood, but it got a whole lot darker when Brent Cockbain received a phone call from home to say his little boy had been taken ill. It was an awful situation. I got on well with Brent and could not imagine what he must have been going through, flying home with that on his mind. Tragically, his boy, Toby, only lived for a few months longer before passing away.

Our thoughts were all with Brent as that South Africa test approached, and we wanted to do him proud. Deiniol Jones took his place in the second row, and Alix Popham was picked to start at Number 8. Mike issued him with an ultimatum before the game, telling him that if he didn't smash Schalk Burger at the first kick-off, he'd never play for Wales again. It was an odd motivational tool, but I guess Mike realised how physical the Boks were going to be, and he decided we had to take the initiative. Burger was more of a ball carrier in those days, and he'd often run down the ten channel attacking the opposition fly-half. Popham was to be Nicky Robinson's bodyguard for the day.

On the way to the ground, we were told we'd have to do a meet-and-greet with a local dignitary. None of the boys were particularly enthusiastic about it. It's one of rugby's ceremonial rituals, in which a visiting team is put on parade for some politician or minor royal to shake hands with and exchange small talk. I've always considered it an unnecessary distraction before a game, and thought this would be no different.

Until I found out it was going to be Nelson Mandela.

That changed everything. I was overwhelmed with nerves.

We lined up on the pitch and Charv, as captain, led him down to introduce him to each of us. I was trembling with anticipation. It seemed unreal. He was one of the world's most iconic figures, and to see him in the flesh was beyond exciting. He was eighty-six at the time, and very frail, but there was a grace about the way he moved and held himself. His exchanges with each of my teammates seemed perfunctory – a handshake and a nodded hello – so I racked my brain for something original to say.

The moment arrived. One of the world's greatest living human beings appeared in front of me.

I proffered my sweaty hand, and mumbled that it was an honour to meet him. Really original, Jones. I expected him to nod and move on, but instead he took a step back, and looked me over with those kind, gentle eyes.

Gesturing to my unruly mop, he said, 'I like your hair. I used to have hair like you when I was younger.'

Eight thousand miles away in Abercrave, my mother was going spare with excitement. Nelson Mandela had chosen to speak to her boy. The others had just had a handshake, but he actually *said* something to me. It's a moment I'll treasure for ever.

The South African anthem is intimidating. The first part is relatively tame. But when the Afrikaans section kicks in, the crowd goes ballistic. Although the white population is outnumbered by ten to one, and the government has introduced quotas to encourage greater participation among the black population, rugby remains the preserve of the white Afrikaner. The crowd response is doubly vociferous up on the high veldt. If there's one place that'll cause even the most mentally strong player to succumb to self-doubt, it's there.

It was an onslaught from the first whistle. Popham didn't smash Burger from the kick-off. Instead, Deiniol Jones – back in the side after a long absence – got poleaxed and had to leave the field after five minutes. It forced an immediate rejig, with the willowy Jon Thomas moving into the second row. Hardly ideal when you're up against the world's biggest pack on their home patch.

We had a scrum on our line. It was Gethin Jenkins, Mefin Davies and myself. We were up against John Smit (a massive hooker), 'Os' du Randt (a mutant of a man) and a giant by the name of Faan Rautenbach. Three twenty-stone monsters. Behind them, they had a massive second row – Bakkies Botha and Victor Matfield. That scrum was a horrible, bristling slab of grist and sinew. I felt like a callow twenty-three-year-old who was very much out of his depth.

We held them out, but I remember nothing of it. The pressure I felt on my head and shoulders was unlike anything I'd felt before. It was like being clamped and crushed by a vice. My vision started to narrow, and tiny worms started dancing before my eyeballs. The noise in the stadium became muted, as though I'd been plunged underwater. I was aware that I was holding my breath, trying to dig in, while those three brutes were trying to bury me in the turf. I was teetering back and forth, barely holding on to consciousness, and began to feel quite delirious.

My next conscious memory was standing at a line-out. I didn't know what day it was, what the score was, or how much time had elapsed since that scrum. A look at the tape later confirmed it was the line-out that followed our clearance kick from the scrum. But it could have been a different game, as far as I was concerned. I had no recollection of getting there. That was my first real taste of South African hospitality.

Popham had been marauding around the pitch as he'd been instructed to do, and as the game progressed he did manage a few big hits on Burger, but they were small moral victories within the wider narrative, which was unfolding with a depressing familiarity. South Africa were bigger, faster and stronger, and were beating us with ease. It reached a point where our backline didn't seem to care. Their shoulders dropped, and their warrior spirit deserted them. Even Popham's kamikaze approach eventually backfired. He launched himself into yet another tackle on Burger, and knocked himself clean out.

Not long after, on about the hour mark, I was taken off. I remember thinking, 'Thank God for that!' It had been a long, exhausting and dispiriting hour.

Mike Wadsworth, the masseur, chucked a jacket over me, said well done, and told me to put my feet up and have a drink. Darren Morris went on in my place. At the next scrum, 'Os' du Randt buried him. It was one of those bittersweet moments. You never want to see the Welsh scrum getting splintered. But when the guy who's getting minced is after your shirt, you're secretly quite happy.

Five minutes later, there's another scrum, and du Randt does exactly the same, drilling hard into Darren. Darren stands up, and gives away another penalty. He's in all sorts of trouble, and I'm just grateful it's him and not me.

But then I get the call. 'Bomb, you're going back on.'

Darren wasn't injured, but they had to pretend he was so I could return and try to shore up the scrum. I'd barely got my breath back. By this point, we were really down to the bare bones. Our reserve hooker, Huw Bennett, came on at openside flanker. Virtually everyone in the pack was playing out of position, and we just defended for about ten minutes until the clock went red. It was admirable the way we dug in, but it was clear we were all knackered.

I'm all for three-test tours, but bolting on a test to South Africa after a series in Argentina was sheer lunacy. If I'd had my way we'd have stopped off in Hawaii for the last leg.

The boys got 'on it' that night. Sometimes you just have to give in to the booze, and drown your sorrows. My sole cogent memory is of Rhys Williams winning a small fortune in the casino. We drank so much that most of the boys were still half-cut during the team briefing the following day, and some pretty heated exchanges took place as a result. The positivity following the second test in Argentina had been replaced by anger that we'd been made to play this final test. It served no purpose other than to shatter our confidence. And as often happens in those situations, things got personal and certain decisions came under the microscope. Clive Griffiths was given a load of fresh grief over his insistence on the blitz defence. Guys like Alfie and Tom Shanklin had never fully bought into it, and if the entire squad isn't singing from the same hymn sheet, you're asking for trouble on the pitch.

The 'blitz' would turn into the 'dritz', with some players preferring the old drift system that Steve Hansen favoured. So you'd end up with some players drifting, other blitzing, and the opposition taking full advantage of the inevitable chaos. I wasn't to know it then, but these cracks in the squad would grow wider with time, eventually developing into yawning chasms that would cause seismic ruptures across Welsh rugby.

Personally, I was enjoying myself. I was being picked. I felt valued and respected, and I wanted no part of the 'sapping' and sniping that was going on behind the scenes. I was younger and perhaps more naive than some of the others, but there's an old adage that the best coaches are the ones that pick you. I was playing regularly so I had no problem with the management.

● ● ●

Things were on the up at the Ospreys as well – we began the 2004/2005 season with a seven-game winning streak – which meant we arrived back in the Wales camp that autumn brimming with confidence. As before, it was a little more 'old school' with Mike Ruddock, with a strong emphasis on the set piece. But there seemed to be a good degree of harmony in the squad this time around.

People have since accused Mike of being too much of a delegator, of not doing enough hands-on coaching, and taking a disproportionate amount of credit when things went well. I totally disagree. The idea that Mike delegated authority to players and then claimed the credit is absurd. What he did was no different to any other head coach I've worked under. He picked his generals and entrusted them with their roles.

Rob Sidoli was in charge of line-outs, and the extra responsibility helped him grow as a player. It didn't mean Mike was ceding authority;

he was investing it. It's no different to Alun Wyn Jones running the line-out now. By their nature, line-out forwards are massive nerds who immerse themselves in that aspect of the game. They study it constantly, and you need that kind of player in that role to give it the attention to detail it requires.

South Africa were up first. It was an obvious chance for revenge, although we were under no illusions about the enormity of the task. We'd only beaten them once in more than a hundred years of trying. Ryan Jones was picked for his debut, which meant there were six Joneses in the starting fifteen. Naturally the press love all that kind of nonsense, so a day of photo shoots was arranged with the six of us, while the usual lazy stereotypes about the Welsh and 'keeping up with the Joneses' were resurrected and spun into ever less imaginative puns by the newspapers.

The game started badly. Ryan missed a tackle and they scored a try. But we fought our way back, and we gave a far better account of ourselves than we had at Loftus Versfeld. Gavin Henson and Sonny Parker played very well together in the centre, and Daf Jones was outstanding on the blindside flank. He was a very good player – perhaps a little underrated by some – and would run through walls all afternoon. He is one of the most passionate Welshmen you could hope to meet. His contribution was summed up during once incident when he found himself with the ball and a one-on-one with South Africa's poster boy, Percy Montgomery. Daf stuck his head down and bulldozed through him, knocking Montgomery clean out. It led to one of Henson's two tries, and rattled the Boks.

Dwayne Peel was another strong influence, taking quick taps, keeping the tempo high and forcing their heavy forwards to run around and tire themselves out. He scored the last try of the game after we marched them back in the scrum on their own line. It wasn't enough to win the game, but it got us within two points and was a damn sight more encouraging than the 53–18 drubbing a few months earlier.

• • •

Our performance against South Africa gave us confidence ahead of the next test against New Zealand. Richie McCaw was captaining the All Blacks for the first time, and a lot was expected of him. He wasn't quite the talisman he's since become, but he was already a master at the breakdown, and we knew that was a key area. Mike picked Daf Jones and Charv at Numbers 6 and 7, and they worked brilliantly in tandem. McCaw admitted afterwards it was one of the hardest games he'd played in.

People have said to me since that the atmosphere in the stadium that day was one of the best they've ever experienced. I have to admit, I don't remember it that way. New Zealand did their customary haka, which always sends a chill down the spine. Our response was to send the opera singer Wynne Evans on to the pitch to sing 'Bread Of Heaven' while waving a Welsh flag. Unless you recognised him from the GoCompare adverts, or were a regular attendee at the opera, chances are you wouldn't have had a clue who he was. The players were all looking at each other and thinking, 'Who's the fat bloke in the baggy Welsh shirt?' It was hardly an appropriate response to a blood-curdling Maori war dance. Perhaps I was a little too much in the zone to appreciate the emotion of it, but it wasn't as memorable for me as it appears to have been for the fans. The All Blacks must have thought we were taking the piss.

The match started brilliantly. Stephen Jones put in a clever kick for Tom Shanklin to chase, and it bounced kindly for us to take an early lead. Joe Rokocoko pulled one back for them, but we went into the sheds ahead at half-time.

Early in the second half, we extended our lead through Mefin Davies (who was playing semi-pro rugby for Neath at the time, following the collapse of the Celtic Warriors). But the All Blacks are arch predators. They prey on the smallest of mistakes and are more adept at spotting mismatches than any other team in world rugby.

It was Joe Rokocoko's vision and pace that ultimately won it for them. He received the ball in his own half and looked up to see myself, Mefin Davies and Brent Cockbain in front of him. Three sluggish forwards. A man of his pace and agility needs no better invitation. We only had about a twenty-yard channel to defend, but he turned on the afterburners and ran around us all. Shanks was scrambling back as the last line of defence, but he got absolutely skinned. Rokocoko cruised to the line in a piece of instinctive brilliance. He was a very special player.

It was the most agonising of defeats. Wales hadn't beaten the All Blacks for fifty-one years, and we lost that day by a solitary point.

It frustrates me to this day that we blew a chance to win the match. We had a line-out fifteen metres from their try line with two minutes to go. Our set pieces had gone perfectly all day. We hadn't lost a single ball on our own throw. We had a so-called 'red' bail-out call which Brent Cockbain would use if he thought he was free. If he called it, it would override the expected move. Brent called it. Jabba responded by throwing the ball directly at him. But Ali Williams saw it coming and leapt high for the interception.

The once-in-a-lifetime chance was lost.

You can't blame Brent. He had the balls to override the call, and it didn't pay off. It happens. But the consequences on this occasion were huge.

CHAPTER 8

Grand Slam Fever

THERE'S no such thing as a weak England side. They have a bigger playing population than any other country in the world and are the envy of every other nation when it comes to strength in depth. So their supposed injury crisis in the build-up to the 2005 Six Nations didn't stir any sympathy in me. Whatever side came to Cardiff for their opening fixture would be a bloody good one. And given their recent record against us, they'd have been favourites whatever fifteen that took to the field.

Having said that, they were missing some big names. The 'big three' back row of Dallaglio, Hill and Back were all out. Martin Johnson had retired, and there was no Jonny Wilkinson. We'd have approached the game with a little more trepidation had those five been playing. (Not that I'd have admitted that to the press.) They based their game around their scrum. Julian White had become a feared scrummager. He was a no-nonsense, aggressive bloke, famed for his reliance on the 'double shove' – a tactic that, if done correctly, can yield penalty after penalty and win games. Very boring. Very conservative. Very English.

But no one loves a scrum more than Mefin Davies. He could lose a game by twenty points but come out on top in the scrum and be happy. For him, a scrum on the march is a far more pleasing sight than a length-of-the-field try. In the week leading up to that England game, Mef held a series of seminars in which he forensically analysed the English scrum, identifying potential areas of weakness. And boy, did it pay off. Mef and Melon squeezed Julian White so tight at every scrum, he was barely able to move. We'd identified their most potent weapon, and neutralised it.

We did a real number on them in the close confines of the scrum and line-out – the tight spaces where the front row forwards earn their crust. In the loose, by way of contrast, I was made to look a fool on a few occasions. Finding myself in the unusual position of chasing up a kick, I made it my business to poleaxe the Englishman waiting to receive it. Fortunately, it was a man of similar dimensions to me – their hooker, Steve Thompson. As a prop, you fear the one-on-ones with the fleet-footed backs, but I fancied my chances of bringing a fellow fatty to the ground. My optimism was misplaced. Thompson caught the ball, looked up and stepped delicately off his right foot, while I launched myself into the space he'd occupied a split second earlier. By the time I'd hauled myself back to my feet, he was twenty yards further down field. He may have been an unusually mobile hooker, but it didn't make it any less embarrassing.

People remember it as 'Gav's game', and they think of three incidents: the two massive tackles he put in on a waiflike Mathew Tait, and the monster penalty kick to win it. All three were classic flashpoints, but it's wrong to reduce his role to a few, admittedly special, cameos. He was in his absolute prime then. He organised the defence and the attack, taking a lot of pressure off Stephen Jones. And he had a confidence and a swagger that few Welsh players had at the time. Generally speaking, we're a modest race. Not prone to self-aggrandisement and egotism. We leave that to the English and the Aussies. But Gav was carved from a different mould. Not many people could strut around with that orange tan and Soul Glo hair, and get away with it. But he did, because he was so damn good.

For my money, the best tackle in that game wasn't one of Gav's but one of Mefin's, on Jason Robinson. He was by far their most dangerous player, and one we knew we had to close down at every opportunity. When he launched an early counter-attack, there was a collective intake of breath from the supporters, all of whom remembered what he'd done to us in the World Cup quarter-final. Mef didn't panic. He kept his position, lined Robinson up and stopped him dead in his tracks. It's what I should have done with Steve Thompson. It wasn't a YouTube moment like Gav's big tackles were. But it sent out a message, and set the defensive tone for the rest of the match.

There was only one try in the game and it was scored, predictably, by Shane Williams. His finish out wide on the left was tremendous, but the scoring pass was even better. Michael Owen – a back row forward – sent a looping thirty-yarder right into Shane's bread basket. You wouldn't come across many Number 8s capable of that kind of sorcery. It was not so much that he *threw* the pass but the fact he had the *balls* to throw the pass. He played rugby with his head up, and it was a pleasure to watch. The way the modern game is going, particularly in the Northern Hemisphere, most Number 8s would stick it up the jumper and truck it up. But he had the vision and the composure to throw a pass any back would have been proud of. I felt sorry for him later, when he was messed around positionally and made to play in the second row. He was never a second row. He didn't have the ballast. Ask anyone who he's scrummaged behind and they'll tell you he's about as effective as a five-year-old boy. But in terms of footballing ability and sheer athleticism, he had few peers.

Gav's kick to win it was unbelievable. Some kickers dread moments like that. It's the moment a team game becomes a lonely, solitary pursuit. The entire game hinged on it. It was the difference between an epic victory and a miserable defeat. That's how narrow the margins can be in international rugby. But there was no reticence from Gav. No hesitation. He was made for that moment. He looks like the star, he acts like the star, and that day he became the star. As much as he comes across as a flash bastard, his work ethic is phenomenal. That's what people don't see. That kick was fiendishly difficult. But he'd done it thousands upon thousands of times before. Never in front of 75,000 people, perhaps, with such a weight of history and expectation bearing down on him. But his dedication to his craft meant he knew he was capable of finding the target.

Watching him line it up, I felt serene. I knew he was going to nail it. And he did.

● ● ●

The Italy game was significant because it was the first time we'd be returning to Rome since the ignominious defeat of two years earlier. Italy had gone well against Ireland in their opening game, but the high we experienced after beating England meant we travelled with confidence.

Whenever you play the Azzurri, you have to approach it with a bit of ambition. They always have a strong scrum and driving line-out, but they rarely have the class out wide that can penetrate well-organised defences. If you can match them up front, you should have the advantage behind. Bide your time, and cut loose when the opportunity arises.

It arose far more quickly than we anticipated, that day. Jonathan Thomas scored early on, and we knew then it was a question not of whether we'd win, but by how much. Four of the six tries were scored by forwards, including a thirty-yarder by Brent Cockbain. God knows how he managed that, because he's slower than me. But when he picked that line, and pinned his ears back, I knew the stars were aligned.

● ● ●

The French game was an altogether different test. It was in Paris for a start, which is an incredibly tough place to play. And that day it was horrendously cold – the kind of cold that seeps into your bones. It was set to be a thorough examination of my credentials, as I'd be up against Sylvain Marconnet, a scrummager of considerable renown. He was one of the best loose-heads in the world, and Mef and I did a considerable amount of homework to ensure I was prepared for what was coming my way. We watched video after video of Marconnet making mincemeat of opposition props, and tried to come up with subtle ways of stopping him.

The first scrum is obviously massive for a prop. No two opponents are the same, and the first time you stare into your adversary's eyes, the first time you thunder into one another with all your force and power, you get a sense of whether or not it'll be your day. You cannot underestimate the importance of a successful first scrum. Your confidence soars, while your opponent's is shattered. Or vice versa. It's an immense psychological blow. On that day, my confidence was shattered to pieces. In the first scrum, and every one that followed, I was hammered. Every time we locked horns, I went down or I went backwards. It was a thoroughly dispiriting experience. My first and most important job is to lock the scrum, and I was failing repeatedly to do it.

It was a pivotal day in my rugby education. Until then, I always tried to play within the laws. I wasn't interested in cheating or in trying to fool the referee. After that, I realised that when the stakes are so high, you need to be streetwise. Rugby is not a game of absolutes. The law book is painstakingly long, and most of the laws are open to interpretation. Did that ball go forward? Was he off his feet? Did he attempt to roll away? And for me, was that scrum collapsed deliberately? Was he scrummaging straight? Was he binding correctly? The referee is under enormous pressure out there and has to make split-second decisions under the scrutiny of millions of viewers.

As Jonathan Humphreys later told me, 'The floor is your friend.' If you feel as though you've lost the hit, and your opposite number has got a shove on, it may be the more noble course of action to try and stay in the fight and attempt to regain the advantage. But the likelihood of you doing so is slim. A scrum going forward is nigh on an irresistible force. As cynical as it sounds, it's better to swallow your pride, collapse the thing, and hope the referee doesn't realise it's your fault. That way, you get the chance to put things right.

Sometimes, though, you just have to hold your hands up and admit that your opposite number is better. That day in Paris, Marconnet was significantly better. Most frustratingly of all, he didn't have to resort to dirty tricks in the way some French players do. He played entirely within the laws, and gave me a proper tuning. I had no complaints.

The first half was diabolical. We were outmuscled and run ragged. Any hubris we may have had following the opening two rounds evaporated in the ice-cold Paris air. The French were menacing and direct, and we were all at sea. There was an enormous gulf in class between the two sides, and our Grand Slam dream began to implode before our eyes. When Dimitri Yachvili took advantage of a sloppy defensive lapse and scored an early try, the writing appeared to be on the wall.

Shane Williams was being terrorised by Aurélien Rougerie. The tall, strapping Frenchman was trampling over Shane every time he touched the ball. Their individual duel was a microcosm of the contest as a whole. We were being bullied. Stephen Jones knocked over a penalty to make it 15–6 at half-time, but it felt like only a matter of time before the dam burst. We couldn't have complained if we'd been thirty points down, such was France's total dominance.

What followed was one of the most complete transformations in test rugby history. There was no panic in the dressing room. No Churchillian speeches from Mike or any of the players. We just talked about how inhibited we'd been. We knew what we were capable of after the Italy game, but we hadn't had the chance yet to express ourselves. 'Get your hands on the ball!' was the order. Go through the phases, go through the patterns. We reminded ourselves that we'd beaten England and run South Africa and New Zealand close in the autumn.

Michael Owen was handed the captain's armband, as Alfie had broken his thumb in the first half, and he was very calm. There were no histrionics, just a pragmatic talk about what needed to be done. His calmness rubbed off on everyone else, and we emerged for the second half feeling as though we had nothing to lose.

I was surprised to see France had subbed Nicolas Mas off, and moved Marconnet to tight-head. It was a bizarre decision, but a very welcome one from my point of view. My arch torturer was now on the other side of the scrum, and from that point on I was fine. Rougerie, who had been so majestic in the first half – all rippling thighs and thunderous charges – suddenly looked clumsy and disoriented. Shane Williams, his rag doll in the first half, had turned into his impish nemesis. A cackling jester nipping, darting and wrong-footing him at every turn.

It was another Williams, though, who was the architect of that victory. The Maerdy Maestro, Martyn Williams, scored two tries in five minutes, totally changing the momentum of the match. The first saw him work a neat one-two with Shane. The second was the work of an arch-poacher. A quick tap penalty, followed by a burrow over the line.

There followed a number of twists and turns, but that period just after half-time set the tone for the victory. For me, though, the critical moments came during the last five minutes, when the French were hammering away at our line. I'd been subbed off by that point so was forced to watch helplessly from the sidelines. The spirit shown in defence was outstanding. We smashed them on the gain line every time they mounted a fresh attack.

When the final whistle blew, we were overcome with joy. We'd beaten France in Paris. Forty minutes earlier, we'd been getting stuffed. But we turned it around brilliantly, thanks to a bit of Martyn Williams magic and a huge surge of self-belief. The reaction at the end said it all. The boys were running around like they'd won the World Cup.

We had a few beverages that night in a little bar off the Champs-Élysées. It's nice to follow up a big win with a few drinks with the boys, as opposed to heading off into the night where the group inevitably splits up into different cliques. As we supped our *vin rouge*, we talked tentatively of the Grand Slam. We knew that we were in with a shout, and it was exciting. None of the squad had been through it before, and there was a real sense that history was unfolding in front of our eyes.

● ● ●

Wales hadn't won a Grand Slam for twenty-seven years. Every single member of that squad was lying when they told the press they weren't thinking about the Grand Slam when we were three wins from three. Of course we were. We couldn't not be. It's one of the biggest prizes in our sport, and to think we were robotic enough to block it out of our thoughts is nonsensical.

In any walk of life, if you have any shred of ambition, you're going to think about what it would be like to reach the pinnacle. It's human nature. And World Cups aside, winning a Grand Slam represents the pinnacle of our sport. Yes, we'd trot out the usual clichés to the press: 'We're not thinking beyond the next game. It's one game at a time. Blah, blah, blah.' But in every Grand Slam campaign I've been involved in, believe me, we've all been talking and thinking about the ultimate prize. The trick is not to allow yourself to be consumed by those thoughts. Three from three is great, but things can easily go tits up.

It was so important for us to maintain our focus ahead of the Scotland game. Some of the younger players thought a win up in Scotland was a formality, so it was up to the older boys to convince them that Murrayfield is a fiendishly difficult place to play. Expectations were soaring among the public and the press, and the positivity was surging through our camp. The feeling was that, unless our standards dropped drastically, we were on course for a clean sweep and Scotland was just a speed bump along the way.

The coaches did a good job of keeping us level-headed. They didn't pour cold water on our optimism, but gently reminded us that Wales didn't have a great record up in Scotland. During one team meeting, Mike Ruddock asked all those who'd won in Murrayfield to raise their hand. Only Gareth Llewellyn did. That was the moment when any complacency disappeared.

Despite the attempts to keep our emotions in check, once we'd kicked off we knew this was going to be our day. Ryan Jones started and finished an incredible try after just four minutes, and the floodgates burst open. Rhys Williams, Shane Williams and Kevin Morgan all scored in that first half, and we were 38–3 ahead at half-time. It felt as though we could do no wrong. Every speculative offload found a pair of hands, and yawning gaps opened up left, right and centre. It was the easiest half of international rugby I'd ever played in.

The second half was a lesson for us. Instead of going for the jugular, we eased off, allowing Scotland to mount a comeback. It happens in rugby a lot. You manoeuvre yourself into a winning position, and then switch off psychologically. You abandon the structure you've been playing to, and errors creep in. Conversely, the opposition feel they have nothing to lose and start to play with reckless abandon. Scotland won that second half convincingly. But it didn't stop us recording a record victory in Murrayfield, by 46 points to 22.

That was the game when the 'new style' seemed to crystallise. This notion of the Welsh way – seeking space rather than contact – was abundantly apparent. Everything that we had trained and practised for clicked in that first half. But the second half, particularly the last twenty minutes, served as a welcome warning. It gave us a few things to work on defensively that we may otherwise have overlooked ahead of the final match. Despite romping to victory, we'd had to make 205 tackles – our highest number in the tournament to date.

● ● ●

We barely trained the week before the Ireland game, because Mike felt we were as fit as we needed to be. The pressure was all coming from the outside. Within the camp we were relaxed. We'd generated so much momentum that we felt invincible. Ireland hadn't lost in Cardiff for twenty-two years, but I was convinced that, come Saturday, their time was up.

The management were very clever in the way they handled us that week. We were encouraged to get away from the rugby environment, to distance ourselves from the hype and expectation. I popped back to Neath a few times to hang out with my mates. In camp, there was no tub-thumping, no rally-crying. Nobody was talking about wanting to smash the Irish. No one was channelling the spirit of Owain Glyndŵr. It was all very calculated, very precise. We looked at their strengths and weaknesses, and came up with subtle ways to exploit them. Brian O'Driscoll was an obvious talisman for them, so Clive Griffiths and Tom Shanklin hatched a plan to shackle him and keep his influence to a minimum. We focused far more on ourselves than we did on them. We were convinced we'd win the game if we played to the best of our ability.

That's not to say there wasn't an appeal to the emotions. Alun Carter, our video analyst, put together a stirring montage of our campaign highlights to the soundtrack of 'Dakota' by the Stereophonics. The blood was pumping and the juices were flowing when we watched it the night before the match. After that, my job was to go on the chocolate run, along with Jon Thomas. We took orders from everyone in the team room, and returned from Tesco with a car boot full of the stuff. The night before the biggest game for three decades was spent slouched in the team room at the Vale Hotel watching films and gorging ourselves on Dairy Milk.

I usually take a sleeping tablet the night before a match, to stop my mind racing about what's to come. Back then, I'd be consumed by nerves in the build-up to a big game. The adrenaline would start coursing around my system early, and I'd start to get really apprehensive about running on to the pitch. Thankfully, I got a good night's sleep, and we were hearing reports in the morning that thousands upon thousands of Welsh fans were pouring into Cardiff city centre. It was a glorious sunny day, and a big screen had been set up outside the civic centre for all those who didn't have tickets. There were predictions that Cardiff's population would swell by about 150,000.

After lunch, the bus arrived bedecked in red bows, and we travelled the ten or so miles into Cardiff with a police escort. It was a journey I'll never forget. As we crawled closer and closer towards the Millennium Stadium, the crowds grew thicker and more dense, until I was convinced the entire population of Wales was crammed into the capital. I imagined that towns and villages throughout the Valleys and beyond were deserted. They all wanted to be able to say, in decades to come, 'I was there.' The sun was beating down, and the beer was flowing. The crowds were excited. Expectant. When they saw the bus they'd go crazy. Cheering, shouting, singing and raising their glasses.

It was humbling to be at the centre of such a swirling vortex of passion and emotion. The fifteen of us picked to wear that jersey had the power to dramatically alter the mood of each and every one of these supporters. The power to dramatically alter the mood of the entire nation. A nation starved of success for so long. Humbling, yes. And a little terrifying at the same time.

The changing room was calm. Gethin Jenkins, the musical dictator, had a playlist going. A medley of hardcore dance music. Nobody else had a say. People tend to think that at this stage players are stomping around, yelling and head-butting walls, but we didn't have any of those types in our team. Michael Owen spoke, reminding us that we'd done our homework, we were as prepared as we'd ever be, and we just had to get out there and execute the plan. He was cool, clinical and precise.

The anthem was a little more passionate than usual. Katherine Jenkins and Charlotte Church sang it with their Welsh jerseys on, but their angelic voices were drowned out by the feral roar of the crowd.

If you ask anyone to name their most memorable moment from that match, they'll inevitably say Gethin Jenkins's try. It was outstanding, but it was his 'celebration' that I remember most fondly. Ronan O'Gara was so frustrated that he'd been charged down and outpaced by a loose-head prop that he stamped on him as he crossed the line. Given the magnitude of the occasion, and the significance of what he'd just done, you'd think Melon could have ignored O'Gara's transgression and soaked up the celebrations. Not a chance. His first thought was to run at O'Gara and throw the ball at his head. Standard Melon behaviour. Always angry, always on the verge of a tantrum – even after scoring one of the most significant tries in the history of Welsh rugby. He missed O'Gara's head as well. Brilliant. It was a hell of a try, though. A prop has no business scoring a try like that. I'm just jealous.

Defence was key. Mark Taylor came in at the last minute for an injured Rhys Williams on the wing. It meant we lost a bit of X-factor in attack, but I don't think Rhys will mind me saying that Tayls was defensively stronger than he was. He did a great job of shackling the dangerous Irish back three. Rhys had been a doubt all week, but Mike was determined to keep it secret. Mark's last-minute inclusion was such a surprise that, about ten minutes in, Kevin Maggs tackled Tayls before getting up, confused and asking, 'What the bloody hell are you doing here?!'

We also stopped their driving line-out. The previous year in Dublin, Shane Byrne had scored two easy tries from driving line-outs, and few things hurt a forward pack's pride more than that. Sometimes these things are about who can cheat the best. We cheated a bit better than them that day. I'd learned a lot under Humphs at the Ospreys about how to bend the laws. I'd love to reveal all here, but I'll be basing my future coaching career on such knowledge. So forgive me if I keep shtum about the specifics.

A monster Gav penalty and another couple from Stephen Jones pushed us into a 16–6 half-time lead, and we knew then we were forty minutes away from history. It was ours to lose. Just before the hour mark, we scored the decisive try through Kevin Morgan after a great midfield burst from Tom Shanklin. 'The Rat', as we call Kevin, has been dining out on that ever since. It kills him that people talk more about Gethin's try. He's like a player from the seventies – constantly living in the past – and will never miss an opportunity to remind people that his try won the Grand Slam for Wales.

I came off after about sixty-five minutes and was forced to watch the climax from the bench. Ireland came back into it with tries from Marcus Horan and Geordan Murphy, and although we had a decent cushion on the scoreboard, it was impossible to relax until the final whistle blew.

When it did, we knew history had been made.

Those 75,000 fans inside who'd got tickets went absolutely berserk. It meant as much to them as it did to us. The stadium felt as though it was shaking. We'd been through some miserable times in that red shirt but now, finally, we'd done it. What an experience, what a ride.

The emotions came flooding out when the trophy was presented. We'd tried so hard to keep a lid on things, to remain calm in the eye of the storm. Now the hard work was over, we could blow that lid right off.

● ● ●

If you're expecting some kind of revelatory insight into how it feels to win a Grand Slam, you won't find it here, because it's impossible to put into words. In decades to come, my reflections may be more revealing, but at the time the emotions are so raw, and so primal, it's hard to intellectualise them. What really mattered to me was getting to share the joy with those closest to me. All of our families piled into the changing rooms after the trophy presentation. My mam, dad and uncle were in there, getting their photos taken with the boys, and – more importantly, for Dad – with Katherine Jenkins. Beer cans were being sprayed open, the trophy was being passed around, and camera bulbs were flashing left, right and centre.

After the euphoria died down a little, my front row buddies and I chilled out with a few beers. Gethin put his shit music on again, and Ryan Jones prowled around desperately looking for a TV camera to talk to. As was the case before the game, nobody was going completely crazy. Shanks was wandering around naked as usual, telling lame jokes, but most of us were just relaxing, admiring our medals and quaffing champagne. There was a real sense of brotherhood among the boys, forged through all those years of adversity. Achieving something like that is one thing, but achieving it with some of your best mates makes it all the sweeter.

All I wanted to do then was hit the pub and start celebrating. I had no time for the post-match dinner back then. I've grown to like them over the years, but in 2005 I saw it as a tedious succession of speeches getting in the way of a good old-fashioned piss-up. After the meal, some of the boys – Shane, Gav, Kevin Morgan – headed into town, and most of the forwards, myself included, headed back to the Vale Hotel to prop up the bar until about seven in the morning. Mefin Davies was with me, and I have this vague memory of him drinking Malibu and milk while the rest of us guzzled gallon upon gallon of ale. Mike Ruddock provided the soundtrack to the night, with his acoustic guitar and his enormous repertoire of American pop songs. 'Is This The Way to Amarillo' seemed to go on for ever. I wished the night could have.

Saturday rolled into 'Super Sunday' and the celebrations continued into another day. The entire squad came out for that, apart from the boys who hadn't played and had been summoned back to their clubs. I felt so sorry for Jabba. He'd been 24th man for every game, so he hadn't got to run on the pitch, hadn't picked up a win bonus, and was now being denied the chance to celebrate. While we were indulging in a second day of drinking and debauchery, he was back training with the Dragons.

It was all fairly uneventful, apart from the moment when Gav chucked a glass off the top of a balcony in a Cardiff bar, like Begbie in the film *Trainspotting*. The more he drinks, the more moronic he becomes. He wasn't being aggressive or spoiling for a fight. He was just being stupid. Charlotte Church arrived within minutes to collect him. After some initial protests, he was bundled into the car and went home to sleep it off.

A few weeks later, I was approached in Neath by a young mother and her little girl who politely asked me to sign her copy of the commemorative Grand Slam book.

As I was flicking through to find an appropriate page to sign, the woman said to her little girl, 'Do you want to show Adam the picture of him in the nude?'

She flicked a few pages on and, sure enough, there I was standing in the shower, washing my hair. Stark bollock naked.

To say it was embarrassing would be something of an understatement. I apologised, signed the cover and shuffled away, leaving them tittering to themselves.

How it had slipped through the net, I'll never know. But suffice to say, the print run was pulled and a second, non-X-rated version of the book was issued. If you do have one of the originals, consider it a limited edition.

CHAPTER 9

Fallout

LET'S get one thing straight. If it hadn't been for Mike Ruddock we would not have won a Grand Slam. Those who claim the 2005 Grand Slam belongs to Hansen and Johnson are conveniently forgetting how much our game changed under Ruddock. Think of the Italy game that year. Victory was based on our determination to keep the ball alive at all costs. Some of the offloading and link play was breathtaking. We were encouraged to do a lot more of that under Ruddock, and we reaped the benefits. We played a lot of touch rugby and a lot of football in training. Forwards' sessions would consist of twenty minutes of football, twenty minutes of touch rugby and twenty minutes on the line-out. To a man, we loved it. It gave us fatties the confidence to express ourselves – and to consider ourselves ball players, as well as just big lumps of meat.

It was a shrewd tactical shift. We weren't a massive team physically, so we were never going to bully other sides into submission. Far more sensible, then, to play with pace and width, and to tire out some of the bigger, less skilful sides. That's not to say the instructions were to sling it around willy-nilly and hope for the best. It was more about imbuing the team with the confidence to play when the time was right. To go for it when you spied a gap.

More significantly than that, Mike Ruddock understood the importance of the scrum. You can have all the skills you like in international rugby, but unless you have a solid platform, you'll spend most of the game defending. Winning the ball, and keeping hold of it, is what it's all about.

For years under Steve Hansen, our scrum had been underpowered. We were soft up front. Teams knew that, and targeted us there. It hadn't been a priority for Steve. We often did scrummaging practice indoors, wearing trainers. Mike was a hard-nosed flanker from Blaina, and he knew that had to change. That's not to say he ripped up what Hansen and Johnson had done before him, but he added a few vital elements that turned a side with potential into a championship-winning side.

In his interview for the job, he was asked to pick his starting Welsh XV on the spot. He made sweeping changes in the pack, where he thought we were vulnerable. He told the board that I should start, as I was Wales' best scrummager, and that I should play at least sixty minutes. No more of this half-hour nonsense. He said he'd stop playing Melon on the tight-head because he didn't belong there. And that he'd put an end to playing people out of position. Michael Owen was being wasted in the second row, and Gavin Thomas — great player though he was — wasn't big enough to play at Number 8. All of those ill-advised selections had made the spine of the Welsh scrum weak.

He was forthright and direct, and it got him the job.

When he picked up the reins, he remained true to his word. Rather than picking the best rugby players and trying to accommodate them, he'd pick the best people in their best positions. He had Robin McBryde and Mefin Davies in his first squad – two of the most passionate scrummagers you'll ever meet – and was able to tap into their expertise. And he'd pick big, heavy, powerful second rows as opposed to lightweight beanpoles. It's all well and good being agile and athletic, but you need ballast to play at test level. His first-choice locks were big men like Rob Sidoli and Brent Cockbain, and you had the likes of Luke Charteris coming through in reserve. Absolute giants.

It's a Northern Hemisphere thing. Up here, there's a lot of emphasis on the scrum. It's not like in New Zealand, where it's just a means of restarting the game. It's a way of getting a psychological advantage, and of milking penalties. There's no point playing a 7 at 8, a 6 at 4, or a 1 at 3. It just doesn't make sense.

People might accuse me of being blinkered, and of supporting a guy who backed me, but the evidence is clear. Under Mike, we won our first Grand Slam in twenty-seven years. That's a fact. Trying to credit that entire campaign to the previous regime, which had left a year earlier, is a fallacy.

● ● ●

Mike's departure was a huge shock to the rugby public. It wasn't to me. Throughout his entire tenure, there'd been a continuous backdrop of sniping. Certain senior players who'd bonded with the previous regime constantly questioned Mike's methods, undermined his authority and made his life awkward. The spectre of Hansen and Johnno hung heavy over the new regime. They may not have brought us much in the way of success, but they had managed to engender an unswerving loyalty among an inner cabal of acolytes who refused to accept that Mike was the boss.

Martyn Williams was a big fan of Steve Hansen. It was through him that I found out about Ruddock's departure. We were in the middle of the 2006 Six Nations campaign, and were getting changed after a routine training session, when Nugget asked if I'd heard.

'Heard what?'

'About Mike. He's resigned.'

I was incredulous. We'd just beaten Scotland quite tidily, and would have won by more if Melon hadn't thrown an interception in the last minute. It seemed a very odd time to go.

Nugget insisted he didn't know the reasons why, but I was aware there had been clandestine meetings going on at the Miskin Manor Hotel between some of the senior players and the chief executive of the WRU, Steve Lewis.

Given our victory over Scotland, I had no idea it was anything more than a few grumblings which could have been sorted out fairly swiftly. The accusation was that Mike didn't really do much. Resentment had been simmering among some of the players that Mike had been awarded the MBE for coaching Wales to the Grand Slam, while they had got nothing. It was an absurd standpoint. Mike is one of the most magnanimous guys you're likely to meet. He did his utmost while in charge to deflect any praise on to the players. The idea that he was swanning around with his MBE and claiming all the credit was an absolute nonsense.

I dismissed the grumblings as sour grapes, and didn't think for a second they would force our head coach out in the middle of a campaign – a campaign in which we were defending champions, no less. If his departure wasn't a huge surprise, the timing of it certainly was. Mike said he was leaving for family reasons. But that has become the stock explanation for almost any club or country parting ways with their coach these days. I wasn't buying it.

Among the chief detractors were Gareth Thomas, Martyn Williams, Stephen Jones and Brent Cockbain. I'm not saying these guys were especially disruptive or manipulative, but it was clear that they were still in thrall to Hansen and Johnson. I'm pretty sure they all liked Mike as a bloke, but they didn't rate him as a coach.

He was definitely more of a 'director of rugby' type. A delegator. That may have looked to some as though he was too hands-off – he didn't have the tracksuit on enough – but most successful coaches are the same. Someone has to step back and see the bigger picture. That's the way Warren Gatland operates. And it's how Clive Woodward had been with England when they won the World Cup. Mike wasn't going to interfere too much in our attack, because Johnno had systems in place that were beginning to bear fruit. And he wasn't going to dictate how to call our line-outs, because Rob Sidoli and Brent Cockbain were in charge of that. But he did transform our scrum, and he wove all the disparate strands together to turn us into a winning team. He assessed what needed to change and made the necessary tweaks. But that wasn't enough for some of the boys, who'd started referring to him behind his back as 'the bus'. Because he wasn't a coach.

Unless I was really green, I wasn't aware of any kind of Machiavellian scheme to oust Mike and anoint Scott Johnson, who'd stayed on after Hansen left. There was a conspiracy theory doing the rounds that Johnno himself had orchestrated the whole thing; that he was whispering in players' ears and turning them against Mike. I think that was a little far-fetched. Yes, Johnson and Ruddock would clash and argue on the training paddock. But then so would Johnson and Hansen. There's nothing unusual about that – in fact, it's the sign of a healthy relationship. Johnno is flamboyant and doesn't try to contain his emotions. Mike is more reserved, and prefers settling differences behind closed doors. Rugby clashes aside, they always seemed to get on really well. Both are massive music fans, and they'd always sit at the front of the bus with Carcass, the physio, bantering about music, exchanging views about their favourite artists and favourite albums. There was no distance between them, as some have suggested. Ostensibly, they were mates. Or that's how it appeared to me.

Johnno definitely had his favourites. Shanks, Dwayne Peel and Stephen Jones were fully paid-up members of his fan club. But that was more a professional respect thing than a clique, because they credited him with bringing their game on. They were backs, and Johnno had given them a licence to thrill. They swore by his philosophy and responded readily to his unique brand of motivational coaching. He was your typical garrulous Aussie. Always smiling, always joking, always ready with a quip. A jovial jester as opposed to a sinister puppet master. I wasn't one of his disciples – partly because I was a forward, but mainly because I wasn't a senior player. He had a strong and persuasive personality and could be an enigma at times, but I don't think he had an evil plan to stab Mike in the back. If he was that type of bloke, he hid it very well.

The other conspiracy theory was that the WRU hierarchy wanted Ruddock out, and manipulated this group of senior players – via secret meetings with Steve Lewis – to spark unrest within the squad. Again, ludicrously far-fetched. The meetings took place. There's no doubt about that. One of the main topics of discussion was payment and insurance. Some of the more militant members of the group thought we weren't getting enough, and they found themselves in a better bargaining position after we'd won the Grand Slam. But clearly other things were discussed as well. I'm not privy to what, because I wasn't invited. But grievances were aired, and they stirred the unrest further.

There wasn't a 'Mike camp' and a 'Johnno camp'. It was never that polarised. But if anyone was going to put their arm around me and play the role of mentor, it was Mike. After that France game, when I'd had a shocker against Marconnet, he sensed I'd lost a bit of confidence. He brought the former Wales prop Stuart Evans in to help me out. He could have done it himself, but he knew that a fresh perspective would have really helped. That to me is a head coach's job. He'd seen I had a problem, and he did something positive to help fix it. He was a simple, straight-up-and-down sort of bloke, and I always knew where I stood with him.

Johnno, on the other hand, loved the mind games. He loved a quote, loved a proverb. One of his favourites was: 'The graveyards are full of indispensable men.' He was making the point that no one was irreplaceable, and that the world – or the team – could survive without you. He also loved a rousing call-to-arms. Before the Scotland game, in 2005, he delivered an emotionally charged speech about the Bell Rock Lighthouse. Some of the boys were visibly moved, but I didn't really get it. With Mike, you got sense. With Johnno, you often got nothing more than riddles. Mike's speeches were more pragmatic, and I preferred them. You don't need Ian McGeechan-style speeches every week, because they'll start to lose their impact after a while.

They both seem to have morphed into caricatures over the years. Johnno as a brash, long-haired Aussie, and Mike as a shy, modest Welshman. Their personalities are obviously more nuanced than that, but those are their defining characteristics. Perhaps Mike should have been a bit more authoritative from the start. Perhaps he should have dished out a few more bollockings when the dissent was beginning to rumble. Perhaps he should have put his foot down earlier with some of the big characters.

● ● ●

Ultimately, the whole saga of Mike's departure depressed the hell out of me. Here we were, the reigning Six Nations Champions, and less than a year after winning the Grand Slam, we were bickering among ourselves. Unfortunately, it's a defining part of the Welsh psyche. We don't handle success well.

We'd rested on our laurels after the Slam, and ended up having a poor autumn during which we were pumped by New Zealand and struggled past Fiji. Instead of using those results as a galvanising force and resolving to improve, certain players just looked around for someone to blame. And that someone was Mike. The Welsh mentality in a nutshell. It was conveniently forgotten that we'd beaten Australia in the final match – for the first time since 1987.

A word that appears to have entered the rugby lexicon over the past decade is 'sapping'. It basically means to sap the energy or positivity from a group. Too many sappers in your squad can bring the morale crashing down and make a head coach's job very difficult. There were more than a few in that squad. They were sapping about Mike's abilities as a coach, and his supposed lack of involvement. But you can guarantee they'd have been sapping about him being too strict and dictatorial, if that had been the case. Once a sapper, always a sapper. It's the way their brains are wired.

I liked Mike Ruddock more than Steve Hansen. I guess that's no surprise, because he picked me regularly and didn't humiliate me by taking me off after half an hour. But beyond that, I found him a nicer bloke. He was more approachable, and a better man-manager. He was decidedly more 'old school' in his approach, and there were those who thought we'd regressed under him. In training we'd do a lot of running up and down the field, ripping, mauling and popping in single file. A lot of players frowned on that, because it was considered old-fashioned.

It was the kind of stuff you'd do in youth rugby, and it hurt a few of the boys' egos to be made to do it again. They were thinking, 'Hang on, we're international rugby players. Why are we being made to do this?' When the Lions coach, Clive Woodward, came down to watch one of our sessions, you could tell some of the boys, like Alfie, were embarrassed. They were thinking what we were doing was so basic, and that England would presumably be light years ahead of us. (This was after we'd played England and beaten them.)

Some of the forwards objected to Mike's motivational techniques when it came to the scrum. He'd stand on the scrummaging machine, getting into you, shouting things like, 'Marconnet's gonna come at you hard! He's gonna smash you. You've got to dig in and hold your ground.' It was standard motivational stuff, and I found it useful. But afterwards, certain players would be bitching about it, saying it was unnecessary and patronising. I'm sure if Hansen had been doing it, they'd have loved it.

Those players I've mentioned weren't bullies, and they weren't actively trying to start a revolution, but they'd ask you what you thought about certain sessions. Did you think they were effective? Were they worthwhile? With every negative thought, and every question raised, they were chipping away at the foundations. The cracks grew wider, and those foundations eventually started to crumble.

Hansen had been more progressive in the eyes of many. Particularly when it came to the 'micro-detail'. He'd spend far more time on the contact area, identifying the best way to remove opposition players from rucks by identifying their weak spots. Mike's approach was much broader – but no less effective, in my opinion. We are seduced by a Kiwi accent here in Wales. Some players automatically assume that a Kiwi knows better. Again, it's the natural Welsh state. Our innate inferiority complex.

Ultimately, when we started to lose under Mike, the wound that had been left to fester opened right up, and arguments became commonplace. After we'd lost to England, in 2006, a lot of the boys wanted to go out into town, and Mike forbade it. He wanted us to stay in the hotel and have a quiet few beers. The Welsh fans were understandably angry at the manner of the defeat, and a number of them were hurling abuse at the team bus as we pulled away from Twickenham. Alfie was quite emotional and wanted to get out and fight them, so Mike understood that going out would not only give the wrong impression but might also lead to trouble. I agreed with him. I had a dead leg, so I wasn't going out anyway, but I think Mike's call was the right one. The dissenters were angry, because they thought they were being treated like children, and a few of them went out anyway.

The fault lines were beginning to turn into deep fissures.

● ● ●

In the immediate aftermath of Mike's departure, things took a surreal turn. Gareth Thomas – for many, the architect of Mike's demise – appeared on the BBC Wales rugby programme *Scrum V*. Rugby being the national sport in Wales, the entire nation felt betrayed by what had happened and wanted answers. To say it was car-crash TV would be a massive understatement. Alfie ended up going toe-to-toe with Eddie Butler, and there was only ever going to be one winner. Eddie is a former Wales captain, former Cambridge Blue, and one of the most erudite pundits on television. It was a mismatch in terms of intellect, and Eddie skewered Alfie on live TV.

Everybody had decided it was player-power that had forced Ruddock out, and nobody seemed to want to admit to it. Alfie was defiant, defending himself and his players to the hilt. But Eddie probed and pushed, causing him to spectacularly lose his cool.

I felt sorry for Alfie, because I really like him as a bloke. He was ill-advised to go on the programme. His intentions were honourable, but he came across as a man with something to hide. He clearly thought he was doing the right thing in the eyes of the rugby public, but many of them had already leapt to their own conclusions.

Why would you chuck a player on a show where they're going to be grilled about player-power? It was a recipe for disaster from the Union's point of view. I'm sure the BBC were happy enough, because it made for compelling television, but in my opinion, Alan Phillips or Steve Lewis should have gone on – someone from the hierarchy who could have been a bit more dispassionate. If you *had* to put a player on there, I'd have gone for someone like Colin Charvis. He's incredibly thick-skinned, and he would have played with a far straighter bat. He wouldn't have worked himself up into a frenzy, like Alfie did. He would have believed he was right in everything he said. As it was, the entire episode meant that the image of Welsh rugby sank even further into the mire.

Johnno took over for the rest of that 2006 campaign after Mike left, and it was a disaster. We got pumped in Ireland, drew with Italy in Cardiff, and lost to France. And for me personally, there was an awful experience of déjà vu. The day before the Ireland game, I was called into his office, where he revealed to me that he'd be taking me off after half an hour again. The humiliation that Mike had helped put behind me was about to return. His justification was that most scrums in the game occur in the first half an hour, and the last twenty minutes. So he'd bring me back on then.

What? How can you actually do that unless someone else is injured?

I couldn't believe it. It was all happening again. After all the heartache

I'd gone through under Hansen, it had come back to haunt me. The hurt and humiliation came flooding back. Perhaps it had been Johnno's idea all along. I argued my case with him, but he was adamant. I was fitter then than I had been in 2003, when it first happened.

I wish I'd had the balls to say, 'What the hell do you know about scrums? You're a backs coach!' But I bit my lip.

It made me realise that he'd probably tried to persuade Mike Ruddock to do the same, but Mike had stuck to his guns. As it transpired, Duncan Jones banged his head and I had to stay on against Ireland, and then ended up putting a full shift in against Italy and France.

It was such a monumental comedown from the euphoria of the year before. We'd gone from Grand Slam champs to fifth-placed chumps, in just twelve months. The environment was riven with mistrust. Unity and brotherhood had given way to bickering and backstabbing. And Johnno was woefully out of his depth as a head coach. The entire drama was so typically Welsh – to be given a glimpse of success, and to destroy it from within.

My biggest fear was that 2005 would be looked upon in decades to come as some historical curio – a random Grand Slam sandwiched between decades of mediocrity and misery.

CHAPTER 10

Warrior From the West

GARETH Jenkins was and is a national treasure, and I love him to bits. His achievements down west as coach of Llanelli speak for themselves. He is, hands down, the most passionate coach I've worked under. With his mellifluous speaking voice and his captivating manner, he's an absolute master of stirring the emotions. Everyone thought he'd be anointed Welsh coach in 2004, when Steve Hansen left. But as we know, Mike Ruddock emerged from the left field. So Gareth was forced to wait, and many speculated that his time had passed. Like his celebrated predecessor at Llanelli, Carwyn James, there were those who thought he was a little too maverick for the WRU. He didn't fit the mould. But his time came after Scott Johnson's tenure limped to an end. For those who'd always believed in him, it was the fulfilment of a destiny.

I didn't know him personally, but the Scarlets players in the squad spoke highly of him – particularly Stephen Jones and Dwayne Peel. Those boys were becoming pivotal figures in that Welsh squad, so I trusted their judgement.

Given what had happened under Mike Ruddock, and the catastrophic fallout that followed, we needed a big personality with a big heart to reignite the flame. From that point of view, there was no better bloke than Gareth. I liked him immediately. His enthusiasm was boundless, and I was looking forward to working with him.

In a parallel with the Ruddock regime, Gareth's tenure began with a tour to Argentina. It was to prove quite a baptism, because we had a long injury list, and there were a lot of new youngsters in the squad. Richard Hibbard, Alun Wyn Jones, Ian Evans and James Hook all came in to add a bit of fresh blood. From a personal point of view, I knew I had to up my game. Firstly, to try and impress the new man. And secondly, because an intense fellow called Chris Horsman had been called up, and he had designs on the Number 3 jersey. My jersey.

It felt like a clean slate after what had happened with Mike. Johnno didn't stick around, and Gareth brought Nigel Davies in – his right-hand man and confidant from the Scarlets. The fallout that had followed the Grand Slam could now be consigned to the history books, and we could set about penning a new chapter. Gareth and Nigel were used to success and felt they could translate that winning mentality to Wales. And my old mentor from Neath, Rowland Phillips, was brought along for the ride as defence coach.

It immediately seemed a happier camp under Gareth. He seemed to galvanise the boys by sheer force of personality, and it was impossible to dislike the guy. His ethos was similar to Mike's in that he was a delegator, rather than a hands-on coach, but nobody seemed to resent him for that in the way they did Mike. There were no grumblings about him not doing enough. Nobody called Gareth 'the bus'.

He set out his philosophy early, but it wasn't wildly different to what we were used to. It was a case of evolution, not revolution.

Mark Bennett was brought in as fitness coach, while Robin McBryde was already there as forwards coach. Nigel was in charge of attack, and Rowland defence. He decided we were a blitzing team, as Neath were at the time. As always with defensive strategy, there were dissenting voices. We were supposed to have been a blitzing team under Clive Griffiths but, as discussed, not everyone bought into it. We would go into games variously with a 'dritz' or a 'blitz' defence. And you don't need me to tell you, if the team aren't all defending to the same system, you'll concede tries. And probably lots of them.

So Rowland had to try and assert his authority on that one – not always easy when you're a renowned joker, like he is.

● ● ●

There is only one place in the world other than Wales where you can hear Welsh being spoken: Patagonia, at the southern tip of the South American continent. And it was there we began our 2006 summer tour. We were to play a test match in Puerto Madryn, where a hardy band of Welsh settlers had arrived in the nineteenth century. It was to be quite an adventure, and I was thoroughly looking forward to it. Rugby offers you unique opportunities to travel, and the older I was getting, the more I was beginning to appreciate that. It was the first time Wales had ever played there.

Hearing Argentinian people speaking Welsh on the other side of the world was an utterly surreal experience. As was seeing Welsh dressers and Celtic-inspired decor inside people's houses. It was one of the finest cultural experiences I've had on a rugby tour. A real once-in-a-lifetime opportunity. Patagonia is a unique place. Incredibly bleak and remote on one level, but breathtakingly beautiful on another. On one memorable day, while we were driving along the seemingly endless coast road, three enormous whales were following our route, breaching over and over again in the shallow waters close to the shore.

The people love their red meat down there, and we were treated to a big *asado* out in the street, where we gorged ourselves on heavenly, juicy steaks while the locals performed their Argentine tangos on the pavement. It was quite a sight, all those smoking carcasses on enormous tables, with slab after slab of tender, succulent meat being carved from them. The accommodation down there was basic, to say the least – particularly when you compared it to what we'd become used to – but that didn't seem to matter. The hospitality and the experience far outweighed any discomfort.

The company was great on that trip as well. There were some good tourists in the squad, like Gavin Thomas, Alix Popham and Matthew J. Watkins – all of them great characters. A lot of the senior boys – Stephen Jones, Dwayne Peel, Alfie and Martyn Williams – didn't tour, which allowed some of the younger guys to come out of their shells. Duncan Jones, my fellow 'Hair Bear', was captain and did a sterling job. I'm happy to report there were no rent-boy incidents this time around.

This was also the tour on which Richard Hibbard – or 'Fatrick Sleazy', as I like to call him – won his first cap. A few of the boys didn't know quite how to take him. He was rooming with Gavin Thomas in Puerto Madryn, and Gav came down to breakfast one morning looking confused, before declaring in his distinctive lisp that he'd woken in the middle of the night to find Hibbard astride him, smacking him over the head with a pillow. He'd apparently been snoring a little too loudly for Hibbard's liking.

Gav was bewildered that some young tyro had had the audacity to do such a thing. 'I don't even know the boy!' he kept repeating, incredulously.

The good spirit on the tour was, in a large part, down to Rowland. His defence sessions were hard work, but they were laced with good humour and mickey-taking, and the young boys lapped it up. Those of us who knew him from Neath had an advantage, because we knew how to read him. Others who were slower on the uptake became his victims. Any little quirks or tics were noted, and used as ammunition against you.

Hibs used to play with his nuts a lot. He rarely wears pants, and likes to 'readjust' himself downstairs frequently. Rowland clocked this early on and every time he did it, wherever we were, he'd shout, 'Honk!' We might be training, at a team meeting, or sitting down for breakfast. He'd sometimes do it in the middle of a speech. Gradually, all the boys cottoned on to what was going on. Everyone was in on the joke – except Hibs. It took him the entire tour to figure out what was going on. And that's only because Dunc and I told him.

● ● ●

The warm Argentinian hospitality didn't quite extend to the test match down in Patagonia. It was played in a football stadium with barbed-wire fences, not dissimilar to the one we'd played in in Tucumán two years previously. And the reception was equally hostile. Ian Evans scored a great interception try in the first ten minutes, not long after Mark Jones had touched down, and the crowd did not like it one bit. The toilet rolls came raining down once again, and the fiery Spanish abuse rose to a crescendo.

We lost Gavin Thomas and Alix Popham to the sin bin shortly after Ianto's try, and Argentina struck back. Once they got their driving line-out functioning, we struggled to contain them, and they ground out a narrow 27–25 victory. It wasn't the ideal start to Gareth Jenkins's coaching reign, but it wasn't a disaster either. James Hook came on for his debut in the second half and scored a try. He'd only signed a professional contract with the Ospreys a few months earlier, so it was a remarkable rise to the top.

The second test was in Buenos Aires and, by then, they'd hit their straps. Felipe Contepomi was back from sitting his medical exams, and his influence was considerable. A late try for Lee Byrne put a bit of gloss on the 45–27 scoreline, but we were well beaten. It was the first time we'd lost a test series in Argentina, but spirits weren't too low. More than twenty front-line players had missed the tour, and we knew we had a bit of strength to call upon when we returned to Welsh shores.

After the test, Ianto was cited for a cheap shot on Agustín Pichot, and the disciplinary hearing was held in the hotel during our post-match function that same night. And when I say in the hotel, I mean literally in the room where we were having dinner. Farcically, they'd cordoned off a section with some rope, but it was happening in full view of everyone. By this time, the dinner had descended into a rather debauched affair. Some of the players were steaming drunk, heckling the speakers and throwing bread rolls at each other. It was no way to behave, given the hospitality we'd received. While all this was going on, the IRB was going about the serious business of dishing out a ban for Ianto. Ludicrous.

As we left the hotel, we passed the All Blacks, who were arriving as Argentina's next opponents. They looked a bit taken aback at the state of some of our players. Some words were exchanged and the next thing I knew, Mike Phillips was squaring up to their back rower – and future Osprey – Jerry Collins, offering him out for a fight. Jerry was a big man, and we could see the way things were going, so a few of us stepped in to wrestle them apart. They laughed about it subsequently, but at the time it felt deadly serious. Mike had had a few and thought he could take on the world. He can handle himself, Mike. There's no doubt about that. But against a gargantuan Samoan-Kiwi like Jerry Collins, he'd have come off second-best.

I like a drink as much as the next guy, but I have to admit I woke up the next morning feeling embarrassed for the way we'd conducted ourselves the previous evening. I'd been brought up better than that, and in a moment of rare anger I stood up in our team meeting and told everyone exactly what I thought. I was angry that we'd let ourselves and our country down. I wouldn't have thought I'd end up being the moral voice of the group, but in the absence of so many senior players I felt the need to stand up in the face of such behaviour.

● ● ●

The expectation that the return of our front-line players would transform us into winners wasn't exactly realised that autumn. We had Australia first up, at the Millennium Stadium, and fancied our chances. We'd beaten them the previous year and had watched the Ospreys beat them three days earlier. We were settled behind the scenes under Gareth, and we had most of the Grand Slam-winning side back in the saddle. The backline was the 2005 vintage, and the pack only had a few changes – Matthew Rees came in at hooker, and Ianto and Ian Gough came into the second row.

But despite our confidence, we could only manage a draw – always an unsatisfactory result. 'Like kissing your mother-in-law,' as Scott Johnson famously said.

Personally speaking, I'd put in a decent shift. We had the Australian front row under pressure for much of the game but, as usual, their backs were a real handful. You couldn't turn your back on them. We did that – literally – for one try. Assuming Matt Giteau was going to kick for goal, we all turned and trundled towards our try line. The crowd groaned in unison, and by the time we'd swivelled around, it was too late. The arch trickster had taken a quick tap and scooted over the line. It was typical Wallaby opportunism. We held the lead for some time in that game, but in the end we had to rely on a late penalty from Hooky to salvage some pride.

So, we were three games into Gareth Jenkins's reign, and still without a win. Despite that, morale remained high. I got on well with the coaches, although I did find Nigel Davies a bit aloof. When you compare him to the larger-than-life personalities of Gareth and Rowland, he came across as a bit glum. I didn't have a great deal to do with him, but I had the impression he didn't rate me and would have preferred someone more mobile in my position. Down at the Scarlets, they'd always had guys like Martyn Madden and John Davies. Big ball carriers, who liked to show up in the loose. I was proved right after the World Cup, when Nigel dropped me for Rhys Thomas. But for the time being, Gareth was keeping the faith.

Training sessions were long under Gareth, and tended to drag. Every coach had to put in their twopenn'orth. There was a lot of talking and, at times, little intensity. We'd go through moves again and again. And if someone made a mistake, we'd keep going until we got it right. Later in my career, Warren Gatland would come in and totally revolutionise that approach, insisting on short, sharp, intense sessions with no room for slack. Under Gareth, sessions might merge into team meetings, and there'd be lengthy discussions that would drag them out beyond an hour and a half. I prefer most of the planning and talking to be done beforehand in the team room. Don't get me wrong, you have to stop and speak sometimes, but those interruptions should be kept to a minimum.

There was a perception among some in the media that Gareth's time in charge of the national side had come too late. That he should have been given the job earlier, when he was winning Welsh Cups left, right and centre with the Scarlets. There was a feeling that Graham Henry and Steve Hansen had brought in a more advanced, Southern Hemisphere way of thinking, and that Gareth was a man out of time. For me, this was the Welsh inferiority complex rearing its head again. The lazy assumption that those from the Southern Hemisphere knew better. For what it's worth, I thought Gareth was very studious in his approach. He scrutinised the opposition and searched for chinks in their armour that could be exploited. Sometimes it worked, sometimes it didn't, but you couldn't accuse him of being underprepared.

As for the inference he was stuck in the nineties, that's a total nonsense. The WRU was always willing to spend money on the national side, so he embraced things like nutrition, GPS, recovery sessions and the dreaded ice baths — all those little one-percenters that can mean the difference between victory and defeat. Mark Bennett was big into his stats, and Gareth would know by heart what your scores had been in the fitness tests. He had an eye for detail, as well as the bigger picture.

We recovered from the Australia draw to beat the Pacific Islanders convincingly in a one-off test, and then gave Canada a bit of a tuning before facing the All Blacks. We annoyed them by not allowing them to perform the haka after our national anthem. That had always been the tradition, but in a show of psychological warfare we declared that we wanted to sing our anthem last. Our stadium, our rules. They were fuming at the supposed lack of respect, and decided to do the haka in the dressing room instead. It was captured by the TV cameras and, it's fair to say, they looked furious.

If it had been a deliberate attempt to undermine them, it backfired spectacularly, because they came out with all guns blazing. Rico Gear had been our arch torturer the previous year, but this year it was the latest off their production line – Sitiveni Sivivatu. He scored a hat-trick as New Zealand slaughtered us 45–10. That was one of the few games in which I ever remember seeing Richie McCaw sent to the sin bin. Their hooker, Andrew Hore, was too. But despite playing against fourteen men for twenty of the eighty minutes, we were unable to muster any resistance. It was a sobering day, and we realised we had an awful lot of work still to do.

A few of the boys in the squad were a bit taken aback at Gareth's response to the defeat. The team dinner was in a Cardiff pub, and as you'd expect, most of the players were a bit down, moping about and crying into their pints. Gareth's solution was to start a mass sing-song in the pub. He got up first and started singing Rufus Thomas's 'Walking The Dog' to scenes of mass incredulity. We'd just got pumped by New Zealand in front of our home fans, and here was our head coach hours later singing comedy songs in a pub.

Personally, I loved it. It was old school, and sometimes you need something like that to lift the gloom and realign your perspective. It hadn't been a dreadful autumn. Had we beaten Australia, the New Zealand defeat might have been a little easier to take. But there was no point wringing our hands endlessly about it. I thought it was the right response to sink a few beers and have a sing-song. Steve Hansen wouldn't have done it. But then he's not Welsh, is he?

Was Gareth a good singer? He was an enthusiastic singer. Let's leave it there.

● ● ●

The Six Nations of 2007 started terribly for me. I missed the opening-day defeat to Ireland through injury, before being picked for the Scotland game in Murrayfield. I got absolutely stuffed by a prop by the name of Gavin Kerr. I'm not a man to make any excuses. He figured me out, and did a job on me. But if I *was* to offer up an excuse, I'd blame my boots. Myself, Duncan Jones and Rob Sidoli were all wearing custom-made boots. We'd had guys down to measure our feet perfectly – the height of our arches, the exact width and length of our feet – even the dimensions of our big toes were taken into consideration. Halfway through the first half, Sid's sole had peeled away and was flapping around like something from a cartoon. The physios taped it up as best they could, but the stitching had gone and he had no spares. Mine weren't quite as bad, but Sid's were ridiculous. He was struggling to get any purchase in the scrum, because his feet were sliding all over the place.

So, Gavin Kerr, if you're reading this, well done on your performance that day. But I'm blaming Sid's boots for my horrendous display.

In all seriousness, though, Kerr smashed me. It came as a big surprise, because I'd scrummaged against him the previous year, and we'd scored a pushover try. It just goes to show that you can never rest on your laurels when it comes to scrummaging. He got the better of me physically to begin with, and then the mental demons started to creep in. Every time I packed down, a voice in my head would start to whisper, 'He's going to do you again, you've got no answers,' and I'd crumble. I was eventually subbed off for Chris Horsman, who also struggled to get any change out of him. I don't know what they'd been feeding him but he was a player transformed from a year earlier.

It was a terrible game. No tries, just penalties. Three to Stephen Jones, seven to Chris Paterson. 21–9 to Scotland. An awful spectacle for the fans, and a depressing outing for us. My performance cost me my place. I was dropped for the next game, and ended up a bit-part player for the rest of the tournament.

I wasn't even in the squad for the game against France in Paris. We found a bit of form in that one, building an early 14–3 lead before losing 32–21. But the low point was still to come.

Italy were having a decent tournament, having beaten Scotland convincingly, and we were a little nervous playing them out in Rome. I was on the bench and came on around the hour mark for Horsman, when we were seven points ahead. But when Mauro Bergamasco went over with three minutes to spare, we were 23–30 down.

Surely we weren't going to lose to Italy again? Cue total chaos.

We were awarded a penalty in a kickable position at the death. It was an easy three points, and would have salvaged a draw, but our captain, Alfie, wanted the win. The referee, Chris White, was asked if there was enough time for a line-out. The answer was yes. Every Welsh fan knows what happened next. James Hook kicked the ball out. The forwards jogged towards the touchline, and the referee blew for full time. I thought Alfie was going to blow a gasket. He went absolutely mental. He tore strips off Chris White on the pitch, and then went hammering on his door after we'd all returned to the changing rooms. White, wisely, declined to answer. Witnessing Alfie in anger mode can be a terrifying experience.

Instead of acknowledging our own shortcomings, we placed the blame squarely on the ref. White apologised publicly a couple of days later for the 'misunderstanding', but it didn't change the course of history. We'd lost for a second time to Italy, and were on course for the wooden spoon unless we could muster a victory against England in the final game of the championship.

With the World Cup looming there were rumblings that Gareth Jenkins might be sacked. Wales had developed a nasty habit of getting rid of coaches before World Cups, and it looked as though history might be repeating itself. It meant the England game – as though it needed any extra intensity – was suddenly a fixture of monumental importance. Significantly, though, there was no negativity from inside the camp. Stephen Jones and Dwayne Peel wielded an enormous amount of influence in that squad, and they were very loyal to Gareth. It was almost like a reverse of the Ruddock scenario. Under Mike, when the results were good and we were winning, people couldn't stop bitching. Yet under Gareth, when the results were poor, morale remained reasonably high. He'd famously said, 'Judge me on the World Cup.' But in Wales, your every move is scrutinised mercilessly. You're judged on everything you say and do.

The pressure valve was released when we beat England. Chris Horsman started that game ahead of me and scored a try, the jammy git. But it was Hooky's performance that everyone remembers. He was a class act. Starting at fly-half in place of the injured Jonesy, he ended up scoring twenty-two points, including a second-minute charge-down try that set the tone for the victory.

It was an enormous relief. The 27–18 win meant we snuck above Scotland in the final table and avoided the ignominy of the wooden spoon in a World Cup year. The overall downward trajectory was worrying, though. 2005: Grand Slam Champions. 2006: fourth. 2007: fifth.

A victory over England is always welcome, but that alone couldn't atone for the miserable string of results that preceded it.

● ● ●

After the Argentina tour, and during the autumn internationals of that year, I'd started to let myself go a bit. I wasn't training particularly hard, I'd stopped doing extra sessions and I wasn't looking after myself. My weight had started to creep back up. I was up to 131kg (or twenty and a half stone) – the heaviest I'd been since turning professional. Looking back, I'm grateful Gareth Jenkins was picking me at all. He'd shown a bit of faith, and clearly had a soft spot for me. But if I'm being honest, I wasn't up to it. I'm not sure why the lethargy set in so badly – I wasn't carrying an injury or anything – but it was easier to slacken off a bit in those days, and I got a bit lazy. It's not like it is now, when you get strictly monitored, and weighed every day. There were scales there, but it was up to you to check yourself. I remember jumping on them one morning when everyone had left, and thinking, 'Bloody hell! How did that happen?'

It may have been something to do with Horey's departure. Mark Bennett was a great fitness coach, but he trusted the players to look after themselves. Horey was more demanding. He was always on at you to do extras. He'd ring you on a Sunday night when you were about to settle in with a cup of tea and a bar of chocolate, and remind you that he wanted you to do this, that and the other the following week.

Mark Bennett had more than just me to worry about. He was working on an overall fitness plan for the World Cup, and he should have been able to trust individual players when it came to monitoring their own weight. I was naturally disappointed to lose my place but, looking at it objectively, I could have had no complaints. Horsman was new, keen and desperate to play. I hadn't really been challenged before, but this guy was a supremely competitive animal.

On one occasion, when I was picked ahead of him under Gareth, he couldn't contain his rage. He thought he was muttering under his breath, but everyone in the team room could hear him. 'For fuck's sake! How can you justify that? I should be playing instead of Bomb.'

He apologised to me afterwards and asked me not to take his anger personally. He was just devastated not to have been starting. I didn't resent him one iota. If anything, I respected it. That's how much you should want to play for your country. And as far as I'm concerned, Wales was his country. Yes, he was English, but he qualified on residency. Those are the rules of the game, and you can't blame someone for exploiting them.

There are a lot of purists who disagree. Some fans think you shouldn't play for Wales unless you can prove a direct lineage to Owain Glyndŵr! But I'm relaxed about it. The Grannygate saga left a sour taste in some mouths, when certain players capped by Graham Henry turned out to have no Welsh connection at all. Martyn Williams and Kevin Morgan would undoubtedly have had more caps if Brett Sinkinson and Shane Howarth had never played for Wales. (And Kevin Morgan will never fail to remind you of that.)

But as long as the three-year residency rule is in place, I say good luck to those who want to qualify. Hors was Welsh, as far as I was concerned, and when he was being picked ahead of me I certainly wasn't moping around thinking I'd lost my place to an Englishman who shouldn't have been there in the first place. Hors may have rubbed a few people up the wrong way over the years, but considering I was competing for the shirt with him, we always got on well. He was a very good player. I felt no sense of injustice, I wasn't crowing to anyone about being better than him. I'd let my standards slip, got a bit fat, and he'd taken his chance. End of.

While playing for my country means everything to me, I'm not one of those players who's constantly trying to impress. I'm fairly philosophical about losing my place, as I'll back myself to reclaim it through my deeds, not my words. Rugby, like all professional sport, is a highly competitive arena, but you can waste energy by constantly sucking up to the coach. There are certain players who'll know where the coaches are at all times, and say things entirely for their benefit. That can be annoying – that needy 'look-at-me, look-at-me' mentality. It might get you noticed in the short term, but it soon becomes transparent. And ultimately, quite irritating.

Heading into that World Cup, all the training was based around weights. There was virtually no cardio-based work at all. For players like me, that was a potential disaster. Slowly but surely, the squad turned into a troop of bodybuilders. It was weights, weights, weights, and some of the boys looked incredible. Sculpted, toned and rippling with muscle. From the end of the season to the start of the World Cup, we can't have done more than five actual fitness sessions that involved running.

The logic was that we were already fit enough, but we weren't strong enough. By the end of the build-up, some of the boys were phenomenally strong. I remember seeing Shane Williams squatting 260kg. It didn't seem feasible. He's a tiny bloke – maybe 75kg – and he was casually squatting more than three times his body weight. You'd see some of them in those ultra-tight jerseys, and they looked like they were tattooed on. Even Stephen Jones looked big! Colin Charvis looked ripped, and he was a man who would do whatever he could to avoid going to the gym.

I accepted the regime and hardly did any extras. I know now that I should have been doing the cardio stuff on my own. I should have been sat on the bike for an hour after the weights sessions to burn off some fat. But my commitment had deserted me, and my fitness levels had plummeted. I'd be so knackered after doing ten sets of squats, I needed a rest.

● ● ●

It had become apparent during the 2007 Six Nations that I was slipping down the pecking order, and that was confirmed when the squad was announced for the Australian summer tour. It was basically a B team going out there, and I was part of it. The perceived first-choice team was kept back with the World Cup in mind. But any trip to Australia is a good trip, as far as I'm concerned, and I didn't feel snubbed. I was happy to be on the plane. It would be tough out there with a second-string squad, but there are few better places to tour. They'd booked us into a beautiful place in Terrigal, to the north of Sydney, and it's difficult to have anything but a sunny disposition in surroundings like that.

This was 2007, but looking back there was still an amateur mentality on those tours. Gareth Jenkins's 'jet-lag protocol' was put into place. On arrival we were told, 'Dump your gear, get straight to the bar, and get a minimum of ten pints down you.' It was an order, and the boys loved him for it. We had two days to acclimatise, and we just did some light training to break ourselves in. Running around on those hard pitches was a real treat. So much better than sloshing through a bog at the Vale of Glamorgan. We suspected we were on a hiding to nothing out there, but it didn't stop us enjoying ourselves.

We had a psychologist on that trip for the first time. A highly rated guy called John Neal, who was rumoured to be on a king's ransom. A lot of the boys were cynical about his presence. He offered individual sessions, but I gave him a wide berth. I didn't want some shrink delving into my feelings. It's funny, looking back, because the current psychologist, Andy McCann, has become a vital part of the Welsh set-up. Guys like Sam Warburton and Leigh Halfpenny couldn't function without him. In 2007, John Neal was either a curiosity or a nuisance, depending on your point of view. I was one of several players in that group who had played at an amateur level before the regions had formed, and before the academies had started. To us, the presence of a psychologist on a rugby tour was absurd. He became a bit of a lone figure, and the boys would resort to heckling him on the team bus after a few beers. The only person I can remember embracing it was Jonathan Thomas. He's always been a positive bloke who'll consider anything with an open mind, especially if it'll improve his game.

We'd been working hard on the blitz defence with Rowland, and it nearly won us the first test in Sydney. Against all the odds, we were ahead with less than five minutes on the clock. Australia had a line-out deep in our 22, but our defence rushed up on their three-quarter line, forced an error, and Chris Czekaj pounced. He scooped up the ball, kicked through, and seconds later Alfie was crashing over at the other end.

Ten minutes later, the Wallabies were on the attack, deep in our territory again, when our defence rushed up and Julian Huxley's pass was picked off by Jamie Robinson. He skinned the scramble defence to score a fantastic try. We were 14–nil up, and scoring a point a minute courtesy of our aggressive defence. The Wallaby backline was standing so flat in attack, they were just playing into our hands.

But you can never rest on your laurels against the Wallabies. They clawed their way back into the game, as they always seem to do. Their heads never drop when they fall a few scores behind. If anything, it galvanises them. There are few sporting nations blessed with more confidence and self-belief than Australia. Halfway through the second half, they manoeuvred themselves into a 22–20 lead, but Hooky dropped a goal to put us back in front with eight minutes left. We hadn't beaten Australia in Australia since 1969. This was a major opportunity.

We had to do something that was quite un-Welsh – grind out the game. We had a scrum in their half in the last minute, and the ball came back cleanly. An 8–9 move had been called whereby Gareth Cooper would kick the ball into the corner, and we'd run the clock down by backing our defence. But Coops didn't put the ball out. He kicked it down the throat of Julian Huxley, who returned it with interest. It was Coops who tracked back to field the ball, but his next clearance didn't have any distance on it, and Australia had a line-out well inside our half. They won the ball after a suspect throw-in, and a few phases later the full-time hooter went. All we needed to do was hold our line, and hold our discipline.

But a wounded Wallaby is a dangerous animal. They swept from left to right and back again, going patiently through the phases until they worked an overlap for Stephen Hoiles to dive over unopposed. It was heartbreaking.

Coops was gutted. He's a perfectionist, and I know he agonised over that kick for some time. None of us blamed him. We all took the piss out of him – don't get me wrong – but that's the way we deal with disappointment. He's a top bloke, and we made sure he wasn't left to stew over what might have been. If he'd been an arse of a bloke, we might have got stuck into him more – but thankfully, there are precious few of those around in the Welsh squad. That might have been the perfect opportunity for the tour psychologist to have come into his own, but Coops was definitely not the kind of guy to go knocking on his door.

The Australian press started talking up the second test as a potentially epic battle, given what had happened. But deep down, we knew we'd shot our bolt. That defeat knocked us for six, and we weren't sure we had the reserves to gather ourselves for another effort. I'd torn my calf, so I didn't play, forcing Ceri Jones to play out of position at tight-head.

It was a shadow of the first test as we surrendered 31–0. It was the first time we'd been 'nilled' in a test match for ten years.

● ● ●

If our performance in that second test against the Wallabies wasn't cause for panic, the World Cup warm-up match against England at

Twickenham was. It was an abject humiliation. We were slaughtered 62–5 on a boiling-hot day. And if that wasn't enough of an indignity, their Number 8, Nick Easter, scored four tries. He was only on the pitch for fifty minutes.

It was a record defeat to England, who hadn't exactly been pulling up trees at that point, and had put out something of an experimental side. We weren't fully loaded ourselves. But with the exception of Will James in the second row, there were few rookies. The only consolation for me was that I wasn't playing. It was a dark, dark day for Welsh rugby, and an appalling way to prepare for the World Cup. I seem to remember Alfie praising the team in the post-match interview for the spirit shown in defence. He must have had a knock to the head.

You have no choice but to write a game like that off completely. There is no point analysing it, no point poring over what went wrong. You just have to banish it from your mind as quickly as possible, and not allow the demons to take hold, because the psychological damage from an experience like that can last for some time. And time was a luxury we didn't have.

Was it because we'd focused too intently on strength and power in our preparations and not enough on rugby? Probably. We hadn't done a great deal of actual rugby training – it was far more about conditioning in that period – but that's no excuse. We'd had one training camp in France, where we focused more on actual rugby and which ended with an unofficial Probables v Possibles trial match. We didn't have enough players to cover all the positions, though, so I ended up playing open-side flanker for the Possibles! I was openside, Richard Hibbard was blindside, and Martyn Williams was Number 8. Hardly the most fearsome back row you'll ever face, and certainly not the most dynamic. Although I must emphasise that I was at openside ahead of Hibbard – I may be big and slow, but I'm not as big and slow as he is. It was amusing to look back on, but not the best preparation for the World Cup warm-ups.

Gareth Jenkins had worked with Clive Woodward on the 2005 Lions trip, and while that was largely considered a disastrous tour on the pitch, Gareth was clearly impressed with the organisation that had gone on off the pitch. The size of the entourage made the whole thing a bit unwieldy, but he realised that to be entirely professional, you need to have back-up. He left no stone unturned when it came to the 2007 World Cup. We were based in a swish hotel just outside Nice, and had the entire place to ourselves. Our nutrition was closely monitored – we had our own private chef who cooked all of our meals – and we'd train on the fields of the local rugby club, which was just down the road. We didn't want for anything. The template for success appeared to be in place.

Gareth didn't coach a lot. He was clearly in charge, but he empowered his coaches to do the hands-on stuff. He'd stand on the touchline bellowing in his deep West Walian brogue, but his skill lay more in his preparation, his tactics and his analysis of the opposition. His rugby brain was an impressive thing to behold, but sometimes his short-term memory let him down. On one occasion, he was reading out the team for the next game – always a tense moment for the players. He went through it from the start.

'Number 1, Duncan Jones . . . Number 2, Matthew Rees . . . Number 3, Adam Jones . . .' When he reached Number 12, he paused. 'Number 12 . . . Number 12 . . .'

Another pause. A sideways glance at Nigel Davies. Nothing.

'Number 12 . . .'

Things were getting awkward. People were looking at their feet. Gareth was going crimson red.

Eventually, Hooky looked up tentatively, and said, 'Is it me, Gar?'

'Yes, yes! Of course it is. Number 12, inside centre . . . James Hook.'

I'm pretty certain he *had* picked Hooky there. But if he hadn't, Hooky would have got the nod through sheer embarrassment.

He was very meticulous, and seeing this at first hand made me realise how underrated he was by much of the outside world. When he was down in Llanelli, he was widely regarded as a genius. The Carwyn James of his era. But for whatever reason, when he got the Wales job, people judged him by different standards and some saw him as an unsophisticated hick from the west, who was out of his depth. Not from my point of view he wasn't. His reign won't be looked upon with much affection by the fans, but the players were as much to blame for any failings as he was.

● ● ●

The Canadians were our first opponents in France 2007. They were tough and abrasive, as always. It was a horrendously hot day in Nantes, and we were sweating copiously into our skin-tight shirts – never a good look for a twenty-stone tight-head. They took it to us up front, and had us on the back foot for large stretches. Guys like Rod Snow and Jamie Cudmore were in their element. They were 17–9 ahead in the second half before they started to wilt in the heat. We eventually ran away with it, winning 42–17.

Next up were the Australians, and a chance for revenge. Because of the boardroom politics that occur during bids for rugby World Cups, our game against the Wallabies was in Cardiff. The WRU were happy to vote for a French World Cup on the grounds they were given a few games. While it was obviously nice to be playing Australia in front of our own fans, it didn't half feel weird flying back from the 'World Cup' in France to play a test at the Millennium Stadium.

I didn't cover myself in glory that day. I'm not the first to have been made to look a fool by a Wallaby back, but Berrick Barnes did me like a kipper within minutes. He sold me a dummy, and I bought it big time. Matt Giteau was on his inside shoulder, and nobody laid a finger on him on his way to the line. It was the first of three first-half tries for them, and we were 25–3 down at the break. Jon Thomas and Shane Williams scored second-half tries, and the final scoreline of 20–32 was respectable enough. But it was clear they were the better side. They were more physical, and more clinical.

I'd like to explode a myth here, while we're on the subject of Australia. There's a commonly held theory that they're soft up front, and deadly behind. The second part is almost always true. The first part is largely bollocks. I've never played against a soft Australian team, and I've played against them a lot. Just last season, the New South Wales Waratahs won the Super XV. You're not going to win that with a rubbish pack, are you? It's annoying as a forward, because the theory has been recycled so much in the press over the years that whenever you play them, you're expected to steamroller them up front. And if you don't, you're deemed to have failed. You're judged against a yardstick that has no foundation in the truth. Yes, there have been occasions in the past when Australian forward packs have crumpled under the weight of superior opposition. But these have been few and far between. When England were in their pomp, they mashed Australia on a few occasions, but then most teams came out second best against England in that department.

The truth is that their rugby philosophy is so markedly different to almost anyone else's. They love to play with the ball in hand, and they love to go through the phases. They don't play a power game, and they don't use the driving maul like other teams do. It's not in their DNA. Where a Northern Hemisphere side will kick for touch and attempt to start a rolling maul from twenty metres out, the Wallabies won't. Because of that, people see them as lightweight, and not capable of mixing it in the tight exchanges. Even on occasions when their scrum has been weak in relative terms, they find ever more imaginative ways of conning the ref and sneaking penalties. They're smart players – and brain is often more than a match for brawn.

They play this way out of choice, not necessity. Rugby Union in Australia is probably the fourth most popular sport behind cricket, Aussie Rules and Rugby League. They're under pressure to keep fans interested. One way of doing that is to play more attack-minded, enterprising rugby. At the risk of labouring the point, I repeat, the Wallabies are not intrinsically soft. Ask anyone who's ever tried to tackle Wycliff Palu.

Victory over Australia had obviously been a target, but we were encouraged enough by our second-half display. We were on an upward curve, with pool games against Japan and Fiji to come. Without sounding arrogant, we expected to win both those games with something to spare.

We had a few decent nights out during that tournament, and it was during one of them that Jonathan Thomas decided to try and 'out' Alfie. It would be some time before Gareth declared his sexuality publicly, but a few of the boys in the squad had long suspected he might be gay. It was one of those rumours that persisted. We'd had a long boozy lunch at a seafood restaurant near Nantes, and stayed on swilling wine late into the night. JT is a really sweet bloke, but he can get a little aggressive after a few drinks. He had his arm around Alfie and kept prodding him through-out the night: 'Come on, mate, haven't you got something to tell us all?'

Alfie, to his credit, maintained his good humour, and kept batting him away. But JT wouldn't let it lie. He genuinely thought he was being helpful, and that Alfie would be grateful for his 'intervention'. We were all gesturing to JT to pack it in, but he kept on and on. He was convinced that he'd somehow persuade Alfie to make the biggest call of his life. JT's one of these wonderful people who can never remember anything about the night before. When I reminded him what he'd done, he was devastated, thinking he'd offended everyone. But it was all forgotten soon afterwards. Alfie was as good as gold – he could have got the hump about it, but he took it in his stride.

I missed the Japan game, because I had a problem with my foot. It looked normal, but I could barely put any weight on it. For three days, I couldn't walk without crutches. Carcass, the physio, could barely touch it without me wincing in pain. Initial scans revealed nothing, and doctors thought it might have been gout. It was eventually diagnosed as a bleed on the nerve. Very rare, according to the medics. It ruled me out of the next two games – including the eleven-try romp over Japan.

Little did I know then that it would be the end of my World Cup.

● ● ●

The final pool match was against Fiji in Nantes, and it was Alfie's 100th cap. He'd had special boots made for the occasion, with '100' embroidered into them.

He gathered the team into a huddle before kick-off to deliver his pre-match speech. He was a great speaker, and always commanded attention. He wasn't a screamer, but he knew which emotional buttons to push, and how to stir the passions. The players were staring intently at him, imploring him to deliver one of his specials. This was a huge game – a career high point for many – and the chance to progress to the quarter-finals of the greatest tournament on earth. The pressure was on.

He locked them all with his steely glare, looked each of his comrades in the eye, and in a hushed voice, said, 'Boys, I know what you're thinking . . .'

There was a nervous pause as he slowly lifted one leg into the circle.

He rotated his ankle to show off his new boot, and shouted, 'Fuuuucking LUUUUSH!'

Classic Alfie. It wasn't one of his more inspirational speeches, but it did a great job of easing the pre-match nerves.

The match that followed will go down as one of the best games ever from a neutral perspective – and one of the worst ever from a Welsh perspective. Our performance, while thrilling at times, was a masterclass in how not to play against the Fijians. The passing of time does not make it any easier to fathom. Fiji are among the most naturally gifted sides in the world when it comes to running rugby. They're the masters of the seven-a-side version of the game. But they've never mastered the intricacies of the set piece, and they're always susceptible there.

So it doesn't take a genius to figure out a game plan against them. Kick to the corners, dominate the territory battle, drive the line-outs, and suffocate them in the scrum. If you starve them of possession, it doesn't matter how gifted they are – you can't score tries if you haven't got the ball. You're probably nodding your head, thinking: so far, so obvious. So why didn't Wales do that on 29 September 2007? The honest answer is, I have no bloody idea.

Their loose-head prop, Graham Dewes, had been playing third-division rugby in New Zealand before the World Cup. Easy meat for someone of Chris Horsman's stature. And, as you'd expect, he was bending him in half at every scrum. Standing on the sidelines, I remember thinking that was the easy route to victory. Smash them in the scrum, and use it to milk penalties. Not the most romantic of rugby philosophies, but this was a World Cup, and the prize was a quarter-final place.

So what did we do? We got sucked into a frantic, frenzied contest of exhibition rugby. It was idiocy in the extreme. The weather was far more

Suva in the summertime than it was Cardiff in midwinter, so everything suited them. The style, the conditions, the pace. Their wingers, Vilimoni Delasau and Isoa Neivua, were devastating. Delasau was arguably the best wing in the tournament, and the two of them were jinking and darting with devilish abandon. Delasau scored one of three first-half Fijian tries, and before we knew it we'd conceded twenty-five points. This was simply not meant to happen. I felt frustrated and impotent up in the stand, but not especially nervous. As with the Canada game, I thought we'd weather the storm, and come good in the end.

The messages were coming on to the pitch from the touchline. Boys! Calm down! Tighten things up, stop playing into their hands.

Just before half-time, our scrum marched theirs back over their line, and Alix Popham touched down for an easy score. That was the way to do it. We scored four more tries in the second half, including a Martyn Williams interception eight minutes from time that put us three points ahead. But there was to be one last dramatic episode. One final Fijian assault. And it was that man Graham Dewes – who'd been so ineffective in his primary role as a scrummager – who flopped over the line at the death, and dumped us out of the World Cup.

It was a thoroughly depressing experience. One of the most embarrassing moments of my career, and I hadn't even played.

People have since raved about the game, describing it as one of the greatest spectacles at that or any World Cup, but I'll never be able to look at it that way. The 2007 tournament will always be a source of misery for me.

Looking back, I was just happy to be in the squad. I wasn't in good shape and I wasn't working particularly hard. I'm not suggesting that, had I worked harder, our fortunes would have been different. But it wasn't a vintage period for myself or the team.

Fiji rightfully received a standing ovation after the final whistle. Oddly, we got a decent reaction too. The players felt obliged to have a bit of a wander on the pitch to say thanks to the travelling fans, and in fairness to them, they resisted the urge to boo. I wouldn't have blamed them if they had. Some of them were clearly clapping through gritted teeth, thinking, 'What a bunch of wankers, you've just lost to Fiji!' But the majority were applauding the effort, and acknowledging Fiji's achievement.

There was no anger in the changing rooms. Just sorrow. It was Alfie's last game for Wales, and he was virtually inconsolable.

A warrior like him deserved a better end to his international career.

●　●　●

Nobody said it at the time, but we all knew that the defeat against Fiji spelled the end for Gareth Jenkins. He'd said, 'Judge me on the World Cup,' and losing to Fiji was simply unacceptable. We all knew the axe was about to fall — it was just a question of when, rather than if. I felt sorry for him. The coach is always the scapegoat. Most of the players would have a chance to redeem themselves in the months to come, but for the coach, that's it. One chance, and he'd blown it.

What followed the end of the Fiji match was one of the saddest things I've witnessed in my life. We fulfilled our press duties and jumped on the bus back to the hotel, where we congregated in the team room. After a short while, Roger Lewis, the WRU chief executive, walked in. He was still fairly new in the post, so not everyone had got the measure of him. What he was about to do illustrated that beneath his avuncular exterior lay a ruthless businessman.

Gareth Jenkins stood alongside him with his head bowed. He'd just been sacked. It was inevitable, but it still felt brutal. Roger explained what had happened in formal, diplomatic language. He said that the two of them had had a frank discussion, and it was felt that Gareth had taken the team as far as he was able to. It was time for someone else to take over.

I've never been a Llanelli fan. The 'West is Best' mantra used to grate on me, growing up. I was brainwashed by Lyn Jones at Neath to despise them. They used to peddle this romantic notion that they were the best team in Wales, and they played the best rugby. Gareth Jenkins, being 'Mr Llanelli', was always inextricably tied up with all of that, so I guess I resented him by association. But my prejudices couldn't have been further from the truth. He is one of the most decent blokes I've ever worked with. And the way he stood there, and took the humiliation, that day will be an eternal credit to him. I'd have been in floods of tears if I'd been in his situation.

After Roger had made the announcement, Gareth delivered a speech of his own. Where Roger's had been rehearsed and dispassionate, Gareth's was off the cuff and emotional. He thanked all the players individually, and talked about how much he'd enjoyed his time as head coach of Wales. There was no bitterness or anger, just genuine gratitude and love. When he was finished, we all gave him a round of applause, and he came and mixed with the boys for the rest of the night, sharing pints and stories until the small hours. He could so easily have gone off to his room and sulked. The fact he chose not to was a testament to his character. He was hurting badly – that was plain to see. It had been his lifelong ambition to coach his country, and it had ended in heartbreak.

He was great company that night. He's a great storyteller, and has a wonderful turn of phrase. He's funny too – often unintentionally so. He sat with Jonathan Thomas and myself for a while and at one point, turning to JT, he said, 'You really remind me of Mike Lewis, a bloke I used to play with in Llanelli. You're big, brawny . . .'

JT nodded smugly at what he thought was a compliment.

'. . . and dull as fuck!'

Classic Gareth Jenkins. Brilliant rugby man, brilliant bloke.

The saddest episode was yet to come. We arrived back in Cardiff the following day, and drove in the team bus from the airport to our HQ at the Vale Hotel. There are two routes into the hotel. One involves driving up the winding driveway, past the golf course and up to the main entrance. The other is a tradesman's route, skirting round the side of the complex and emerging at the indoor training barn. When we reached the junction of these two roads, Gareth asked the driver if he could stop and get off.

He knew the press would be at the hotel reception en masse, roaming around like hyenas picking at a corpse, and he couldn't face the inevitable inquest. The bus slowed to a halt. Gareth stood up, with his bag of duty free in one hand – a couple of Toblerones and a bottle of whisky – and he bade us all farewell. No valedictory speech this time. Just a brief thanks, and he was gone. He walked up the lane on his own, wheeling his suitcase and clutching his plastic bag. It was a scene dripping with melancholy. He looked smaller, less commanding, like the whole experience had robbed him of his vitality.

CHAPTER 11

Pride

MY suspicions that Nigel Davies didn't really like me as a player were realised when I was left out of the South Africa game in the autumn of 2007. It was the sole autumn test that year, and Nigel was a lame-duck coach. He'd hung on in the aftermath of Gareth Jenkins's sacking, but Warren Gatland had already been appointed as his permanent successor.

The phone call came from Robin McBryde – the forwards coach, and my old mate. Chris Horsman was injured, so I was a little surprised.

'We're going with Rhys Thomas,' was his explanation. 'Because he's a big ball carrier.'

Fair enough, I thought. But you're playing South Africa. Maybe you need a decent scrummager as well?

So for the first time in a long while, I watched a Wales international from the outside, as a fan. I went up to Glasgow to stay with my mate Andy Newman, and we watched it together.

I spoke to a few of the boys, though, and the preparations for that game sounded a bit random to say the least. They did their team run a day early, on the Thursday. And on the Friday, they went on an outing to Big Pit – an underground mining museum in Blaenavon. It's an old working mine, and any visit there involves travelling down the mine shaft and crawling around the tunnels. Guys like Alun Wyn – who's six foot seven – spent two and a half hours bent double, scrabbling around underground, the day before the test. Unsurprisingly, his back was bent in half twenty-four hours later. Not the best preparation for going up against Bakkies Botha and Johann Muller.

It was a good game to miss. Rhys Thomas was given a right old going-over in the scrums by CJ van der Linde, and we were comfortably beaten 34–12.

During the anthems, Andy Newman and I were a little bemused to see the boys all dramatically clutching the three feathers on their chest. Apparently, it had been a three-line whip from the management. They were told they had to. Along with the trip to Big Pit, it was some kind of strange attempt to get the team in touch with its inner Welshness; to tap into their latent cultural pride. I've nothing against grabbing your badge in principle, if that's what floats your boat, but it has to be spontaneous. You can't manufacture that kind of national pride. It should exist anyway. There's no greater pride than being asked to represent your country. Grabbing your badge and going to Big Pit doesn't make you any more Welsh.

Everyone should sing the anthem, though. That should be a given. It annoys me when Richard Hibbard doesn't. He says it's down to nerves, but I'm not buying that. I can forgive you if it's your first cap, and your stomach's churning, but otherwise, it's your duty. You don't have to be like Alun Wyn, or Leigh Halfpenny – belting it out with tears streaming down your face – but you should at least know the words. I know it's in Welsh, and not all of the boys are Welsh speakers, but it's easy enough to learn. (Although it proved beyond John Redwood when he was Secretary of State for Wales.) It was something I learned from a very young age. My mother would insist that we all stand in our living room and sing it before watching Wales play.

Years and years ago, I read in a Welsh rugby album of mine that the former Wales captain Mike Hall's two proudest rugby moments were when he got to sing 'God Save The Queen'. Once when he played for the Lions. And once when he played in the Varsity Match for Cambridge.

I was livid. What was he thinking? No Welshman should ever think that. Or if he does, he should keep it to himself.

I could never sing the English anthem – never in a million years – and if I'd ever been asked to do so on a Lions tour, I'd have refused. I know it's technically the British anthem, but it's English as far as I'm concerned. We've got our own, thank you very much. When Craig Bellamy, Ryan Giggs and Aaron Ramsey played for Team GB at the London Olympics, they all made a pact saying they wouldn't sing 'God Save The Queen'. Too right!

Singing the anthem with pride is a rugby thing. I remember hearing Craig Bellamy say how envious he was of the Welsh rugby team when they sang the anthem. The football boys don't come close to it in terms of passion and emotion. There have been times when I've been filling up with tears, biting my lip and struggling not to lose control, but I wouldn't have it any other way. It makes you realise that although the game is pro-fessional, and we're getting paid to play, pride is still the primary motivator.

People have told me they feel embarrassed to sing the anthem. That's pathetic. If you can't do that before a game, you shouldn't be pulling the jersey on.

I'm a massively proud Welshman. I come from a mining background which gave earlier generations a sense of resilience and perseverance that's made me proud. I've seen at first hand how the closure of the mines has affected people's livelihoods, and their sense of self-worth. When I line up to sing the anthem, I'm not just representing my country. I'm representing my mam and dad, my wife and daughter, and my grandparents whose lives were so much harder than mine. I'm representing Abercrave and its rugby club, and all the teachers and coaches who've inspired me and mentored me through the years.

For a small country like Wales, it's enormously empowering to be able to express yourself through sport. We can't compete financially with countries like England, but we can beat them on the rugby pitch, and that really matters to a nation whose identity is inextricably linked with sport. It's woven into our culture.

I'm a little concerned by the shifting sands in international rugby, which allow 'time-servers' to come over to Wales, get residency and end up playing for Wales. They're not Welsh, so that's not right. People say those are the regulations, and any coach worth his salt will exploit them for the benefit of the team. But playing for Wales is sacred, and caps shouldn't be cheap. I don't mean to sound hypocritical, because I've mentioned before that I didn't hold anything against Chris Horsman (who was English born and raised). But what makes me uneasy is seeing South Africans coming over here and expressing a desire to play for Wales before they've served their residency, and before we've even seen whether they're any good or not. It's cynical and soulless. I could never do that.

There's only one international team I'd ever want to play for. If I wasn't good enough for Wales, then I'd have to miss out. I wouldn't go looking for another side that might give me a run. It's black and white. If your country of origin isn't picking you, work harder! Moving to the other side of the world, trying to shoehorn yourself into another international set-up, is mercenary and it's wrong. You could argue that times have changed, and that it's the nature of modern rugby, but I think it's a sad indictment of the game and its administrators.

Parentage is an entirely different thing. A lot of fuss was made when Gareth Anscombe was brought over to Wales from New Zealand and given a dual contract. Yes, he was born and raised in New Zealand, but his mother is Welsh. Believe me, I've been out for dinner with the family, and she's as 'Cardiff' as they come. I have no problem with that.

It's very different to someone like Hanno Dirksen, who plays on the wing for Ospreys. He's South African but was brought over here by Scott Johnson, who saw him playing in America. He ended up in Truro College in Cornwall and then transferred to Neath Port Talbot College, whereupon his 'Welsh residency' commenced. He's now eligible for South Africa, the USA and Wales, and has expressed his desire to play for Wales. Whether he ever will or not is something we can't predict, but the whole scenario doesn't sit comfortably with me.

I've got nothing against Hanno – he's a good boy – but the system that allows him to pick his nationality seems flawed. It's not like flitting between clubs. You should only really have one option at international level. Perhaps two, if your parents are of a different nationality from each other. End of story.

CHAPTER 12

The New Messiah

'WE'RE a blitzing team. And if you don't like it, you can fuck off.'

I'm paraphrasing, but those were more or less Shaun Edwards's first words to the Wales squad. Warren Gatland had brought him in as his trusted lieutenant from Wasps, and he was to head up our defence. He was a Rugby League legend, and most of the boys were excited about working with him. The rest were terrified. He is a terrifying man.

As he sat there, scowling at us, we all silently consented. It was a remarkable show of authority. Bear in mind that Clive Griffiths and Rowland Phillips had been trying to instil a blitz mentality for the past four years, and it had met with varying degrees of indifference and downright hostility from some quarters. There was to be no such dissent under Shaun Edwards. That was made crystal clear from day one. It suited the Ospreys boys down to the ground, because it was a system we employed at club level. And it's probably why thirteen of us made the starting line-up for the first 2008 Six Nations match against England.

I'd been an international for four years by the time Warren Gatland arrived. But my recent omission from the team, and the fact we'd bombed out of the World Cup, made me wonder whether I was even on his radar. My confidence took a further nosedive when I heard him mention to the press that we didn't have much depth at tight-head. He said he was looking at the eligibility of guys like Duncan Bell and Jason Hobson, who were playing in the English Premiership.

Gatland's energy and enthusiasm were evident from the start. He accepted an invitation from Lyn Jones to come and do a few sessions with the Ospreys, and he ingratiated himself with the players quite early on. You'd spy him up in the stand, watching impassively, making mental notes. He was a man of few words, so when he did speak to you, you paid attention. After a European game against Gloucester, in which we squeezed them in the scrum, he sidled up to me and said, 'Good game tonight.' I took it as a sign that I was in his plans. Shortly after, I was selected in his first Six Nations squad. I was back in the fold.

There was a big emphasis on ball-in-play time. It was one of his theories: keep hold of the ball, and tire the opposition out. A sea change from the Northern Hemisphere's 'kick first' mentality. It was a clever ploy against England, because they had such a strong driving line-out. Warren's solution to combat that wasn't to come up with a way of stopping the line-out from generating momentum, but stopping it happening in the first place. Simple, really. And how do we achieve that? By not kicking the ball out and giving them line-outs. Keep it in play.

We were also introduced for the first time to 'the pattern', which has since become Gatland's hallmark. Again, it's not rocket science, but it involves picking up from the base of a ruck and 'folding' around the corner repeatedly until you've sucked in enough defenders to launch an attack. It's an approach that has its critics, particularly in recent years, when former internationals like Gwyn Jones have lambasted it for being predictable and one-dimensional. But when done well, it is incredibly effective and has brought unprecedented success for Wales.

Gatland insisted that we work harder than any other team in international rugby. We were going to be so fit, so determined and so strong that we were going to put opposition teams under unbearable pressure. Pressure would lead to mistakes. Mistakes would lead to mismatches. That's effectively what the 'pattern' is. It was a brave new world for me. I'd never heard of words like 'regeneration' in relation to rugby, but that was one of Gatland's buzzwords. We'd pick and drive on the blindside for phase after phase after phase, narrowing the defence on that side of the pitch. Then, when the time was right, we'd switch to the openside, and you'd see the backs sprinting round to the opposite flank to launch an attack. Or 'regenerating', to use the parlance.

As a front-five forward I was told I needed to hit ruck after ruck after ruck. I was given targets of numbers to hit during a game, which I'd be measured against. If I hit thirty rucks, on top of performing all my usual roles in the scrum and the line-out, that would be considered a good shift. Melon would always show off and hit forty-odd, but thirty-plus would be enough for a pat on the back from the head coach. They were definitely counting.

We'd practise it intensively in training. The 'minute drill' became a dreaded sequence. Nine defensive players would be dressed in full body armour suits, and split into three groups of three. Then I'd be in a group of four who'd have to run around smashing into the armoured players, clear out, then run to the next, clear out, and so on until the minute elapsed. A minute doesn't sound like a long time. But believe me, in those circumstances, it felt like an hour. It was exhausting, lung-busting stuff, but it fitted into Gatland's philosophy of short, sharp, intensive sessions. At the end you'd be – excuse the expression – hanging out of your arse. It was all about replicating the live game. If you added up all these drills, it'd probably total ten minutes of contact work. Under previous regimes we'd spent up to half an hour kicking the shit out of each other, but it was nowhere near as focused and disciplined. We'd never worked this way before, and it felt genuinely revolutionary.

Forwards were expected to carry the ball and were expected to turn up at first receiver as part of a relentless battering ram to soften up the opposition defence. Gats expected you to peel away from a line-out and to be there at the next ruck, offering yourself as a ball carrier. If you did make it, and the scrum-half didn't use you, it'd be him getting the bollocking. Gats was big on rewarding forwards for their hard work. It all made sense to me. It was both simple and complex at the same time, and it made me look at rugby in a different way.

The training sessions would never last more than forty-five minutes, which was unheard of in Wales. The norm before was around an hour and a half – double the length, but probably half the intensity. These new sessions were knackering. You'd be properly blowing at the end, and there was no place to hide. If you stopped and chatted for a quick debrief, it would be for a maximum of a minute while the water came on. There was no hanging around or time-wasting. Every second of every minute was productive. It reminded me of the old Muhammad Ali adage about training harder than you play.

Critically, there was no dissent. No one was grumbling about the intensity, or questioning the motives. They were just getting on with it and following orders. The new coaching group had a natural authority. Gatland was the overseer – a man who said little but chose his words wisely. Rob Howley and Neil Jenkins were held in high regard because of their own playing pedigrees. And Shaun Edwards ruled by fear. They'd forged a successful template through their time with Wasps – a template that had won them trophies galore.

●　●　●

We hadn't won in Twickenham for twenty years. And if we were to lift that hoodoo, we were going to have to do it with a club team. I was picked to start, along with twelve of my Ospreys colleagues. The only non-Ospreys in the side were Mark Jones of the Scarlets and Martyn Williams of the Blues. Gats picked the team based on the game plan we'd spoken about, and gave another chance to people who'd fallen out of favour under Gareth Jenkins. People like myself. I was feeling fitter and stronger, and was part of a front five that could do some damage physically. It was me, Duncan and Huw Bennett in the front row. Ian Gough had been restored to the engine room – the man with the thickest neck in world rugby, according to Will Greenwood. Goughie can just about catch a ball, and will never be picked for his footballing ability. But if you want someone to run around smashing rucks and wreaking havoc, he's your ideal bloke. You wouldn't see him in a team that wants to play high-octane, running rugby – because if he turned up in midfield, he'd be guaranteed to drop the ball or knock it on – but he was tailor-made for Gatland's game plan. If you're reading this, Goughie, it's a compliment. Honestly.

The captaincy was awarded to my old mate Ryan 'Jug Head' Jones. No one loves the camera more than him, and Gats rightly assumed that giving him the skipper's armband would take a bit of pressure off the other boys. After our miserable World Cup campaign, and the defeat to South Africa, no one was giving us a prayer. But it's amazing what good coaching can do for your confidence. This group had got into our heads, and they'd convinced us we were world beaters.

Training had gone brilliantly, and we arrived at Twickenham with a bit of a swagger. We'd lost some experienced generals like Charv and Alfie, but this felt like a new Wales, and we were determined to start with a bang. It may have been the World Cup finalists against the World Cup flops, but we were excited, and had no fear.

I've never been a massive fan of M People, but the journey down to London put me off them for life. It's a little-known fact that Shaun Edwards used to be married to Heather Small, the singer from M People, and they have a son together. It was one of the most incongruous couplings I'd come across – a hard-as-nails Rugby League legend and a glamorous pop star. They'd split up by this time, but Tom Shanklin thought it would be hilarious to play M People songs on the bus all the way to London. And I mean *all* the way. What began as a joke ended as a form of torture. Even their most loyal fan would have been dying inside by the time we pulled up at Twickenham. Shaun was at the front. We'd all been watching the back of his head, and getting increasingly nervous about the moment when he'd inevitably erupt. It was a risky thing to do to your new defence coach who has anger issues, but Shanks loves the banter.

Eventually, Shaun cracked, swivelled round and shouted in his thick Wigan accent, 'You ought to try living with her! She's a bloody nightmare.'

The boys collapsed into nervous laughter. He'd seen the funny side. For a while there, I'd thought he was going to rip Shanks's head off.

As a Welshman you always want to beat England more than any other side. It's part of your DNA, and has been reinforced since birth – through your parents, the media, your sense of history and, to an extent, your education. I'd like to think we've moved beyond that 'as long as we beat the English' mentality, but that doesn't mean we won't continue to take more pleasure in beating them than we do anyone else. Back in the seventies, when Phil Bennett delivered his famous speech before playing England, the match represented a class war. Working-class Welsh boys against public-school-educated Englishmen. Those boundaries have blurred over the years, but that's not to say you don't still bristle walking through the Twickenham car park past all the posh English fans in their claret cords and Barbour jackets, eating prawn sandwiches out of the back of their Mercedes. It's a far cry from your average Welsh fan stumbling down Westgate Street with a pasty and a pint.

As with most games, you can pinpoint a moment when the axis shifts. Sometimes it's obvious, sometimes more subtle. In that England game it was the period just before half-time. We'd been under severe pressure defending our own line. They'd been trying to squeeze us through their scrum and driving line-out, trying to force cracks in our defence. But we held firm. It was enough to make us believe this game was still a contest. Up until then, we'd been second best. They'd carved us open a few times, and we were turning the ball over needlessly. Halfway through that first half, they'd crafted a brilliant try. Wilkinson lofted a perfect cross kick to Lesley Vainikolo, who outjumped Mark Jones on the left wing, and pulled off a sweet little offload to Toby Flood. It was 16–6 at half-time, but it could have been more.

There was a feeling in the changing room that England had emptied their tank. They'd thrown everything at us, and only managed to build a ten-point lead. That can be a lot in international rugby, but we felt we were within reach. The calm, measured approach of the coaches was a factor in our confidence. They knew what it took to win big matches, and they instilled in us that we could still win this one. Their belief was unswerving, and it was contagious. Games like that inevitably break up a little bit, and gaps start to appear. We knew that when that happened, we had some world-class game breakers to call on: Shane Williams,

James Hook and Martyn Williams. And Lee Byrne was at that point the best full-back in the world.

It was fitting, then, that he got us back into the game. Hooky went on a little blindside snipe, beat three defenders with some magic footwork, and offloaded to Byrney, who sprinted over. The conversion drew us level, and you could see the panic in England's eyes. Their composure deserted them, and they started throwing loose, speculative passes. Even the unflappable Jonny Wilkinson looked rattled. Moments after Byrney's try, Iain Balshaw attempted a rushed clearance, and saw it charged down by Mike Phillips. We piled through, Melon scooped it up, passed to Nugget, and Phillsy looped round to finish off the move he'd started. It went to the video ref, but we knew from Phillsy's reaction he'd got it down. Hooky nailed the touchline conversion and the victory was in the bag.

As part of the post-match review, our analysis team printed out individual stats. It was like getting exam results. You'd know roughly how you'd got on, but this laid it out in black and white. Everyone would have an individual sheet of A4 with their name, photo and a list of statistics: rucks hit, tackles made, carries, etc. And there'd be a space beneath for notes.

Everyone's sheet was vaguely complimentary, apart from Jonathan Thomas's – he'd been knocked out by Jonny Wilkinson in the opening quarter. He'd offered himself as ball carrier off Mike Phillips and ended up getting smashed by Wilkinson. Knocked out by a fly-half. That in itself is embarrassing, but his humiliation was complete when he read his stats. His sheet was empty apart from the words: 'Serves you right for running the mutes line, inside the 15s off 9.'

He'd disregarded the rules of 'the pattern'. JT is a dynamic back row forward, and had been encouraged to offer himself as a ball carrier – but only in certain areas of the pitch. Specifically, the narrow outside channels in between the touchlines, and the 15-metre lines. Those were the strict parameters. In the England game he'd had the audacity to pop up as first receiver in the middle of the pitch and, as far as the coaches were concerned, had got what he deserved. It was tongue in cheek, but it quickly taught us two things: Warren's game plan was precise to the point of being scientific, and you were judged according to very exacting standards. The poor bloke had been knocked out and could have been forgiven for expecting a little sympathy. None was forthcoming.

It summed up the attitude from the coaches. We'd just beaten England at Twickenham for the first time since 1988, but we weren't allowed to get carried away with ourselves. Everyone was delighted, but our excitement was kept in check by the knowledge that it was just one victory. A significant one, yes, but the hard work was yet to come. We were told to enjoy the win but to ensure we didn't rest on our laurels. There were no wild celebrations.

●　●　●

The team for the next game against Scotland would be decided in training, and it was made clear that nobody's place was safe. We approached that game with more trepidation than you might imagine. Scotland weren't a bad side, and we were terrified that the euphoria from the England game could disappear during the next eighty minutes in Cardiff.

Gatland did make some changes. Tom Shanklin reclaimed his place in the centre from Sonny Parker, and Jamie Roberts made his debut on the wing, which diluted the Ospreys contingent a little. But as was so often the case, it was the Williams boys who came to the fore. Two tries from Shane and a man-of-the match performance from Martyn put us on the road to a comfortable victory.

Shane's first was pure class. A trademark incision into the line from Byrney, followed by a slightly wayward pass that Shane gathered at pace, before stepping inside and scoring. Hooky then crossed in the second half after seeing Euan Murray and Ross Ford in front of him. There was only one winner there.

Shane's second try was the best of the bunch. He looked up, saw a congested field of would-be tacklers, and thought, 'Let's have a crack.' He left the first line of defence for dead with his lightning acceleration, before stepping and shimmying his way past everyone else. There were few players in world rugby as capable as he was of making the opposition look foolish. His footwork alone could transform the most agile of defenders into leaden-footed oafs. There was a bit of controversy surrounding that try, as replays suggested he may have been in touch, but it would have made no difference to the result. Shane was coming into his own during this period. His confidence was sky high, and he had the touch of an alchemist. I can't tell you how relieved I was to be playing with him, rather than against him.

There was a fortnight between the Scotland and Italy games, so we had a couple of days off to relax before reporting back to camp on the Wednesday. The forwards were called in first. We didn't know what was in store for us – perhaps a little fitness session to get our lungs going a bit, or some light drills.

Nothing could have prepared us for what happened next. Warren Gatland assembled us in the team room and introduced us to a little Northern guy called Paul Stridgeon. He was a physical conditioning coach and a former wrestler. And as we were about to discover, a bit of a sadist. After a brief preamble, he explained we'd be doing something called 'power endurance'. It was all about using energy systems that you'd never used before, and pushing yourself to the limits of your physical capability.

Prior to this, we'd maybe do some casual weights on a Wednesday – three sets of ten bench presses, with a rest in between, before moving on to the next at your own pace. It was just pure strength work. This was a whole different level. It was relentless – no rests, just constant sets until you were on the verge of collapse. Ten bench presses, followed by ten chin-ups, followed by ten squats, ten step-ups, and ten shoulder presses. Then back to the start, and do it again, and again, and again, and again. It was absolute torture. That was phase one.

Phase two was a combination of shuttles, wrestling and tug of war. Ianto claimed afterwards that he'd had an out-of-body experience. He honestly thought he was going to die. In his defence, he did get the raw end of the deal by being paired with Robin McBryde – a former winner of Wales' Strongest Man, and a man who prides himself on his strength and physical fitness. Looking back, it was comical – a lanky six-foot-eight beanpole being ragged around on the end of a rope by a grisly hooker with the strength of an ox – but no one was laughing at the time. They were too busy puking or gasping for breath. Alun Wyn spent half the session with his head in the bin.

Ianto couldn't move for at least half an hour afterwards. He was like a felled giant. He lay on his back looking like an enormous spider, with his long spindly limbs splayed out in different directions. The boys were ripping into him, but he was so wiped out he couldn't even raise a smile. He was absolutely in bits. McBryde had shown him no mercy, and during the whole session Gatland had been patrolling the perimeter like some evil dictator, saying, 'Get used to this, boys. This is how it's going to be from now on.'

That was when my heart really sank. I'd persuaded myself it was just a one-off to test us. But it was clearly the start of a new regime.

The only person who seemed to take it all in his stride was Huw Bennett, the smug bastard. Once you'd completed phase one in the gym, you had to go and wait in the barn for the second phase. He finished long before anyone else and ended up casually strolling around in the barn while we wheezed and spluttered our way through it. I don't know how he does it, but he appears to be built from different components to the rest of us.

The backs arrived as we were finishing up, and I'll never forget the looks of horror on their faces. We were splayed out all over the floor, in various states of distress, coughing, gasping and retching. It must have looked like a scene from a zombie movie – like we'd all contracted some deadly plague and were dying before their eyes. If we were able to derive even a shred of satisfaction from the situation, it was in the knowledge that the pretty boys had it all to come.

Until I reached the twilight of my international career, I always felt insecure about my place in the squad. I always felt as though the coaches were looking for someone better. It was as though I'd do for the time being, until they unearthed someone with real potential. So whenever I was left out, paranoia would set in a little. I'd convince myself this was the beginning of the end.

I was pulled aside before the Italy game and told I wouldn't be involved. 'You're not dropped,' they insisted. 'We just want a look at what Rhys Thomas can do.'

I was disappointed. Even when you're given a solid reason, you feel gutted. You train to play, not to train some more, and when you're left out of the match-day squad you can't help but feel empty. It's an occupational hazard of being a professional sportsman. All of us have a competitive streak. It shows up more strongly in some, but you don't reach this level without being competitive. No one likes being told someone else has been chosen ahead of them. But that's sport – without competition, you wouldn't strive to get better. And once you get over the sulk of being left out, that's exactly what you do.

The blow was softened by the fact that I wasn't the only one. Gatland changed the entire front row – with Melon and Matthew Rees coming in for Duncan and Huw Bennett – and in the backs Hooky and Phillsy had made way for Stephen Jones and Dwayne Peel. It was clearly a chance to test the depth of our squad, so I didn't feel overly aggrieved. At least not until the end of the campaign, when I realised the Grand Slam bonus was paid pro rata. The fact that I'd missed a game meant mine came up about seven grand short! But we're getting ahead of ourselves.

It's an odd experience watching your team play when you're not injured and not on the bench. Of course you still want them to win, because it's a squad effort – and at that point in time, it was a particularly harmonious squad – and you certainly don't wish ill on the person who's taken your shirt. But I'd be lying if I said I was rooting for Rhys.

Scrummaging is my thing. It's what I pride myself on above all else. So if a few Welsh scrums had been shunted backwards in that game, you may have seen me smiling inwardly. It's human nature – and before you judge me, it'd be the same in any position. If a fly-half is left out, he won't mind too much if his replacement misses a kick or two. If a flanker is dropped, he won't be too bothered if his replacement falls off a few tackles. But despite those feelings, I've never felt resentful towards a player who's been picked ahead of me. I went to find Rhys Thomas on that occasion to wish him good luck, and that's the way it should be. The onus should be on the player who's lost his shirt to do that. Rugby has always had deep-rooted values, and that is one of them. You might be hurting, and you might not necessarily mean it, but it's important that you go through the ritual.

History will tell you that we beat Italy comfortably that year, but we were in no way complacent about it, having lost to them the previous year. It was tense for twenty minutes, after Martin Castrogiovanni bulldozed his way over for a try, but we cut loose in the second half. Byrney and Shane ended up with two tries each, and Shanks snaffled an interception to score on the occasion of his fiftieth cap. I've never seen him run so fast.

Shane's second try was sensational – he showed his usual jinking footwork to dance around a few tacklers before turning on the afterburners and scorching his way to the line. The TV cameras cut to the coaching box and captured a disbelieving Shaun Edwards shouting, 'What a player! What a player!' It's what we were all thinking.

So we'd played three, won three, and the whispers of another Grand Slam were beginning to grow louder. We'd been criticised in the past for not finishing teams off when we had them by the jugular, but no one could accuse us of letting our foot off the gas on that occasion. If the championship was to come down to points difference, we'd just accumulated a hatful.

● ● ●

The next game was the Triple Crown decider against Ireland in Croke Park. The press were obsessed with the supposed bad blood between Warren Gatland and Eddie O'Sullivan. They'd worked together when Warren had coached Ireland between 1998 and 2001, and Eddie ended up succeeding him. Rumours abounded regarding an internal coup that had seen Gatland displaced by his assistant, which meant the Triple Crown match had an extra layer of spice. Warren – who's not averse to lobbing a grenade or two when he chooses – played every O'Sullivan question with a straight bat. It became something of a soap opera, but it suited the team down to the ground because it took all the pressure away from us. The gaze of the media was elsewhere, which allowed us to go about our business without the degree of scrutiny that would normally have applied to such a massive game.

Personally, I was so relaxed during the build-up, I decided to braid my hair. It was an odd decision, but it'll probably come across as an even odder one when I reveal that it was Shaun Edwards – the bald, no-nonsense northerner – who suggested I do it. He wandered over during a break in training and, apropos of nothing, asked if I'd ever considered braiding my hair.

Bewildered, and suspecting it was some kind of practical joke, I said no, I never had.

'I think you'd look really good with braided hair, Bomb.'

I glanced around, looking for Ianto, the squad's biggest wind-up merchant. Seeing nobody, I began to think that Shaun was being serious. There was part of me that was still a little star-struck in his presence, and I thought if he's recommending I do this, it must be a good idea.

So the next day, I went and got my hair braided into cornrows at some African beauty parlour in Swansea. Two and a half hours it took, and it fucking killed. But it was worth it, because I turned up for training the next day and Shaun Edwards's first words to me were, 'Looks fookin' ace, lad!' It was the equivalent of giving an apple to your favourite teacher. I'd pleased one of the coaches, and it felt good. It was the only positive reaction I had, mind. Pretty much all of the boys spent the entire session ripping the piss out of me, as you'd expect. But Shaun loved it.

To this day, I don't know why he suggested it – or whether or not he was taking the piss. Perhaps it was a command from Gatland, who was fed up of my long hair flailing around during games and getting pulled in rucks. He was constantly on at me to cut it. Maybe this was seen as a compromise.

I'm asked about the long hair all the time, as though it's some kind of bold personal statement. People assume I'm into heavy metal — or motorbiking, or something. But that's not the case. It all started during the Under 21s World Cup in South Africa, in 2002. Myself, Duncan Jones, Luke Tait and Ryan Jones were bored one afternoon and decided to go and have streaks put into our hair. It looked terrible, and we were left with two options. Grow it out or shave it all off. I just kept growing it and growing it. Duncan's girlfriend at the time loved his new look, and insisted he keep his hair long. So I followed suit.

There was no pact between us, but it didn't half lead to some good headlines. We became known thereafter as the Hair Bears. It was a nickname that endured, especially during the period when we were both starting for Wales on either side of the scrum. Also — and crucially for a man who plays in my position — it hides the cauliflower ears. Most rugby fans would have struggled to pick us out of a line-up before the Hair Bears period, but our profiles soared in the aftermath. I was accosted by a bunch of young Leicester fans in the Ospreys car park once. They chased me down, shouting, 'There's one, there's one!' I felt like an animal in a safari park.

I might have to get it cut one day, but it'll be the onset of baldness that makes that decision for me. I wouldn't do it for charity, and I wouldn't do it to satisfy a coach, but I won't be one of those middle-aged men walking around with a few spindly strands swept back into a ponytail. That's not a good look by anyone's standards. And my wife certainly wouldn't tolerate it.

I've had my fair share of stick over the years, especially from former Wales front rowers like Graham Price and Bobby Windsor who thought that my image didn't lend itself well to the long line of tough, uncompromising bruisers that have worn the jersey over the years. They made no secret of the fact that props should strike fear into the heart of the opposite number, and not give a shit about personal appearance. But my hair isn't a vanity thing, it's just a personal preference. And I like to think as long as I'm playing well, it doesn't matter what I look like. Hopefully my critics have come to realise that over the years.

●　　●　　●

Anyway, back to the Grand Slam. None of us had played at Croke Park before, and we were under no illusions as to how tough it would be. It was bigger than Lansdowne Road, at around 80,000, and the history of the place seemed to push Ireland on to another level – especially against England, as we had witnessed the year before. They destroyed the English that day, and we were conscious that something similar could happen to us if we didn't stand up to the hostility of the crowd and the occasion. To me, it was one of those places, like Wembley, where you don't get a chance to play often. So I tried to take it in, and to enjoy it.

They had a fantastic side. It was the classic blend of a Munster-based forward pack – all strength, guile and brawn – and a classy Leinster-style backline, marshalled by the world-class axis of O'Gara, Trimble and O'Driscoll. The Irish provinces were going great guns in Europe, and there was a feel-good factor running throughout Irish rugby. Their squad was being dubbed the 'Golden Generation' by the press on the other side of the Irish Sea, but we were confident. We were unbeaten, and getting better.

I got an early introduction to Tommy Bowe, a man who'd later become my teammate and friend. But he wasn't as polite that day as I would come to know him in later life. As a prop one of your roles when your team is receiving a kick-off is to run a 'lazy line', to get in the way of a chasing winger. Not a block as such, but a line that stops him generating full speed and building momentum. Ryan Jones was in position to catch the ball, and I was trying to stop Bowe from reaching him and putting in an early hit. One moment I was focusing on Ryan, the next I was splayed out on the floor after receiving a sharp elbow to the head.

As I looked up, I heard Tommy intone, in his distinctive Ulster brogue, 'Get out of my way, you fat bastard.' Welcome to Croke Park.

Ronan O'Gara kicked Ireland into an early 6–0 lead and Shane Horgan came within inches of a try, but for a heroic smother tackle from Mike Phillips. That was as close as Ireland got to crossing the line in the entire game. From that point on, any fears we may have had began to fade. We were holding our own in the tight exchanges, picking-and-going effectively. And whenever we put a bit of width on the ball, we sensed that our runners had a bit more gas than theirs. Shane Williams and Lee Byrne were fizzing and darting about, and some gaps were starting to appear. We should have gone in 6–6 at half-time, but a penalty was reversed when Mike Phillips was spotted dropping his knee on Marcus Horan. Yellow card. Temper, temper, Mike!

Their equivalent of our Mike Phillips was Ronan O'Gara. Lovely bloke off the pitch, but mouthy and objectionable on it. He was his usual gobby self that day, barking orders at his teammates and hurling insults at us, but it was largely in vain. On one occasion, when he was ambling back, I jogged up behind him and shoulder charged him into a ruck. He didn't like that one bit, and I was on the receiving end of a tirade of abuse, most of which is unrepeatable here. Suffice to say he used the word 'fat' a lot.

His kicking game that day was as accurate as ever, but our back three were so solid that Ireland were getting no change at all out of the aerial game. And as the second half wore on, it felt as though they'd exhausted all their attacking options. We were creating far more chances, but just falling short of the try line, until Shane, once again, pulled a rabbit out of the hat.

There was no overlap when he received the ball on the wing, just the tiniest of gaps between Andrew Trimble and Tommy Bowe. That was enough for Shane. He accelerated between them, leaving both flapping at thin air. He was virtually untouchable at that point, and almost definitely the best winger in the world. I'm lucky enough to have played with him since the start of his career in 2000, and I always knew he was a rare, rare talent. He just needed someone to show a bit of faith, and he was repaying Warren Gatland many times over. Not many people of his size can have such a dominant influence on games, but he was the scourge of the opposition for that entire campaign. It's his strength as well as his pace that's the key, and he demonstrated it with that try. For a little fella, he can certainly handle himself, and he'd never back down from a fight. In fact, he claims he's an unbeaten amateur boxer. Three fights, three wins, if you believe what he says. I've never seen any evidence, but it wouldn't surprise me. He's an angry little fucker. Because of who he is, he often gets targeted on a night out. He never goes looking for a fight, but if someone decides to pick on him, believe me, he can handle himself.

He's mentally tough as well. To overcome as many knock-backs as he has illustrates the character of the man. He never gave up when people told him he was too small, and worked incredibly hard in the gym to improve his physique. He only put on about 5kg, but it was 5kg of pure muscle. When you looked at him in 2008, and compared him to the waiflike figure that ran on for his debut in 2000, it was apparent what a specimen he'd become.

For my money, he's the best winger ever to have worn the Welsh jersey. It's not something I say lightly, because there are a number of world-class contenders, but when Shane was on song, he was beyond compare. I've played alongside some of the best players of my or any era – Brian O'Driscoll, Paul O'Connell, Alun Wyn Jones – but Shane was head and shoulders above them all. Pound for pound, he was the best. He was frighteningly good. Crazy good. Take-the-piss good.

Not long after Shane's try, we lost Nugget to the sin bin. Ireland had launched a threatening attack, and we were scrambling back to defend. Eoin Reddan was running a good supporting line, and Nugget – like all good sevens who play on the edge of the law – tripped him from behind. It was a definite yellow card, and it meant if we were going to win this game, we'd have to do it playing with fourteen men for twenty of the eighty minutes. But we'd survived Mike's period in the bin without too much drama, and backed ourselves to do the same.

The scrum had gone well all game. I'd played against Marcus Horan a lot over my career, and he was a good, wily operator. John Hayes was almost universally rubbished, but anyone who's played that many times for Ireland, and won that many Heineken Cups, must be good. I could never understand why he was considered a weak link. Every time we had a meeting before an Ireland game, we were pretty much told, 'Run at O'Gara, run at John Hayes. Neither can tackle.' In 2009 I would pipe up, pointing out that we said this every year, and that to my knowledge it had never worked. It's a myth, and we should be showing them a bit more respect. I never understood the 'weak scrummager' tag either. John Hayes is no mug. He's six foot four, and twenty stone of strong, sinewy farmer muscle, who could more than hold his own in the scrum. I never saw him get an outing playing against Wales, and he didn't give us any change in 2008.

And as for running down O'Gara's channel, I always thought that was a bit basic. I despair of commentators who say things like, 'Why doesn't he just run down the fly-half's channel?' Modern rugby is slightly more sophisticated than that. There are ways to defend those tactics. (Think of our game against England in 2009.) The pre-game mantra was, 'Run hard at Charlie Hodgson,' and Jamie Roberts was our weapon of choice. England had seen it coming a mile off. Joe Worsley stood opposite Jamie all game, said, 'Screw the line-out,' and spent the afternoon smashing him backwards. Hodgson had his bouncer, and the '10 channel' was out of bounds. Flankers and inside centres look after their tens. And they did so with O'Gara that afternoon in 2008, and every time we've played them before and after.

In the end, it was our new-found maturity that won us the game. With minutes left on the clock, and a four-point cushion on the scoreboard, we reverted to a very 'un-Welsh' style of play – keeping possession, and going through the phases. It wasn't pretty, but it was effective, and Ireland – to their obvious frustration – couldn't lay a hand on the ball. We had lost too many matches from winning positions, and were determined not to do it again. There was no need for a heroic final flourish, we just had to grind it out. And we did. The clock ticked over to 80. Mike Phillips booted it out, and the celebrations began.

As we were coming off the field, I remember saying to Gats, 'You must be landed, getting one over on Ireland after the history between you and Eddie O'Sullivan.'

'Bomb,' he said, 'it means nothing to me.'

He said it was all about us players, and that we shouldn't get sucked into the petty jealousies that the press were intent on exaggerating. We'd just won a Triple Crown in his first season in charge, and that in itself was reason enough for celebration.

When Ryan Jones held the Triple Crown trophy aloft, it felt real. He'd been an excellent skipper. Calm, measured, and very much his own man. He wasn't afraid to disagree with Gats, if he thought he had a point – and that's not always easy to do, especially in your first campaign as captain.

He loved the attention that was being lavished on him as well, and he kicked the arse out of the media. He'd lost some of his dynamism on the field, but he was a very solid presence. And that was exactly what we needed at the time.

He was never a screamer or a shouter, either on the pitch or in the changing room. He didn't see the need, and neither did I. We left all that to Huw Bennett, who'd be bellowing loudly in his hybrid Somerset-Valleys accent, while the rest of us were trying to focus. He was largely on his own. Not many of the pack were 'rip their heads off!' shouty types. Me: no. Melon: definitely not. Matthew Rees: no. Goughie: didn't know what day it was half the time. Alun Wyn: no. Nugget: far too laid-back. JT might go bonkers every now and again, but that was about it. None of the backs were crazy shouters either. Stephen Jones would get twitchy and excited, but not in an aggressive way. It was mainly just Benny. He'd get so wound up, he'd make himself sick. And that would set Jug Head off as well. We'd often be preparing to run out to the soundtrack of those two chucking their guts up in the toilets.

We allowed ourselves a good few pints of Guinness that night, but were careful not to go overboard because the Grand Slam game against the French was just a week away. I spent a good few hours in the company of the Irish boys, and Tommy Bowe in particular. He apologised for his indiscretion at the start of the game, we shook hands, and we've been great mates ever since.

● ● ●

France had a very good team that year. They were the defending champions, and in Nicolas Mas and William Servat they had two of the finest front row forwards I'd ever played against. The tension in the build-up was getting stronger by the day. It was different to 2005, when it took everyone by surprise. We were expected to win this time. We could lose the match and still win the championship, but no one was contemplating that. We wanted to do it in style. France would have to win by twenty points if they were to steal it from under our noses.

We were worked hard on the Monday and the Tuesday in training. Two days of no-holds-barred full contact. It was that kind of commitment that had got us this far, and we weren't about to slacken off now. We hung our hats on our levels of intensity. In our minds, it's what separated us from the rest. That said, the coaches always knew when to draw the line. Their man-management was outstanding. We knew they were in charge, but they empowered us just enough to make us feel valued. We were lieutenants rather than just infantry.

On the Thursday, Warren asked Gavin Henson how long he wanted to train for. Gav suggested half an hour, and Warren agreed. He'd singled out Gav to give him a bit of responsibility, and to get him out of his shell. It was a clever ploy. Gats knew he could do what he needed in half an hour, and the players felt they weren't being needlessly flogged. We were all in a good place. We had our captain's run at the Millennium Stadium on the Friday, and then we knew we could just chill out. All the hard work was done, and we felt as prepared as we'd ever be.

We returned to HQ, and Nugget and I went out on the chocolate run. That was my favourite part of the week by some distance – the last twenty-four hours. A chance to hang out with your mates in the team room and get excited about the challenge ahead. The two of us filled the boot with chocolate. No one was worrying about calories, because we knew we'd burn it all off and then some the following day. Stephen Jones demolished a box of Guylians, Melon hoovered up a giant bag of M&M's, and I ploughed through a metre-long bar of Galaxy. The game was at the back of our minds constantly, but we tried to distract ourselves with a film and a couple of episodes of *EastEnders*.

Some of the boys wanted to watch the Under 20s game, while others wanted to avoid thinking about rugby. Not everyone hung out in the team room. Some would head home to their families for an hour or two, others would pop out to see their mates, but I always loved that time in the nerve centre on the eve of a big game. It's where the bonds were really forged. We were confident. That confidence was bred from the way we'd played. When you win every game comfortably, self-belief surges. It's a cliché, but winning is a habit. And we'd become used to it.

It was damp and drizzly in Cardiff when Saturday dawned – a far cry from the spring sunshine of 2005, when we were last going for a Grand Slam. But our spirits would not be dampened, and emotions were running high. Ian Gough led the team out for his fiftieth cap, and he emerged from the tunnel with Ray Gravell's two daughters, Manon and Gwenan. Grav – one of the greatest Welshmen to have lived – had died the year before, and the sight of his two daughters leading the team out on the occasion of a championship decider was enough to send even the sternest of bottom lips quivering.

I can honestly remember very little about the game, but one moment stands out for me in vivid technicolour. France were attacking our line with sixty-five minutes gone, and were ten points behind, when they were awarded a scrum. We were in the shadows of our own posts. It was a critical juncture. Had they scored from that, they'd have seized the momentum and who knows what might have happened. Their players were talking to each other, plotting some back row move, and whispering conspiratorially. Our defence was set, but instead of bracing ourselves for the desperate French onslaught, we backed ourselves to do a job on them in the scrum.

All eight of us in the pack aligned perfectly, timed our hit to perfection, and drove them clean off their own ball. It was a beautiful feeling, marching a grizzled French pack backwards and seeing them buckle under the weight of some good old Welsh brawn. Jug Head picked up from the base, and Phillsy cleared. People will remember the tries, but we front row forwards will be reminiscing about that moment, and that moment alone, in fifty years' time. I could wax lyrical about Shane's magnificent try, but I've already showered him with enough praise. That scrum is what really won us the Grand Slam! John Humphreys later told me that, at that point, I should have run off the field and high-fived everyone in the crowd. I was never going to score a fifty-yard try, so that was my equivalent.

It would be churlish not to mention Shane's try at all, though. It was another absolute gem, just like we'd become accustomed to. We'd begun the second half with fourteen men after Gav had been sin-binned for a high tackle. We may have lost a player but we didn't lose any confidence. The intensity of our training, and our improved fitness, meant we'd finished all our games strongly so far, and had scored most of our points in the second half. This game proved no exception. We struck on the hour mark, by which time Gav had returned to the field.

Our defence had been exceptional all tournament, thanks to the incredible attention to detail of Shaun Edwards. The blitz had been working like a dream, and we'd only conceded two tries. It was causing France problems all day, and was the catalyst for Shane's try. David Skrela threw a wayward pass that missed its target, and Shane was on it in an instant. He fly-hacked through, and showed the kind of footballing skills that Lionel Messi would have been proud of to dribble it to the line. The bounce was kind, but his skills were out of the top drawer. It was his 41st try for Wales and took him ahead of Alfie at the top of the charts. What a time to break the record.

If Shane was charmed, our other wing, Mark Jones, was the unluckiest man in rugby. He nearly scored one of the greatest tries in the history of the tournament. Nearly. Alun Wyn stole a line-out in our 22, and Boycey set off on an incredible mazy run. He glided up the pitch and looked for all the world as though he was going to go from one try line to the other, but he was hauled down inches short. Shane had won all the plaudits during that campaign, and was player of the tournament by some distance, so it would have been nice for Mark to have had his moment in the sun, but he was denied by the tiniest of margins.

Nugget put the seal on the Slam, picking up from the base of a ruck, and sprinting twenty-five yards unopposed to the line. I was on the bench by that point, but I leapt to my feet, pumping my clenched fists in the air, just like the 75,000 other supporters in the stadium. It was an incredible feeling. There was to be no edgy finale, no shredding of the nerves. We were out of sight, and the celebrations could begin.

It was regarded as less of a flash in the pan than the Grand Slam we won in 2005. Because of the way we were playing, and the mentality the coaches had instilled, we were beginning to be seen as a very good side. The feeling was that we were going to go on to bigger and better things. The previous September, we'd been knocked out of the World Cup by Fiji, but Gatland's aura had rubbed off on us all. We'd gone from laughing stock to Grand Slam champions in the space of five months.

People always ask me what it was like in the dressing room afterwards, imagining it was the scene of some kind of wild party. But we were so physically and emotionally drained, it was actually quite quiet in there. Prince William popped in to offer his congratulations and pose for a few photos, and Shaun insisted we all join in for a chorus of 'Saturday Night At The Movies'. But my abiding memory is of me, Ryan and Alun Wyn Jones sitting on the floor in the middle of the room, quietly sipping a can of beer and chatting. It was a fantastic moment. We'd been through so much together as friends, and this was an opportunity, in the eye of the storm, for a bit of quiet reflection. It sunk in then that we'd done something special.

And that feeling really hit home when we got off the team bus at the Hilton for the post-match function. Hundreds upon hundreds of fans had gathered on the pavements and in the hotel foyer. Camera flashes were going off everywhere, and people were tripping over themselves to touch us and shake our hands.

Welsh rugby fans are the best in the world. They've been through some awful times, and kept the faith throughout. It was nice to be able to repay some of that faith, and to see how much it meant to them all.

CHAPTER 13

The Lions Roar

I'D never felt pain like it in my life. It was searing through my body. My shoulder felt like it had been smashed with a sledgehammer. I was slipping in and out of consciousness. Howls of agony were escaping through my gritted teeth. Several strangers were wrenching my right arm in and out of its socket. As my vision began to blur, I was vaguely aware of the crowd noise swelling to a crescendo outside. I was in South Africa. I was aware of that much. And my Lions tour had just come to a catastrophic end.

Rewind six months, and I was at the Millennium Stadium packing down against a fearsome young prop forward by the name of Tendai Mtawarira. You may know him better as 'the Beast'. I was winning my fiftieth cap for my country. He was winning his second for his. This was my manor, and I didn't much care for the hype surrounding this supposed young superstar. This was my domain. I'd just run out on my own to milk the adulation of the crowd on the occasion of my half-century, and I wasn't about to let this upstart spoil my party. I kept him firmly in his box all afternoon. The Beast barely raised a snarl. He was good, but not quite worthy of the pedestal he'd been placed on.

While I won my personal battle, the outcome of the game was familiar. Another defeat against the Springboks – this time by a narrow margin of 20 points to 15. But valiant defeats weren't good enough any more. Gatland was furious that we'd spurned so many try-scoring opportunities. We went on to lose to New Zealand a fortnight later, but we finished the autumn on a positive note with a 21–18 victory over Australia. A confidence-boosting victory to take into the 2009 Six Nations. That autumn series was also notable for the emergence of Jamie Roberts as an inside centre. He'd been a full-back and a wing for the Cardiff Blues, but Gatland thought his size and bulk would be better suited to 12, and as we've seen over the years, he's become a vital cog in Warren's game plan.

Our Six Nations title defence didn't go according to plan. It started well enough with wins over Scotland and England. But a narrow defeat to France meant there was no chance of another clean sweep. We limped to an unimpressive 20–15 win over Italy, and faced Ireland on the final day as one of four sides that could still technically win the championship. They were going for a Grand Slam, but if we beat them by thirteen points, we could still snatch the title. As it was, the game came down to a ridiculously nervy exchange of drop goals in the dying moments. Stephen Jones nailed one to put us 15–14 ahead with five minutes left – a scoreline that would have secured us the Triple Crown, if not the championship. But two minutes later, O'Gara dropped a goal of his own that gave them a 17–15 lead. They were three minutes away from only the second Grand Slam in their history. But we were determined to spoil their party, and our chance came in the final act. We were awarded a penalty on the halfway line. The very outer limit of Stephen Jones's range, but he stepped up for the challenge. The ball sailed good and true, and appeared to be on course, but it dropped agonisingly short, giving the game and the title to Ireland.

We ended up finishing fourth. Such are the fine margins of the Six Nations. If Leigh Halfpenny had been on the pitch, we'd probably have won. It was a hell of an effort from Steve but he didn't have the range of 'Pens', and it's not easy taking a kick from that distance when your legs are burning from eighty minutes of test rugby. You need massive balls to take these kicks, and I have nothing but respect for those who do. It hadn't been a spectacular fall from grace, but history will suggest that the 2008 Grand Slam champions were mere also-rans the following year.

It was disappointing obviously, but I still felt we were a very good side. A very good side that hadn't had the breaks. Following the defeat in France, the French players and supporters had gone crazy. French victories over Wales in the past had been met with a kind of Gallic indifference – but not this one. They knew they'd got out of jail that day, because we were better than they were. Our scrum was massively on top, and Andy Powell was punching holes in their defence for fun. Their ecstatic reaction at the final whistle made me realise how good we were. France – a team who'd been the dominant force in Northern Hemisphere rugby for some time – were over the moon to have beaten Wales.

I was devastated after the Ireland game, as you'd expect. No one likes losing, especially in that manner, but I was cheered when Paul O'Connell sidled over, offered his commiserations and said in his thick Limerick accent, 'Hopefully, see you in June.' He was favourite to captain the Lions out in South Africa, so I saw this as a good omen. Earlier in the campaign, Warren had dropped a similar hint, telling me how fit I was looking and suggesting that I'd look good in red in the summer. We had lost our Six Nations title, but there was an enormous carrot dangling on the horizon.

● ● ●

The call came in April. I was training with the Ospreys as the Lions squad was being announced live on television. Shane Williams was on the sidelines nursing a knock and monitoring the squad announcement. He was trying to communicate with me via very basic sign language, which consisted of him giving me the thumbs up and pointing. But I didn't know whether that meant I was in, or he was in, or one of our Ospreys team-mates was in. I couldn't concentrate on training at all, and it wasn't until the session finished that I found out for sure. I *was* in. I'd had the call to represent the British and Irish Lions – the highest honour a Northern Hemisphere rugby player can achieve. It was me, Tommy Bowe, Shane, Alun Wyn, Byrney and Mike Phillips. Six Ospreys in the Lions squad. Five Welshmen, and a rogue Northern Irishman.

When we'd emerged from the showers, the press and photographers had arrived, and we each had our photo taken with the Lions jersey. I was beyond proud. The texts started flooding through from family and friends. My parents were over the moon, as was my wife, Nicole. I'd been gutted not to have been selected for the previous Lions tour in 2005, but I knew this time that I was a much better player. Four years earlier, we'd won the Grand Slam and a lot of people thought there should have been more Welshmen on that tour, but I was far more ready for it this time. I'd had an enormous kick up the arse from Gats, and Craig White – the Union's new conditioning coach – had helped transform me into a much fitter, leaner player. He was going on the tour as well, which gave me added confidence that we could do well. The other tight-heads selected were Phil Vickery and Euan Murray, both of whom were very good at the time. If I was honest with myself, I was going out as third choice. But I knew if I worked hard, I'd have a chance of getting in the team.

The day of the first squad-meet in Pennyhill Park, all the Welsh Lions got the bus up together from our Vale of Glamorgan HQ. Talk about a clash of cultures. A busload of Welsh rugby internationals bundling out into the leafy, genteel surroundings of a mansion house in Surrey. We all met Rala, the kit man, who dished out the stash. Shirts, shorts, tracksuits, fleeces, coats, blazers, polo shirts, shoes – an entire new wardrobe. Every item emblazoned with the unique Lions badge. It had all been organised with military precision.

Then we were all told who we'd be rooming with for that week. That was the weirdest part of the day. Although we all vaguely knew each other, and had played against each other, we were only on nodding terms with many of the other players, and some of them we actively disliked. It was like starting at a new school. Everyone was a bit shy, a bit nervous, and keen to make a good impression. I looked at the list, and discovered that I'd be rooming with Andrew Sheridan, the English behemoth that I'd propped against many times. It had never been a pleasant experience. There were always scuffles between us when we played. A punch here, a sly headbutt there. Typical of the animosity on the pitch between the Welsh and the English. Suffice to say I wasn't too chuffed about the prospect of sharing a room with him. I rushed to judgement, thinking he'd be arrogant and boring. Just some big mutant of a bloke, clomping around, getting in my way. I couldn't have been more wrong.

He was already in the room when I wandered in and said, 'Alright, butt?'

I was taken aback when he replied in Welsh, 'Bore da. Shwmae?'

It turned out his wife is from Builth Wells, and he was down with the lingo. Within five minutes, all my prejudices had melted away and it became apparent that he's one of the nicest, most self-effacing blokes in rugby. The polar opposite to what I'd imagined. I thought he'd be gruff and monosyllabic, but he's very articulate and softly spoken. I thought he'd be rugby obsessed, but he spent most of his spare time strumming his guitar, singing and writing songs. I'd be lying there chilling out, and Sherry would be sat coaxing these delicate melodies from his guitar and singing softly to himself. Such a bizarre contradiction. He's got these big meat hooks for hands, yet he can play the guitar with such finesse. He never asked me to sing harmony with him, though. Perhaps he feared that I had a better voice than him. As the week progressed, a routine unfolded whereby we'd crash in the room after training, and Sherry would lightly serenade me throughout the afternoon.

Another Englishman who turned out to be the opposite of what I'd expected was Joe Worsley. I'd always thought he was a total pillock. During that 2009 game when he'd man-marked Jamie, I thought he was just a grunting, Neanderthal hardman. At one point in that match he disagreed with a refereeing decision, and patronisingly drew a square in the air, suggesting that it should have gone to the TMO. JT and I looked at each other at the time, and JT mouthed, 'What a prick.' Again, I couldn't have been more wrong. He's a brilliant bloke. Really funny, camp as Christmas, and a big softie at heart.

I can safely say that everyone on that tour was a good guy. There were no bad eggs at all, and no danger of any cliques forming. Much of the credit for that should go to the management. You had two Lions icons running the show in Gerald Davies and Ian McGeechan. And the coaching staff were professional in the extreme. Any animosity that may have existed between the four nations washed away in an instant once we'd arrived at Pennyhill Park.

I also witnessed early on the commanding influence Paul O'Connell had over his Irish colleagues. Gerald was giving one of his trademark speeches over dinner one evening. It was classic Gerald – full of drama, passion and emotion – and delivered with the poise and eloquence of a Shakespearean actor.

Tommy Bowe, who'd probably spent too much time in the company of the Welsh boys by then, turned to a group of us once Gerald was done and said, sarcastically, 'Bloody hell, you could tell that was for the cameras, couldn't you?'

Paul tore a strip off him. He was furious. 'Have some bloody respect, will you? This guy is an absolute Lions legend. How dare you mock him like that!'

Bowie sunk into his chair like a naughty schoolboy.

●　●　●

Training was hard. The intensity was ferocious – like nothing I'd experienced before. There were times when it felt more intense than an actual game, so desperate was everyone to impress. You can't help but focus on your competitors for the shirt at times like this. I was doing weights with Phil Vickery, and I'd be determined to do more than him. After a running session, I'd comb through the results to see if I'd outperformed Vicks and Euan Murray. I'm sure they were doing exactly the same.

We spent a lot of time trying to instil a defensive system that everyone was happy with, and sorting out the line-out. It was the first time I'd worked with Paul O'Connell, and it was easy to understand why he was so good. They were doing stuff we'd never done, and their attention to detail was meticulous. With Wales, we'd walk into the line-out with one call, and one contingency in our back pockets if we thought the opposition had figured us out. Ireland would have a minimum of two calls, and then three 'bail-out' calls for the front, middle and back of the line-out. So there were five possible destinations for the ball. The decision would be made by Paulie when he was standing there and could check out where the opposition were standing, and who they had decided to mark. It was so much more intricate than what I was used to with Wales.

And in Stephen Ferris, Ireland had one of the strongest rugby players I've ever encountered. I was lifting Paul O'Connell with him in the line-out, and Ferris just launched Paulie about thirty feet in the air. No wonder their line-out had been so good. He was so unlucky with injury. Had his career been longer, he may have become the greatest blindside flanker ever to have played the game. He was freakishly good. An absolute specimen of a man.

The night before we were due to leave, we had a team dinner at the Natural History Museum in London, and plans had been put in place for a team bonding session the following day. I think it involved sailing a yacht or something. No one was really up for it, and there was a lot of 'sapping' going on at the dinner. I can understand why these sessions are arranged, but most players see it as 'forced fun', and they're often a bit cringeworthy. Paul O'Connell had picked up on the negative vibes and had a word with the management. By ten o'clock, we were all back in our rooms at Pennyhill Park preparing to turn in for the night. As Sherry and I were brushing our teeth, we both received a text from the Lions management telling us to get our arses to the bar. They'd organised a lock-in, and the entire squad ended up getting blind drunk. The bonding session had been cancelled, and this had been hastily organised to take its place. It was a great call. In my experience, the best way to get to know your colleagues is just to sit at the bar, have a few beers, get pissed and swap stories.

● ● ●

I was desperate to be picked for the first game on tour. I remember watching the *Living with Lions* DVD from the 1997 South African tour, and hearing Ian McGeechan say that the first team up is a special one. It was something I'd striven for, and my dream came true when I was selected to start against a Royal XV in Rustenburg. I knew then that, barring any disaster, I would be a Lion. The Royals weren't a recognised team, but I didn't care about the opposition. I was just excited to be representing the Lions, and getting a chance to put a marker down. Most of all, I wanted to do the jersey proud. Geech was big on Lions history. He reminded you constantly of the responsibility that lay on your shoulders. I thought about all the world-class props who had worn the shirt before me: Graham Price, Dai Young, Paul Wallace, Jason Leonard. I was in exalted company.

Things didn't go entirely to plan. I was knackered after about half an hour because of the high altitude, and we played poorly as a team in what was an unconvincing victory. But I was there for my scrummaging, and that went well. Sherry was on the loose-head, and we kept our opposite numbers quiet. I was taken off after an hour, whereupon my stomach went into frightening convulsions. I'd leaned over in the changing rooms to undo my boots, and the next thing I knew, I was keeled over and wailing in agony on the floor. I thought my stomach was about to explode. A big lump had appeared, and I was starting to freak out. The team doctor ran in and got me up on to a recovery bed, and moments later I had three men – Prav and Pasky, the two physios, and James Robson, the doctor – massaging me. My first Lions tour, and there I was after one game, top off, being massaged vigorously by three men. They reassured me that it was just cramp, and kept rubbing until the lump went down.

I was embarrassed. It wasn't the best start to the tour. A limp victory, followed by a massage in front of the boys, during which I was a groaning, sweaty mess. But despite all the anti-climactic elements – the poor performance, the stomach cramps, the fact there weren't many people there watching, the fact it was played in a rickety old stadium in the middle of nowhere with wild animals roaming around – despite all of that, I was a Lion. And no one could take that away from me.

Geech had been consistent in his message that he was going to give everyone a chance of making the test team. He understood the need for harmony among the players and did everything in his power to prevent cliques being formed. I knew that Vicks would start the next game with Euan on the bench, and that Euan would start the third game. We were on fire in that second match and smashed the Golden Lions 74–10. Jamie and O'Driscoll's centre partnership was starting to gel. But more importantly, Vicks played really well, which kept the pressure firmly on me. And then Euan put a decent shift in during a tough game against the Cheetahs, which went down to the wire.

I knew that the next game against the Sharks was my big chance. It was effectively a trial match for me. Up against a big team, in a big stadium, against a front row that contained some contenders for the test side – the likes of Jannie du Plessis and Deon Carstens. There was a familiar face in that side in Stefan Terblanche – my old mate from the Ospreys. Bizarrely, he was taking their kick-offs. He couldn't kick for toffee at the Ospreys, so he'd obviously gone home and worked hard on that. But his new-found ability in that department didn't help his team on the night. After a tight first half, we pulled away to win 39–3. They couldn't live with our pace and physicality.

I was much happier with my performance in Durban than I had been with my debut in Rustenburg. Having said that, I felt that Vicks was probably first choice in the coaches' minds, particularly given the Wasps connection with him, Gats and Howlers. They gave him the captaincy for the fifth game against Western Province, which further cemented him as favourite in my eyes.

Fate intervened, as it often does in rugby. Euan started the next game against the Southern Kings, which was the last match before the first test. He looked in imperious form, and at one point he helped drive the opposition scrum back about fifteen yards. That scrum alone may have dropped me to third choice. But not long afterwards, Euan turned his ankle and put himself out of the tour. It was a cruel twist of fate, but one that elevated me almost immediately into the test squad. I'll never know whether I'd have made it otherwise, but you have to seize an opportunity when it arises.

He wasn't the only injured player that night. The Kings had obviously been told to try and bash us up. There were cheap shots, stray elbows and swinging arms coming from all angles, and not just from the over-exuberant youngsters. Experienced players like De Wet Barry were marauding about like possessed demons, shoving heads into the turf and kneeing people in the privates. Hooky was a significant casualty, having to go off after a nasty blow to the head. And we didn't get much succour from the ref that night – a certain Nigel Owens, who turned a blind eye to several of the Kings' 'indiscretions'. Cheers, Nige! Nothing like a bit of Welsh solidarity on tour!

The doctors worked overtime that night, stitching up all manner of cuts, and massaging some bruised and battered bodies. We'd been determined not to sink to their level. The management had hammered home the need for discipline. A needless yellow card could mean the difference between victory and defeat. The best way to combat South African aggression was to be better than them. To out-scrummage and out-maul them. To run at them, through them and over them. Nothing wounds a South African rugby player's pride more than that. New Zealand have done it for years. If they can't match them physically, they can almost always outsmart them. That was our aim on this tour, and we had some intelligent players to back it up. Geech summed it up best when he said we had to dig in for the physical stuff, and make sure we were clever when we got the opportunities.

We knew they'd be picking the test squad when we got back to the hotel. We returned at about seven o'clock and were clapped back in by the boys. When we assembled for the team meeting, I was really nervous. Back then, there was only one prop as cover on the bench. I thought Vicks would start at tight-head and Melon at loose-head, so it was a decision on whether to pick a loose or a tight as the replacement. That probably meant a straight choice between Sherry and me. Even though I'd resigned myself to the fact I wouldn't be starting, I was still gutted when Geech read Phil's name out. I just had to pray I was on the subs bench.

And I was. The runner-up prize. Not a bad consolation.

● ● ●

I'd always been slightly in awe of the All Blacks and the Springboks. For me, they'd always seemed a class apart, and I was now in a position where I'd be playing against the Boks in the biggest match of my career. As much as I tried to suppress it, there was still the timid voice of the fan inside me, thinking, 'These guys are awesome.' In the build-up to that first test, I was given the best advice I've ever received from the unlikeliest of sources. I'd been going on about Bakkies Botha to Mike Phillips, remarking how powerful and intimidating he was, when Mike snapped at me:

'You know what your problem is, Bomb? You give these guys too much respect. You put the New Zealanders and the South Africans up on a pedestal, and you think you're not as good. Well, you *are* as good, and you're going to prove that on Saturday. So stop moping around.'

It was short, sharp and succinct, but it really hit home. I'd never had Phillsy down as a motivational speaker, but he nailed it that day. It was exactly what I needed to hear, and it's probably the most sensible thing that's ever come out of his mouth. Well done, Michael.

The crowd in Durban seemed less hostile than at other venues, and when I ran out for the warm-up, there were thousands upon thousands of red jerseys up in the stands. It was a strange sensation. I was chomping at the bit, desperate to play and expend my nervous energy, but I had no idea when – or if – I'd be going on. It was a difficult first half to watch from the stands. John Smit went over for a soft try in the first five minutes, and the Boks were awarded a string of kickable penalties, mostly from the scrums. We were being destroyed up front. On the rare occasions the ball found its way into Brian O'Driscoll's hands, it looked as though something might happen. He was our sharpest attacking weapon by some distance. But we were living off scraps, and possession was proving hard to come by.

The problems with the scrums deepened as the half progressed. Vicks was getting a mauling from the Beast, and giving away penalty after penalty. People who know little about scrummaging interpreted it as a straight shoot-out between a dominant loose-head and a struggling tight-head. But scrums, like line-outs, depend on a contribution from every individual forward. What mystified me was the position of the locks. Traditionally, you have your biggest, heaviest lock on the right-hand side of the scrum, behind the tight-head. Alun Wyn Jones is a much bigger man than Paul O'Connell. It may not seem immediately obvious, but believe me, he is. He's around nineteen stone, six foot six, and very powerful with it. I'd have definitely preferred Alun Wyn behind me in the scrum. That's nothing against Paulie, but as the tight-head, you're the guy under the most pressure, and you generally prefer the bigger man behind you. I've had Alun Wyn behind me for most of my career, and I know how much that's benefited me. But Paul was locking on the right – presumably because that's where he plays for Ireland, and he was captain. If I'd been Vicks, I'd have insisted on them swapping, just for that extra bit of ballast and support. Every little helps.

The Beast was being quite clever. He was going outside Vicks a bit and then driving straight across him. 'Boring in', to use the scrummaging parlance. According to the letter of the law, you're not allowed to do that. But the referee was either being very lenient, or hadn't figured out what was going on. And once he'd got it into his mind that the Beast was winning that contest, the decisions kept on going his way. Vicks popped up in one scrum, which is never a good thing if you're trying to convince the referee you're comfortable. At that point, I was thinking, 'Shit, I could be on after half an hour here.'

We were 19–7 down at half-time. Graham Rowntree approached me in the changing room and told me to get warm. A subtle hint, meaning I'd be on sooner rather than later. Shaun Edwards was going ballistic about the Smit try. He was incensed that someone that big and cumbersome had got around the corner faster than any of our defenders could reset. Any try that came from a defensive error was a personal affront to him.

I came on at 44 minutes and 27 seconds, or thereabouts. I wasn't counting. History has been kind to me – suggesting my presence, and that of Matthew Rees at hooker, provided the impetus that changed the game – but it wasn't quite as immediate an impact as that, because as soon as I arrived, we conceded a try through their driving line-out. Those were the last points we conceded, though, as we went on to mount a steady comeback.

The set piece was much more stable after I came on, and I was credited with 'taming the Beast'. While it was nice to win the plaudits,

I realise that sometimes the stars just align in your favour. I'm shorter than Vicks and more dumpy, and that can make all the difference. It meant I was able to scrummage lower, and prevent the Beast going about his destructive business. It had been going so badly in the first half that anything I did would have been lauded as game-changing. It's not as though I came on and started driving them back fifty yards – I was just doing my job. I managed to get a little bit of a nudge on in my first scrum, and that probably persuaded Bryce Lawrence, the ref, that I wouldn't be leaking penalties like Vicks had been doing. I didn't come on and start destroying him. I merely helped steady the ship, and provide a more solid platform.

It gave us a foothold, and allowed us to start playing on the front foot. Crofty scored his second. And Mike Phillips crossed for a third with five minutes left, making the final scoreline far more respectable. If you take into account all the chances we blew – Mike came agonisingly close with an earlier opportunity, and Ugo Monye was twice denied over the line – we ended up gutted by the fact we hadn't won. I'll always look on that match as one that got away.

The first thing I did afterwards was go and see Vicks. Rob Howley and the analyst Rhys Long had both told me how much the game had changed once I'd gone on. It was obviously nice to hear, but I knew how Vicks must have been feeling and I didn't want to compound his misery by strutting around like some kind of hero. He was a legend who'd played for his country more than seventy times, and I held him in the highest regard. There wasn't much I could do apart from say, 'Hard lines, butt,' and tap him on the arse. But I know from experience that small gestures like that are important. A prop's pride is a fragile thing, and being subbed off early can damage it critically. I know that only too well. The changing room can feel like the loneliest place on earth if you've had a bad game.

Vicks was inconsolable. He looked up at me with a pained expression, and told me solemnly that I'd be starting next week.

Being an essentially shy Welshman, I dismissed it out of hand. 'Don't be silly, butt, you'll be back.' But of course, I desperately wanted the start.

There was certainly no gloating. A lot of the fans had assumed the Welsh boys would have been lording it over the rest, claiming we were the only ones strong enough to stand up to the Boks. Myself, Matthew Rees and Gethin Jenkins became the first all-Welsh Lions front row for more than fifty years, which was a nice historical footnote, but the idea that we'd be parading around claiming credit for the turnaround couldn't be further from the truth. The squad was so tight that the only thing on everyone's mind was the defeat. I've played with players who don't mind losing by thirty points, as long as they score a try. There was no one like that on this tour. They were all team players.

It was the first time I'd been asked to do post-match media when I'd been a sub. I could understand why, because the scrums had been a major talking point, but it was a surreal experience. I was hit by a barrage of questions about the first-half scrums, which I obviously hadn't been involved in. It was clear that some of the journalists were trying to goad me into saying that Vicks and Lee Mears had been shit. But that wasn't going to happen. I backed them both to the hilt, and ended up just blaming the ref.

Paulie was alongside me, and eloquently explained that there are significant differences between the way Northern Hemisphere and Southern Hemisphere referees officiate at the scrum. It was a more subtle way of making the point, but he was essentially blaming the ref as well!

● ● ●

My exploits were enough to earn me a starting place for the second test, alongside my Welsh colleagues Matthew Rees and Gethin Jenkins. Smiler and Melon. Simon Shaw was selected ahead of Alun Wyn, which I thought was unfair on Al. But Shawsy held the record for most Lions games without a test start (seventeen), and no one was going to begrudge him his moment. He was also a massive bloke, and would provide us with a good bit of ballast. In training that week, I was mightily relieved when he packed down on the right-hand side of the scrum behind me. Paul O'Connell switched to the left to pack down behind Melon. It's where he should have been during that first test.

I was rooming with Lee Mears in the week between the first and second tests and, like Vicks, he was incredibly down. His mood was far removed from his normal cheerful demeanour. He was tying himself in knots, analysing his performance, and kept asking me if I thought he'd played badly. I honestly thought he'd had a decent game, but no matter how many times I told him, it wouldn't sink in. I kept reminding him of his cheeky pop pass to David Wallace that nearly resulted in a try, but all he could think about were the scrums. He was having nightmares about bring crushed by a marauding pack of Springboks. Like Vicks, he was beyond consolation.

I was 24th man for the Tuesday-night game against the Emerging Springboks, and it was bucketing down with rain in Cape Town. I knew my parents were in the crowd and I was scanning the stands for them when Vicks sidled up alongside me to ask who I was looking for. When we eventually found them, he started waving as enthusiastically as I was, shouting, 'Mrs Jones! How are you, Mrs Jones?' to my mother. A few days earlier, his pride had been shattered, yet here he was, as jolly and outgoing as ever, waving to the parents of the man who took his place. If that had been me, I'd have still been sulking. My mother has loved him from that day onwards. I always suspected she had a crush on Jason Leonard, so she clearly has a soft spot for burly English props. We drew the game 13–13. It wasn't the best preparation, but there was a bigger challenge ahead.

The attention that was focused on me ahead of the second test was unreal. I'd done the press conference before the Sharks game, and it had been just Eddie Butler and me doing a low-key interview in the corner of a room. On the Thursday before the second test, I was swamped by journalists, all thrusting their microphones and Dictaphones in my face, and furiously scribbling down everything I said. The South African journalists appeared slighted by the fact I'd given their precious Beast a hard time, and were insinuating that I'd had an advantage because he'd been tired by the time I'd come on. How will you handle him from the start? was the crux of their questioning. I tried to be as diplomatic as possible. It's always best to blow some smoke up the arse of your opponent in these situations, whether you believe it or not. The whole charade was quite enjoyable, and I was left in no doubt how significant this second test was. I'm naturally quite shy, but my ego was tickled just enough by all the attention, so it came out to play.

The drive to Loftus Versfeld in Pretoria is quite an experience. The fans park their cars on the road leading up to the stadium and set up their *braais* alongside them. It's like a more aggressive, testosterone-fuelled version of the Twickenham car park. More stubby shorts and cargo shirts than claret cords and Barbour jackets. And little evidence of prawn sandwiches either – just enormous slabs of meat, sizzling away. The hostility hung heavy in the air, mingling with the barbecue sauce and the smoke from the grills. The South African fans appeared to be waving as our bus approached, but as we got closer we realised they were all doing the 'wanker' sign. You didn't have to be fluent in Afrikaans to get the gist of what it was they were saying. I was the most nervous I'd been up to that point in my career. If we'd been outside, I'm sure they'd have happily ripped our heads off. The mood on the bus was solemn. Everyone was in their own head space. The silence was unnerving. Shaun Edwards was the only one moving – sitting up at the front, rocking back and forth as though he was preparing to play.

The pre-match speeches were dripping with an emotion bordering on desperation. Brian O'Driscoll spoke well, as he always does, reminding us of the enormous significance of the game. To switch off for one second would be the difference between victory and defeat. We were to be as focused as we'd ever been in our lives. Geech was as passionate as ever. And Paulie was a seething, prowling ball of barely contained anger. He can be scary when he builds up a head of steam, but he never rants and swears for effect. It's always targeted and focused. His eyes bore through you to the depths of your soul, and he commands your total attention. With Paulie it's never overblown empty rhetoric, because he always backs it up on the field. He's the ultimate warrior. Geech talked about the significance of the shirt. If we won, he said, we shouldn't swap shirts with our opposite numbers. A winning Lions shirt is a rare and treasured possession.

The noise inside the stadium was deafening. Reassuringly, though, the chants of 'Lions, Lions' were as loud and vociferous as anything coming from the Springbok section of the crowd. The number of red shirts was mind-blowing. Some old friends of mine from Abercrave were there among the thousands who'd made the pilgrimage. They'd been saving for four years for this. It had cost them a lot of money, and it meant everything to them. They couldn't wear the shirt that was on my back, so I was representing them all. It was a humbling moment.

During the South African anthem, the hair was standing up on the back of my neck. I'm not indulging in cliché – it was *literally* standing up on the back of my neck. Only the Millennium Stadium can match Loftus

Versfeld for sheer volume. It was a full-on sensory assault. Noise, heat, passion, chaos. We gathered in a huddle for Paulie's final address, and no one could hear a word he was saying.

• • •

The game began controversially. It was less than thirty seconds old when Schalk Burger shoved his fingers into Luke Fitzgerald's eyeball. An act of extreme thuggery that has no place on a rugby field. The referee bottled it by only giving him a yellow card. Never has the case for a sending-off been more conclusive. Rugby can be brutal and uncompromising, but eye-gouging undermines all its core values of nobility and respect. Sticking your finger in someone's eye is unforgivable. Broken bones can heal, and bruises can fade, but if you lose your sight, it's never coming back. (It's happened to me once in my career, and it's a sickening feeling. I was playing for Neath against Leicester when I felt a finger slide between my eyeball and the socket. It sends a shiver down my spine thinking about it now.) The slow-motion replays on the big screen confirmed that Burger's actions were deliberate and malicious, but he escaped with just ten minutes in the sin bin. It was a shameful dereliction of duty on the referee's part.

The incident set the tone for an explosive opening quarter, and there were a few early dust-ups, most of which were started by Mike Phillips. We scored ten points in Burger's absence – three from the ensuing penalty, and another seven from Rob Kearney's converted try. He was back on before the game's first scrum – something I'd been anticipating with a mixture of relish and fear. I knew there were high expectations after what had happened the previous week, and I was shouldering the hopes of four nations. South African crowds love a scrum. There was an audible hum of expectation as we packed down, like a crackle of electricity before an explosion. The front rows faced off, grunting and snarling at one another as steam rose from the chewed-up pitch. Crouch. Touch. Pause. Engage. The two packs thundered together, and began twisting and wrestling to try and get that all-important psychological advantage. There was little in the way of movement until the Beast popped up. I chased him hard, shunting him backwards, and Shawsy and Tom Croft pushed through behind me. Advantage Lions.

Halfway through the first half came the scrum that changed my career. It was five metres from our try line, and the Springboks were sniffing blood. Once again, the ominous hum came from the increasingly restless and bloodthirsty crowd. I think it's safe to say I was shitting myself. I knew they'd be going for a pushover try. And if they pulled it off, I'd look a right mug. All that talk of the 'Beast tamer' would be forgotten in an instant.

As soon as the front rows collided we knew we'd won the hit. Big time. The Boks buckled, and slid backwards. Their monstrous hooker, Bismarck du Plessis, popped up, followed immediately by John Smit. Popping up is the equivalent of a boxer throwing the towel in. It's an admission that you've lost. We showed no mercy, and continued to drive them backwards, stripping away a little bit more of their manhood with every powerful thrust. It felt like the crowd had had all the air sucked out of them. Here were their beloved Boks – the very essence of virility in South Africa – being outmuscled and brutalised by the Lions. There is no better feeling for a front row forward.

That scrum has written itself into Lions folklore. The whole team ran in to congratulate us as we stood triumphantly over the collapsed Springbok pack. Symbolically speaking, they all knew how important that was. My rugby career changed overnight. It was that pivotal. It turned me from a curious-looking tubby bloke into the 'world's best tight-head prop'. I had a text afterwards from a mate back home joking that I could now put an extra £100,000 on any future contract I'd negotiate.

We clearly had them rattled up front. If you believe in conspiracy theories, you'd think they must have come up with a plan at half-time to deal with it. Within five minutes of the second half starting, Melon and I were both lying seriously injured in the medics room. Our tours were over.

Most of my friends and family have never forgiven Bakkies Botha for what happened. I was bent over at a ruck, trying to seal the ball off, when he appeared from nowhere and *smoked* me. I knew immediately that something was wrong. The pain was acute and excruciating. My shoulder was smashed out of its socket, and my right arm was locked outwards in a strange saluting position. I went to go back at him, hearing Shaun Edwards's voice in my head. He had little sympathy for injury victims. Unless you were unconscious, he expected you to get back in the defensive line. I've only ever seen one exception, and that was when Ianto pulled virtually every ligament in his knee against New Zealand. But when I tried to stand, I realised I was in a world of trouble. My vision narrowed and I collapsed in a heap. I was only vaguely aware of Paulie standing over me asking if I was all right.

Was it a cheap shot? I know he'd have gone in there with the intention of hurting me. That's the way he plays the game. But you can hurt people legally in rugby, and I'm not convinced it was a deliberate piece of foul play. Alun Wyn prides himself on his ability to hit rucks, and smash defenders out of the way, but that doesn't make him a dirty player. It makes him a hard player. Bakkies Botha had built his reputation on his no-holds-barred aggression. I just happened to be the wrong man in the wrong place. I didn't feel individually targeted. I'd have felt flattered if I had been – if someone thought I was so influential that I needed to be singled out for special treatment. But I never felt bitter about it. If anything, I felt like it was my fault because I was in the wrong position. If I'd latched on better, and my arms had been tighter to my body, I wouldn't have come out of it so badly. It was a Lions test match, and my technique let me down. Fair play to him, he caught me a peach.

Because I'd grown up watching the Lethal Weapon films in which Mel Gibson's character routinely dislocates his shoulder and pops it back in by slamming it against the nearest available surface, I never thought it would be such a big deal if it happened to me. Boy, was I wrong. I was escorted to the medics room, and the first thing I heard was a series of anguished cries along the lines of, 'Arrrrggh! My fucking cheek!' It was Melon. He'd come off just before me with a fractured cheekbone, and was writhing around in agony. Seeing Melon in that much pain made me feel a little bit better about myself.

My precious Lions jersey was cut off with a pair of scissors, and a team of doctors spent the next fifteen minutes yanking and tugging my arm, in a vain effort to put my shoulder back in. It was hellish. I was inhaling gas and air, and feeling sick and light-headed. One of the doctors stood astride me on the bed, pulling my arm up towards the ceiling and shoving it back down again. They just couldn't get it back in.

The next person I saw was Phil Vickery. He was 24th man, and had come in to see if there was anything he could do to help. He ended up taking my boots off and gathering all my gear together for my inevitable trip to the hospital. He even phoned my wife to let her know I was OK. I cannot speak highly enough of that man. They bundled me into an ambulance, gave me something a little stronger than the gas and air, and I passed out within minutes.

By the time I came to, the game had long finished. I woke up on a ward surrounded by my injured teammates. Jamie Roberts was there, along with Brian O'Driscoll, Tommy Bowe and Melon. All key players. More fodder for the conspiracy theorists. My shoulder, mercifully, had gone back in, and I was sat up with my arm in a sling.

The first person I spoke to was Richard Wegrzyk, the team masseur, and the first thing I said was, 'What was the score?'

'We lost, Bomb.'

I couldn't believe it. I was devastated. We'd been so dominant, so much better than them. I've never watched the second half to this day. I couldn't bring myself to. I didn't want to believe it had happened. It remains a disappointment of monumental proportions, and a horrible way to end the tour of a lifetime.

● ● ●

A couple of days later, Drico and I were drowning our sorrows at the bar. His tour was over as well. As I was taking a sip of my beer, one of the management came over to tell me my flights home had been booked for the following day, because the Ospreys wanted me back. I went to my room, called Nicole, and burst into tears. I'd had such an amazing time, and enjoyed it so much, that I didn't want to leave.

The prospect of flying home without the rest of the boys left me with a horrible, empty feeling. I couldn't understand why I had to go. Leinster weren't summoning Drico home, and the Blues seemed happy to let Jamie and Melon stay. But the hierarchy at the Ospreys insisted I come home, because they'd booked me in for an operation on my shoulder the following Monday. They'd seen the scans and wanted the surgery done as soon as possible, to give it enough time to heal ahead of the next season. They paid my wages, and they wanted me home.

My emotions were undoubtedly raw at the time, but it felt like an unreasonably heartless decision. All I wanted was to see the tour out with my mates, and to support them for that third and final test.

I ended up watching it on TV back in Merthyr with my wife and my parents, but I didn't last more than five minutes before rushing out of the room and bursting into tears again. I felt so sad that I wasn't there. The bond that we'd all forged was so strong that it left a gaping void in my life when I returned home.

For the record, my mother has never forgiven Bakkies Botha for that hit. Wales trained against Toulon in 2014 before our trial match, and by that time he'd joined their travelling band of 'Galácticos'. I saw my mother later that night, and she asked if he'd had the gall to come and speak to me. I replied that he'd shaken my hand, asked how I was, and that we'd had a civilised chat.

She was disgusted that I'd given him the time of day. Mothers never forget.

CHAPTER 14

Just a Fat Kid From Abercrave

IT won't have escaped your notice that I'm slightly on the larger side for a rugby player, even for my position of choice. That's meant that my battle with fitness has been a constant theme of my career. As I've alluded to, there have been periods when I've pulled the ripcord and allowed my weight to balloon. Those lapses follow a pattern, and almost always happen after a significant setback – 'half-hourgate' during Steve Hansen's reign being the most obvious. Comfort eating has been my coping mechanism, my most damaging vice. And the longer my career's gone on, the harder it has become to get away with it. That's largely down to the pervading influence of fitness and conditioning coaches. Those all-seeing, omnipotent overlords who monitor every morsel of food that passes your lips, and stalk you with their instruments of torture. As rugby has hurtled headlong into the professional age, their role has become increasingly vital. There isn't much between the teams at the very top level, so the tiny percentages can make all the difference.

I've worked with many fitness coaches during my career – all of them unique in their own way – and despite appearances to the contrary, it's a part of my life I've really enjoyed. I may never appear on the cover of *Men's Health*, and I may never find my hidden six-pack, but no one who knows me well will accuse me of not trying. Those aforementioned lapses aside, I've been one of the most committed and assiduous trainers in any of the squads I've been a part of. I consider my fitness coaches to be very important to my development. And as such, I'd like to introduce you to a few of them.

STEVE RICHARDS (Neath)

Steve was my first fitness coach ever, and I was undoubtedly his most challenging project. I first met him when I signed for Neath, and my weight was hovering around the twenty-two stone mark. Needless to say, he wasn't impressed. Horrified was probably closer to the truth. His first move was to ask me to monitor what I ate for a week and write it all down, so he could make some changes. He changed at least 95% of my diet overnight. Out with the chips, the pizzas, the pasties and the junk food. In with the dry jacket potatoes, boiled veg and unseasoned chicken. For every bloody meal. Every now and again I'd make a 'man salad', which was basically just bacon, egg and lettuce, in a big bowl.

He was a proper 'Valley Commando' from up the Rhondda, and the boys loved him. He was an incredibly fit bloke himself, as you'd expect, and put a huge emphasis on running. The energy-sapping Merthyr Mawr sand dunes were a favourite venue of his – and nine times out of ten, he'd be out in front by some distance. I lost more than two stones in three months with 'Ritters' – largely from diet, and an endless programme of running. It was a very 'old school' regime compared to what I've become used to now, but it was exactly what I needed. Ritters had a great manner about him. He worked you hard, but was encouraging with it. He was loud and aggressive, but never a bully. He'd stick with you when you were about to hit the wall, and coax you through it. His wasn't a particularly scientific method – it was more about relentless hard work and commitment – but it was very effective at that time. That Neath team was very fit.

Every player was a decent runner. If we weren't down at Merthyr Mawr, we'd be out running through the Gnoll woods behind the ground. There are tracks up there that weave through the trees and round the ponds, and lots of steps to jog up and down. In terms of pure cardiovascular fitness, it was arguably the fittest I've ever been.

He had a mate who'd written a book about the SAS, and he had quite a military manner about him. This was amplified by his big old sergeant-major moustache. His favourite phrase was, 'SAS it out!' which basically meant do what the SAS would do. We'd have finished our session at Merthyr Mawr with a run up the steepest dune – the 'Big Dipper' – and he'd say, 'Back up again, boys. Do it again.' The minute anyone protested, he'd shout, 'SAS IT OUT, BOYS!' Nutter.

I knew that I'd been given a chance at Neath, and it was a life-changing one, so I was determined not to mess it up. If it hadn't worked out, I'd have had to look for menial work at the DVLA or the army camp up in Sennybridge. It was the prospect of failure with Neath that drove me on.

Ritters eventually left for Pontypridd, which was something of a homecoming for him. But he'd been such a loved figure at Neath that it was inevitably an emotional goodbye. Or it should have been. During his farewell speech in the home changing rooms, the tears began to well in his eyes. Had it been any club but Neath, the boys would have stayed respectfully silent, and maybe shed a tear or two with him. But the Welsh All Blacks didn't deal in such soppy sentimentalism. The minute his voice began to quiver, a hail of piss-taking and abuse rained down on him.

Thanks for the memories, Ritters.

HUW BEVAN (Ospreys)

Bevs was excellent. A real dyed-in-the-wool rugby bloke, who later took his expertise to the England cricket team. He was my fitness coach with Wales Under 21s, and then with the Ospreys. As a former hooker himself, he had an obvious soft spot for the fatties in the front row. He was the first person to introduce me to so-called 'functional intervals'. He also loved Merthyr Mawr, and was obsessed with heart-rate monitors. He'd have us down the dunes with the Under 21s on a Sunday morning for a beasting session. Being young boys, we'd inevitably turn up rough, hungover, and dreading what he had in store. I lost count of the amount of times Ryan Jones spewed over the dunes in those days.

His big thing was the 3km time trial. Seven and a half laps of the athletics track. He'd split us into three groups – slow, medium and fast. Have a guess what group I was in? Your clue is that it contained me, Andrew Millward and Duncan Jones. Bevs always appointed himself pacemaker for all three groups, which meant that he did the trial three times in a row. The behaviour of a show-off, a sadist, or an absolute fitness fanatic.

He knew I needed a bit more attention than many of the boys, so even after a hard fitness session, he'd make me go on the cross trainer for half an hour to burn off an extra 600 calories. He also brought in a lot more rugby-specific things – like tyre-flipping and picking up logs – that were designed to replicate the kinds of things you'd do on the pitch, especially as a front row forward. Shifting a big, heavy tyre was the equivalent of clearing a big, awkward player out of a ruck.

Another favourite of his was interval training, which involved a lot of flat-out running on the treadmill. Unless your heart rate was really high, you weren't trying hard enough. He'd know full well if you'd been cheating. Hibs and I used to train together as two of the resident fatties, but our attitudes were poles apart. I would crack on and push through the pain barrier, whereas Hibs – who was young, and opposed to any kind of authority – would look for an easy way out. Say we had to do ten intervals on the running machine, Hibs would get off after four, and do the rest on the bike, because it was easier. He didn't realise that your heart rate doesn't stay anywhere near as high on the bike. So when his stats were printed out, and the graph mysteriously plummeted down after an initial spike, he had some explaining to do. Nothing would get past Bevs. Absolutely nothing. His reliance on science meant there was no place to hide.

After the 2005 Grand Slam, I felt as though I wasn't firing on all cylinders and my fitness was in decline. Sometimes I'd go home after a tough day and eat an entire packet of biscuits, undoing all the hard work I'd put in. I told Bevs I wanted to be fitter, and he was happy to help me out individually with extra sessions. In addition to the three fitness sessions we were doing a week, he'd take me mountain biking up at Afan Argoed near Neath. It was a brilliant way to get off site and do something more interesting and fun. It worked an absolute treat, and by the autumn of 2005 I was at least 10kg lighter than I'd been during the Six Nations. It meant I could keep up with the likes of Tandy and Humphs when we'd go for a run.

There were few things worse than Bevan's look of disappointment, and I was on the receiving end of it more than a few times, notably on one occasion in Toulouse after we'd played them in the Heineken Cup. Andy Newman and I got the munchies late at night, and went out on a snack run. Back in the team room in the early hours, Andy was tucking into a massive bag of salted crisps, and I was eating Nutella from the jar with my fingers when Bevs walked in. I looked like a guilty child, with chocolate all over my hands and around my mouth. He wasn't impressed. There was no bollocking, just a shake of the head and a withering look of disappointment. Newman tried making some quip about his body fat being pretty good at that point, and Bevs just barked back at him, 'It won't be after this, you fat bastard!'

ANDREW HORE (Wales)

Your relationship with a fitness coach is different to that of a head coach. The line between boss and friend is more blurred, and that's why I got on so well with so many of them. You'd spend so much time in their company that you'd almost inevitably become good mates. That's what happened with Andrew Hore. He took an immediate shine to me when I joined the Wales squad. He could see that with a bit of gentle encouragement, I could make massive gains. He invested a lot of time with me, drawing up an individual programme and often sitting with me during a bike session when the rest of the boys had gone home, chewing the fat and spurring me on.

He was a real all-rounder, and introduced a whole variety of methods from other disciplines. We played a lot of touch rugby to work on our core fitness, for example. And he brought Mark Jones's wife in as a netball player to help us with things like spatial awareness and agility. She'd put us through drills involving hopping, sidestepping, backwards running and switching direction on 90-degree angles. It wasn't my forte, if I'm honest, but it kept things varied and interesting. These things would have been unheard of a few years earlier. Some of the players were more receptive than others to the 'alternative' sessions. Boys who'd honed their rugby skills on muddy fields by knocking seven bells out of one another took a bit of persuading to attend Horey's yoga classes on a Wednesday, or his 'pool power' sessions on a Thursday. When I say pool power, I mean aqua aerobics. But I think we can agree it sounds more manly?

If I needed to sum up Horey in two words, I'd say 'organised' and 'angry'. And 'short', if I'm allowed three. I've never met someone as disciplined as him. And, by extension, someone who gets as angry as he does when things aren't in order. He's very precise, very exacting, and very thorough. And he demands that from others. No one was immune from his anger. He'd vent on coaching staff as much as players, if he felt they weren't raising the standards. He expected detailed plans to be drawn up and adhered to. If they weren't, he'd blow his top. Nothing could be ad hoc or spontaneous.

But he was also the kind of bloke who'd be consumed by guilt if he went too far. If he had a go at me personally, it wouldn't be long before he'd come back, put his arm around me and apologise. He'd explain that he was only angry because he had my best interests at heart. His job was his life, and he left no stone unturned in his quest for perfection. He'd ring you on a Sunday night to outline your plan for the week. I wasn't the only one he'd call, so that might mean thirty-odd phone calls from him – and at a time of the week when most other people would be relaxing with a glass of wine.

He was held in such high regard by everyone in Wales that we chaired him off the field after his last game. When he gave his farewell speech, virtually everyone in the room was biting their lips and trying not to cry. I'm not exaggerating when I say I loved the guy. I genuinely thought the world of him. My main motivation for me wanting to improve my fitness after the 2005 Grand Slam was to please him. I knew he was leaving that autumn, and I didn't want his lasting impression of me to be as a big fat slob. I wanted him to be proud of me before he left for New Zealand. My relationship with him broke down somewhat during his unlikely return as Ospreys CEO, but back then I couldn't have thought more highly of him.

MARK BENNETT (Wales and Ospreys)

Hard as fuck. Crazy as fuck. Scary as fuck. That's how I'd describe Benny. I loved him, though. He was a good boy. The polar opposite of Horey. For him, everything was about weights. He loved power cleans, loved key lifts and loved bench presses. All the stuff that I wasn't particularly bothered about. In a nutshell, weights are for people who need to put on bulk. As you can imagine, that's never been an issue for me.

As with previous coaches, Hibs and I were his two main targets. He was a big believer in having the right diet, claiming that nutrition was far more important than actual exercise. He didn't put much stock in fat-burning routines like long bike sessions. According to his theory, if you were eating the right things, you shouldn't be carrying excess fat.

Instead of embracing variety, like Horey, he was a fan of paring things down to the bare necessities. He told me that if I mastered the power clean, I wouldn't have to do any other weights. It was a whole-body exercise that covered all the main muscle groups. So if I got it right, it's all I had to do. That sounded great to me, in principle, but I've never got my head around power cleans. I just haven't got the flexibility in my wrists. Benny would have me stretching my fingers constantly so I'd be better at it, but it never worked for me.

Some of the boys loved all that stuff – 'chucking the tin', as they'd call it. Jonathan Thomas, Huw Bennett and Alun Wyn all threw themselves into the heavy weights, spending hours in the gym, religiously doing their power cleans, while grunting, sweating and panting like cavemen. Ianto and I would be sat in the corner potching about until Benny walked in, whereupon we'd leap to attention and pretend to be doing some bench presses. I've never enjoyed weights. I'm not sure why. It's a lot easier than running, but running would always make me feel better. Weights were just a necessary evil to me. Fine if it was a short, sharp session. But anything longer than fifteen minutes I'd find tedious and repetitive. It's definitely a vanity thing for some boys. I can understand why power cleans would help you become a better rugby player, but sitting in front of the mirror doing bicep curls all day – like Bradley Davies does – is largely pointless.

I share the view of many that modern rugby players spend too much time in the gym at the expense of being out on the field. New Zealand are consistently the best in the world because they spend more time on rugby, and are better footballers as a result. They're not the biggest side in the world. Their forwards are nowhere near as big as South Africa's or England's but they're usually a damn sight smarter. Brain almost always beats brawn. Going into that 2007 World Cup, we were bigger and stronger than we'd ever been. The shape on some of those boys was hugely impressive. Huw Bennett looked like Arnold Schwarzenegger with his shirt off. But we got knocked out by Fiji. Says it all.

Benny was understandably obsessed with fitness, and read widely around the subject. If you ever challenged him on anything, he'd be able to quote the science back to you and put you in your place. It was pointless starting an argument with him. He studied all other sports religiously and applied his findings. If we were doing a speed session, he'd be quoting the biomechanics of people like Usain Bolt and Maurice Greene. And he'd always be the first to spot a new trend. When kettle bells first appeared, he declared them the best thing ever, and restructured our entire gym routine around them. Then 'Cross Fit' came in, and that trumped everything.

He was borderline OCD – his mind was always active, always whirring – and the boys ribbed him about it. During the Argentina tour in 2007, we were doing a pool recovery session. Gavin Thomas was drinking from a cup of water when Benny walked past, and he casually asked him how many cups he thought it would take to fill the pool. It was a deliberate wind-up, but he knew Benny wouldn't be able to resist. That night, at dinner, he came to find Gav, and he'd figured it all out. He'd gone back to his room, calculated the dimensions of the pool, and come up with the mathematical equations to work it all out. I'm not sure he knew Gav had been taking the piss.

MICK MCGURN (Ospreys)

Belfast Boy. Funny fucker. Mad as a box of frogs. He came over to watch a couple of training sessions before he took the reins, and his first words to the boys were, 'You're the most skilful team I've ever seen. But you're also the fattest.' This was at a time when we had Marty Holah, who didn't have an ounce of fat on his body, and people like Gav and Byrney who prided themselves on their fitness. So he was obviously referring to certain members of the cast, and I think we all knew who.

Unlike Benny, fat-burning sessions were high on his priority list. Where he deserves credit is that all those fat-burning sessions involved rugby – so you'd be running flat out, but passing the ball at the same time. Either that or he'd have you in boxing gloves, smashing into the punchbag. It meant you'd have a proper, lung-busting workout, but you'd be distracted enough by the rugby not to notice. He understood that the tedium of long cardio sessions could be relieved with a bit of variety. I returned to my Andrew Hore levels of fitness under Mick.

He was a great motivator. On occasions, when he thought the boys were just plodding along in the gym, he'd burst in, crank the stereo up and go bonkers. He'd be striding around ranting and raving in his impenetrable Belfast accent, and geeing everyone up. The first time he did it, he got more than a few weird looks, but it didn't take long for us all to warm to him.

Mick slept on my floor for months on end. I'd moved in with my wife's parents at this point, so I offered to let my place to him. I went round after a week or so to check he'd settled in, and discovered he'd been sleeping on the floor in the living room. There was a perfectly serviceable bed upstairs, but he insisted that he preferred the floor. Prior to that, he'd been sleeping on a fold-out bed in the physio room at the Ospreys training base in Llandarcy. A poky little windowless room next to the management offices. Like I said, mad as a box of frogs.

CRAIG WHITE (Wales and Lions 2009)

I loved Whitey from the start. We struck up an immediate bond which lasted from the first training camp we had in Wexford to the minute he left. He knew exactly how to push my buttons, knew how much playing for Wales meant to me, and he used that desire to motivate me. He noted early on how much my weight fluctuated, and he persuaded Gats not to pick me if I exceeded a certain amount. It was cruel but extremely effective. Nothing motivated me more than the thought of losing my beloved Wales shirt. I spent an awful lot of time in the sauna during that period. I even experimented with using laxatives as a more maverick method of weight loss.

Whitey specialised in training front-five forwards, and it was obvious that I was to be his pet project. In my testimonial brochure he wrote that he thought he'd come to the WRU to turn around the fortunes of the entire squad, and ended up spending 90% of his time with me. He was always on to me about my diet, telling me he didn't want me to return home from the Lions tour with any regrets. He bollocked me once after I was 'papped' drinking a can of Strongbow on TV during an Ospreys game. I wasn't playing, I hasten to add. He didn't mind me having the odd pint, but only in moderation. And definitely not on television.

Everything Craig did was rugby-specific. He knew that as a front-five forward, leg strength and explosive power were the things I needed the most. He declared early on that it was his intention to 'blow my legs out' during every session. If I could walk properly I hadn't worked hard enough. That camp in Wexford was where I was introduced to an instrument of hate that's haunted my dreams ever since. The Prowler. A sledge packed with 140kg of weight that we had to push relentlessly round an athletics track. Thirty metres would take around forty seconds. We'd take a minute's rest, and then push it thirty metres back to where we'd started. And then back again, and again, and again. Ten times in total. The track was lumpy and squishy underfoot, which made it doubly difficult.

Only three of us were singled out to do it: myself, Rhys Thomas and Ianto. The rest of the forwards were deemed fit enough. Huw Bennett joined in because he wanted to, the nutcase. It's a perfect exercise for a prop, because it gets you pushing at exactly the angles that you'll need to in a game. Similarly, he devised a routine whereby you'd lift a 50kg weight repeatedly over a tackle bag, before sprinting off to do the same at another point on the pitch. It was a form of weight training, but was designed to replicate a forward's work at a ruck – clearing players out, and then reloading for the next breakdown.

He was obsessed not only with what I ate, but with everything I put into my system. He once arranged a five-hour seminar where he lectured the entire squad on the perils of ingesting certain liquids. We were only to drink full-fat milk, because the skimming process was not to be trusted. Tap water was to be avoided at all costs, because of the excessive levels of fluoride and the potential presence of pesticides. We were either to drink bottled water, or have filters installed in our houses. Deiniol Jones made a fortune off the boys because he had an interest in a water filtration company. And even certain bottled waters were to be avoided if the plastic wasn't of a certain quality.

Certain foods were out of bounds too. If Whitey had had his way, none of us would have been allowed to eat bacon. Why? Because pigs eat rats. And rats carry disease.

It was revelations like these that exposed the more eccentric side of his character. And while I indulged him with some of his more left-field suggestions, I drew the line at the invitation for me to stay at the Vale Hotel for five weeks one summer as part of his 'colonic irrigation' experiment. I loved Whitey to bits, but not that much.

CHAPTER 15

Isla

I wasn't exaggerating when I said the two Lions tests in 2009 changed my life. My contract at the Ospreys was up for negotiation when I returned, and I was in a considerable position of strength, as I was being talked up as the world's best tight-head. I was being recognised everywhere, and my profile expanded beyond just rugby circles. But perhaps most importantly, my reputation soared on the pitch. Reputation means everything to a front row forward. In a murky world of cheating, gamesmanship and dirty tricks, being regarded as one of the best means fifty-fifty decisions are going to start to go your way. Humphs told me as much the minute I returned home.

I had more autograph requests in the weeks following the Lions tour than I'd had in my entire career. And I lost count of the number of times I answered the question, 'How did you tame the Beast?' The mystique of the Lions had really captured people's imaginations. While I enjoyed the attention, and the positive press, I never allowed the 'world's best tight-head' tag to go to my head. Principally because I didn't believe it. I thought guys like Carl Hayman, Nicolas Mas and Martin Castrogiovanni were equally as good as, if not better than, me.

My shoulder injury kept me sidelined until December that year. But I made history as the first water boy to receive a standing ovation at the Liberty Stadium. I jogged on with the bottles during a break in play against Leicester, and was aware of a light swelling of applause. By the time I'd returned to the dugout, the entire crowd had risen to its feet and were heartily clapping me off.

Unfortunately, my return to the actual playing field wasn't as triumphant. The mystique surrounding the Lions, coupled with my long absence, had lent me an almost mythical air. I swear people thought I was some sort of cartoon superhero who could reduce opposition front rows to rubble. As such, there was a fevered sense of anticipation surrounding my first scrum back in an Ospreys jersey.

We were playing Treviso in the Heineken Cup. The ball was knocked on, a scrum was called, and the moment of truth arrived. The crowd fell silent. They were expecting me to destroy my opposite number, to squash his head into his torso and bury him in the ground. The ball was fed in. I slipped, collapsed the scrum, and gave away a penalty.

● ● ●

It wasn't long until the Six Nations, and I was desperate to get back in a Wales jersey. I was also determined not to let my standards slip. I'd gone up a few gears and I liked the way it felt. The flip side was that people would be targeting me now, wanting to bring me down a peg or two. I was under more pressure than before, because I had further to fall.

I did enough in my short time back from injury, and was selected for the first game against England. I'll remember that game for a number of reasons. Firstly, because I scored a spectacular try. OK, I scored a try. Secondly, because Tim Payne told Gats afterwards that I was the best prop he'd ever played against. And thirdly, because it marked the start of a strange and unlikely acquaintance with Boris Johnson. Hopefully, these three incidents will help gloss over the fact that we were well beaten that day.

If you go on to YouTube and search for my international tries, you'll find one piece of footage lasting eighteen seconds. That includes replays. Suffice to say, neither try was a fifty-yarder. They were probably a combined total of five yards, and I can't watch without cringing with embarrassment. Against England, I found myself out on the wing when Alun Wyn passed me the ball. I panicked and looked for Shane to pass to. By the time I found him, I was already over the line. I did a shit dive, and was immediately surrounded by my teammates. Instead of expressing the usual joy that greets a try – especially against England – they were all just laughing hysterically. It was the funniest thing on earth that I'd scored. Shane was absolutely pissing himself. Alun Wyn tried to be a bit more supportive, but you could tell even he was laughing on the inside.

So while it failed to earn the respect of my teammates, it did earn the respect of a certain Mayor of London, who was moved to write a letter to a friend of his at the *Telegraph* describing me as 'Cro-Magnon Man' and his new favourite player. The journalist had met Nicole during the World Cup, so he forwarded the letter on. Now, dear reader, you're probably aware of the meaning of Cro-Magnon man, but I had to Google it. I discovered the following: 'Cro-Magnons were robustly built and powerful. The body was generally heavy and solid with a strong musculature' (source: Wikipedia). I thought, 'Fair play, Boris, I'll take that.'

It may sound weird – a working-class boy from a mining village in the South Wales Valleys corresponding with a Tory mayor of London – and I hope I'm not offending some of the staunch Labour supporters in my family, but I was chuffed to bits with the letter, and took it as quite a compliment. I've never been particularly engaged politically, so I wasn't principled enough to take a stand. I was just excited that my exploits had raised the eyebrows of a powerful politician all the way over there in London town.

● ● ●

You'll excuse me if I don't dwell too much on the rest of the 2010 Six Nations. Despite the promise of the first two campaigns under Gatland, we ended up an underwhelming fourth after suffering further losses against France (narrowly) and Ireland (convincingly). I can't really put my finger on why. We didn't feel as though we'd gone backwards, and we hadn't suffered too badly in the injury department. We just didn't manage to put together a decent run like in 2008 and 2009.

I missed most of the rest of the season with an elbow injury. It happened during an Ospreys match against London Irish. It was the first time I'd come up against a young loose-head by the name of Alex Corbisiero. He was a tough customer, and the tight-head was a South African monster called Fran Rautenbach. He drove across during one scrum, the whole thing collapsed, and my left arm got bent 45 degrees in the wrong direction.

It was a bad time to suffer such an injury, because we were heading into a World Cup year, and one of my rivals for the shirt, Craig Mitchell, would now have the chance to prove himself during the 2011 Six Nations. At the start of the campaign, I was still confident I could hold on to my number one status despite being stranded on the sidelines. But Mitch played well, and as the tournament progressed, I started to get nervous.

Gats is never one to offer reassurance in such circumstances. As it panned out, Mitch got injured just as I was returning to fitness, and Gats was asked in a press conference whether he'd be giving me a call. His answer was something along the lines of, 'Well, I hope he's been spending a good bit of time in the sauna, because we can't have him coming in carrying too much weight.'

But call me up he did, and I was back in for the final game against France. My first taste of any rugby action for seven weeks. I'd gone from a fan to an international in the space of a week, after watching the Ireland game in the stand with Nicole. I'd wanted to go incognito to avoid all the inevitable attention, so Nicole bought us both giant daffodil hats. But it only took one person to spot me and, within minutes of the kick-off, I'd posed for nigh on a dozen selfies and fielded numerous questions about my pending return to fitness.

We won that game after Mike Phillips scored a controversial try from a quick line-out. The Irish were furious, because he had technically used the wrong ball. But the most significant moment of that game for me was Craig Mitchell's shoulder injury after quarter of an hour. I knew then that I'd be summoned back for the last game against France.

It wasn't too daunting a prospect because I'd spent the previous seven weeks being beasted by physio-cum-conditioner Brian O'Leary, at the Ospreys. That's the thing with an elbow injury – it doesn't stop you from doing any conditioning work. So you can arguably get fitter while you're injured, because there's no rugby training to get in the way. That said, there was part of me that didn't want to be thrown back in at the deep end in the last competitive match before the World Cup. Especially against such a strong side as France, and such a quality player as Thomas Domingo.

As it happened, I was fine. But as a team, we were shocking. It turned out to be the Lionel Nallet show. The big lock scored two tries and played the game of his life. We went into that game with a chance of winning the championship, and ended up coming fourth. Again. Fourth for three years running after our Grand Slam.

It wasn't quite the upward curve we'd predicted for ourselves, but equally none of those campaigns were considered disastrous. They all showed how fine the line had become between success and failure in this tournament. In 2009, we were a missed penalty away from the Triple Crown and ended up fourth. In 2011, one bad defeat on the final day meant the difference between winning the title and coming fourth. It wasn't the last time the championship would swing on such fine margins. It's what makes it so compelling, and the envy of the Southern Hemisphere.

So while three fourth-place finishes amounted to an extremely modest return, we weren't feeling that deflated heading into the 2011 World Cup. Gats's philosophy has always been that the longer we're together, the better we become. And we had a long build-up ahead of the World Cup.

● ● ●

That tournament was a big date in the diary, but an even bigger one for me personally was the due date of my daughter.

Experience has taught me that if you're willing to incur the wrath of your pregnant and hormonal wife by playing rugby on the day of your firstborn's arrival, then it helps if you have access to a private jet. I was training with the Ospreys on a Thursday ahead of our PRO12 semi-final against Munster, when Nicole called to say her waters had broken. I didn't know what the hell I was supposed to do, and flew into a panic.

It took a pep talk from Ryan Jones to calm me down, after which he ordered me to get my arse back home. The management were fully supportive, and virtually shoved me out of the door. Jonathan Humphreys's wife was expecting too, and there was a chance he'd be called away in a similar fashion. As I was skedaddling out of the door, Scott Johnson shouted good luck, and told me Mike Cuddy had arranged for a private jet to fly me out to Munster if I missed the flight the following day.

Fifty-one hours later, at 10.20 on the Saturday morning, Isla Jones emerged into the world. Our beautiful daughter. I'd slept for a total of forty-five minutes since leaving the Ospreys training session two days earlier. I can't imagine how exhausted Nicole must have felt. But at that point in time, with the adrenaline flowing, I couldn't have felt more alive.

I sent a flurry of text messages to my closest friends and family, one of whom was Andy Lloyd, the Ospreys team manager. He replied with a short message of congratulations, before asking if I could get to Cardiff Airport by midday! I didn't know what to do. My daughter had just been born, and now my employers were on at me to get to work. I thought they must have really needed me.

Nic was drugged up to the eyeballs, and silently mouthed her permission. Her parents and mine agreed it was OK, so my dad whisked me off to Cardiff Airport, where Mike Cuddy's private jet was waiting on the tarmac. Humphs and I ascended the stairs to be greeted by Mike's wife, Simone, who had a bottle of champagne on ice. Humph's wife, Vicky, hadn't yet given birth, so he didn't want to jinx anything by raising a toast.

We landed in Limerick at around one o'clock, four hours before kick-off. Lloydy greeted me at the hotel, and told me to go straight to my room to get some kip. But I'd gone beyond exhaustion, and was buzzing about being a father. My eyelids were drooping but my mind was racing. I lay there staring at the ceiling and smiling to myself for a couple of hours before being summoned to the bus.

By the time I ran out on to the pitch, I was in bits. Absolutely knackered. The adrenaline had left my system, and I felt like a broken man. Nigel

Owens was reffing, and he penalised me at the first scrum. I gave him a withering look and said, 'Come on, Nige, give me a break!' He knew the situation I was in because he'd congratulated me before the game. But he wasn't about to show me any mercy. It occurred to me then that I was of no use to anybody. I should have been at Nicole's bedside, not on some rugby pitch in another country. My mind was elsewhere, and my body had shut down. I ended up contributing less than nothing to a losing cause. It was Jerry Collins and Marty Holah's last games for us, and we pretty much rolled over without firing a shot.

Within fifteen minutes of the final whistle, I was in a taxi bound for Limerick Airport. I was back at the hospital with Nicole by nine o'clock. Less than nine hours had passed since Isla had been born, and during that time I'd flown to Ireland, played a rugby match, and flown back.

Days later, it all felt like a dream. I'd been on autopilot and had followed orders like a sleep-deprived zombie. If I had my time again, or if anyone in a similar situation asked for my advice, I'd say don't go. I was useless out in Munster, and if Nicole had been a little less drugged up, and a little more compos mentis, I wouldn't have got away with it.

I appreciate it was a big game, but nothing is worth leaving your newborn child for.

CHAPTER 16

The One That Got Away

ACCORDING to the powers that be, the secrets of our success at the 2011 World Cup were the brutal training camps in Poland. I'd argue it had more to do with the fact we unearthed a generation of world-class players. Sam Warburton, Taulupe 'Toby' Faletau, Leigh Halfpenny, Jonathan Davies and George North all came to the fore at that time, and transformed Wales into world beaters.

Spała seems to have entered Welsh rugby folklore as a watchword for pain and brutality, and some of the boys like to perpetuate that. But it wasn't that bad. There's a perception that the camp was some sinister communist-style outpost in the middle of a bleak forest where all sorts of evil doings went on, but it was actually a relatively modern university campus. It *was* in the middle of a forest, but it was picturesque rather than foreboding. If anyone was to blame for conjuring this image of torture and brutality, it was the fitness coaches. Adam Beard had a streak of sadism running through him, and took great pleasure in telling the boys that we'd be training eight times a day. *Eight* times a day.

That was a minimum. As I was to find out on day one, there would be a cruel system of punishments, which would add yet more sessions to our daily regimen. When the camp began, I was still in new-dad mode. Isla had been keeping us up all night, and I'd been getting far less sleep than I was used to. Ironically, I'd been looking forward to Spała, because I thought it would give me an opportunity to rest! As such, I slept in as late as I could on the first day, and chose not to 'self-monitor' in the morning. It's something you're expected to do – weigh yourself, answer a few questions about the sort of night's sleep you've had, how you're feeling, and the mood you're in. Given my situation, I allowed myself the morning off. As did Jamie Roberts. Mistake.

After a long and intensive training day, the two of us were pulled aside and told we'd face punishment for failing to self-monitor. We were to spend fifteen minutes in the sandpit. It doesn't sound particularly torturous, but it is. Dan Baugh took us over there, apologising as he did so, and explained that he'd been forced to do so by the powers that be. He barked at us like a military commander, as we were forced to crawl around in the energy-sapping sandpit like naughty schoolboys. We were then forced to do an extra pool session. Ten hundred-metre swims, followed by ten fifty-metre swims. Times three. Gavin Henson joined us for this one, as he'd transgressed some other hidden rule during the day. I was plodding along, trying to get it done, but Gav – never the best swimmer, and a natural rebel – got out halfway through and stormed off. He was ordered back in but refused. Secretly I admired his refusal to buckle to authority. In my mind, the training was hard enough as it was without this childish system of punishment. Payback came later in the week when Adam Beard was late for something and incurred a penalty of half an hour's wrestling in the sandpit. The audience for that one swelled to include the entire camp. The tables were briefly, but satisfyingly, turned.

Alun Wyn and Ryan Jones were chucked in the sandpit together later in the week as punishment for fighting. Things had got a little heated between them during a line-out session, and it escalated into a brawl. I'm not sure any punches actually landed. There was a lot of 'windmilling' and flailing around, but little real action. They're both big men, but they're not natural fighters. Not that I can talk; I'm definitely not a fighter. But it would have been an altogether different scenario if Paul James and Richard Hibbard had been squaring up to one another. That would probably have resulted in a hospital admission rather than a sandpit punishment. Both can handle themselves. But regardless of the nature of the 'fight', it was the fact they'd lost their rag that incurred the punishment. Gat's rationale was that if they did the same in a game, they could cost the team a yellow or a red card.

Spała was also where many of the boys encountered the dreaded cryotherapy treatment for the first time. Another Adam Beard innovation, these awful, hideous chambers were kept at mind-boggling temperatures of −140° Celsius. The theory is that they help your muscles recover more quickly, and enable you to train longer and harder. Hence the ambition to cram eight sessions into a day. If you hate the cold, they're something you need to avoid. If you hate the cold, and suffer from claustrophobia, they're your worst nightmare. And for a few of the boys, it was like a scene from a horror film. Barely thirty seconds had passed before Nugget and Gavin Henson were battering on the doors and yelling to be let out.

Because this is my book, I can say I was a lot braver! I've never been a fan of them, and there have been occasions since when I've doubted their effectiveness. You sometimes emerge feeling energised and alert, but at other times you feel no different to when you went in. Regardless of how it makes you feel afterwards, when you're in there, it's horrendous. You start in a 'cold' room, which is quite toasty at −70°. You're wearing clogs, long socks, gloves, pants and ear muffs. All your extremities are covered up to avoid frostbite. Nine times out of ten, you go in after training, so you're a bit sweaty, and we all know how much worse the cold is when you're wet. When the light goes off, you move into the big one, and the real horror begins. Your body becomes overwhelmed by the extreme cold, and every bone and muscle starts to throb. You can feel your damp hair crystallising and turning to ice. Your skin turns an alarming shade of blue. Your face starts to hurt, and you have to pace around the chamber just to stay sane. You use up all your psychological and physical reserves to dig in and tough it out.

And just as you're starting to feel pleased with yourself for showing such resolve, a random elderly Polish couple will stroll in and stand nonchalantly with their hands on their heads. It's good for the joints and for circulation, so the locals swear by it. It was also used regularly by long-distance runners, who'd wander in with the same casual attitude. There'd be a bunch of us supposedly macho rugby players hopping around frantically, on the verge of tears, next to these stoic skinny guys toughing it out with a minimum of fuss. And bear in mind we were all big men with a substantial amount of muscle and — in my case at least — body fat. These guys were just skin and bone. They were a different breed. Proper hardcore athletes.

We were only ever in there for three minutes at a time. But boy did they go slowly!

• • •

While Spała was hard and uncompromising, there were elements that were fun. The management understood that eleven days of relentless beasting would take its toll mentally, so they ensured things were sufficiently varied to keep us interested. In addition to the fitness work, there were a lot of skills sessions with Neil Jenkins and Rob Howley. They'd test reaction times and spatial awareness by firing tennis balls at us. Jinks and Howlers would have a racquet each and would spend half an hour batting balls in our direction. It's times like these when the competitiveness kicks in, and everyone wants to win. Tip: if you *do* want to win, make sure Lou Reed's not on your team. He didn't catch a single ball, and I don't think he would have if he was still there now.

The diet wasn't particularly inspiring. It was all breaded chicken and breaded pork, mixed in with various unidentifiable Polish delicacies. And the nightlife was non-existent. Our location in the middle of an isolated forest meant we had to come up with our own entertainment. When I first came through as a professional player, the team room was a hive of activity – a real social hub. The whole squad would congregate there, playing board games and chewing the fat. But over time, the curse of the laptop has crept in, and most of the younger boys now spend hours in their rooms on their own watching endless box sets. In Spała, it was left to the unlikely figure of Gethin Jenkins to tighten the social bonds. He appointed himself quizmaster and put on regular quiz nights, complete with music and movie clips. He threw himself into it with the kind of zeal you wouldn't associate with such a grumpy git.

The management would get involved, which would ramp the competitive edge up a few notches. Prav, the medical manager, was a good all-rounder, Jinks was a rugby encyclopedia, and Carcass fancied himself as a left-field intellectual. Gats wasn't much cop. He didn't know much about anything. Without blowing my own trumpet, I was the one people wanted on their team. Myself and Jonathan Davies (affectionately known as 'Foxy' to the boys, because his parents used to run a pub called the Fox and Hounds). He's a really bright bloke – a prefect type – the sort of annoying guy at school who was good at every sport, as well as being academically gifted. Jamie Roberts was decent at general knowledge and music, but not so hot on sport. And at the other end of the scale, you'd have guys like Justin Tipuric, Taulupe Faletau and Leigh Halfpenny who would offer nothing at all. Nothing. You'd be lucky if they even opened their mouths.

It was a noble effort to keep the quizzes going, but they would inevitably descend into farce, when people started accusing Melon of getting the answers wrong. Mobiles would be whipped out to check erroneous facts, and arguments would escalate. It would always end with Melon defending himself against a flurry of accusations about being a shit quizmaster. You've got to credit him for making the effort, though. And for taking the abuse.

Before we left Spała, the squad had to be trimmed down. A euphemism for players being dropped. That was really tough for those who didn't make the cut. We knew around eight of us would be deemed surplus to requirements, and were desperately hoping we wouldn't get the dreaded summons to the coaches' quarters. Most of those who were cast aside were big characters – Jonathan Thomas, Lou Reed, Andy Powell. There's no easy way to do it, and the management thought it'd be best to tell them on the last night of camp. My heart went out to them, because they'd poured their heart and soul into the eleven days, only to be told their World Cup dream was over before it had begun.

If there's one thing that can put being dropped into perspective, it's a visit to Auschwitz. We went there on our day off. I spent a long time in silent contemplation as I moved around the museum. The images of the victims' hair and personal possessions are now indelibly imprinted on my mind. We'd heard a lot of moaning in training that week, but we all felt totally humbled after our visit. It gave me a few hours to pay my respects, and to think deeply about how lucky we are. The complaints we'd all been making evaporated into insignificance. In the emotionally suffocating atmosphere, I realised exactly what I was – a pampered rugby player being paid handsomely to play and train for a game I loved.

Whether the visit was a Gatland masterstroke or not, I can't be sure. But it made a lasting and permanent impression on me.

● ● ●

The first two World Cup warm-up games were against England, home and away. Naturally, I wanted to be involved in both, especially as I'd missed the majority of the 2011 Six Nations. If I was to miss them, it would have to be for a very good reason – not, for example, for dropping a plate on my big toe. Embarrassingly, that's what happened. So while I sat on the sidelines with a swollen toe, Craig Mitchell got another two chances to further his claim. We lost the first one away, and won the second in Cardiff. Both were close, and a far cry from previous World Cup warm-ups against England, where we'd got into a habit of being spanked.

I got my chance in the third warm-up game, against Argentina. It was a decent test against a grizzled front five containing my old adversary, Rodrigo Roncero, and I more than held my own. I played the full eighty minutes, which pleased me immensely. Those eighty minutes had hopefully restored my status as number one in Gatland's eyes.

So that was it. The World Cup was nigh. We were off to New Zealand.

I was very excited, but for the first time in my life I had the unusual sensation of saying goodbye to my child. I always missed Nic when I was away, but I felt really emotional bidding farewell to Isla. I knew they'd be joining me in a fortnight, but at that point it felt like a lifetime away.

When we arrived in New Zealand, I went out for a coffee and was approached by two women in their sixties who wanted to tell me how beautiful my daughter was. They'd seen a video on the news of me giving her a cwtch before getting on the plane. It hit home then, how big a deal this World Cup was. It wasn't going to be like Australia in 2003, when you could keep your head down and avoid the scrutiny. Not only did everyone here know who you were, they also knew who your five-month-old daughter was as well.

They absolutely *love* their rugby in New Zealand. It was time to buckle up for the ride.

From the moment we arrived in Wellington, we were portrayed in the local media as a virtuous band of travelling ambassadors – an image that contrasted sharply with that of England's gaggle of misbehaving hoodlums. As with most things the truth lay somewhere in between. Part of the reason we had such good press was our 'choir'. Warren encouraged us to start one so we had something to do at official events in response to the haka. Our repertoire was limited. 'Ar Lan y Môr' and the occasional 'Calon Lân' – that was about it. Craig Mitchell and Alun Wyn Jones were the choir masters. They're both genuinely good singers, and passionate about it too. Leigh Halfpenny was decent as well – very much in the virtuous choirboy mode. As with a lot of things like that, you have your cynics who stand at the back, miming unenthusiastically, but I loved it. As we've established, I'm a proud Welshman, and when you're away from home for long periods, it's important to keep morale up.

The other main reason we were given good press was that our 'poster boys' like Sam, Leigh and George were all clean-cut and ultra-professional.

None of them drank, stayed out late, swore, or offended anyone. And this image rubbed off on the rest of the squad. If Sam said that he hadn't touched a drop of alcohol, the press assumed we were all God-fearing teetotallers. It was a load of nonsense. I'm not saying we were out boozing it up all the time, but the likes of myself and Phillsy had our fair share of nights out. We just weren't subjected to the same degree of scrutiny as the English. They were judged harshly on everything they did, and a succession of misdemeanours added up to a damning charge sheet by the time they'd boarded their flight home. I won't indulge in any mud-slinging here, but throwing dwarves and jumping off ferries are probably things professional sportsmen should seek to avoid.

The New Zealand rugby public is incredibly well educated. Wherever you go, you get sucked into a conversation about rugby, and it's more than just surface-level stuff. You can be queueing for a coffee, and before you know it, you'll be deeply engaged in some tactical discussion with a total stranger. A frail elderly woman approached me in a cafe after the Samoa game and told me earnestly that we weren't kicking enough – that we were playing too much rugby in our own half. She probably had a point.

● ● ●

We didn't fear South Africa. After the hell of Spała, we felt ready for them. We'd played them a lot in the four years since the last World Cup, and knew what they were about. In contrast, we felt we had an element of surprise, with some new guys like Taulupe Faletau just beginning to emerge. We were better than them on the day, and should have won comfortably. But sport doesn't always reward the better side, and the defending champions knew how to get over the line. Frans Steyn scored a try within the first five minutes, and a defensive lapse in the second half allowed Francois Hougaard in. That aside, we matched them in every department. I played the full eighty minutes, and again ensured that the Beast wasn't allowed out of his cage. People still talk about Hooky's controversial penalty in the fourteenth minute that appeared to have gone over but wasn't awarded. It was a bit of a sickener, but you can't allow yourself to dwell on such things.

We should have won regardless. As it was, we fell to a 17–16 defeat. Played one, lost one.

It meant we absolutely had to beat Samoa. They're a team that sends shivers down the spine of every Welsh fan. Twice before we'd lost to them at World Cups – in 1991 and 1999 – and on both occasions they had been enormous upsets. We had a week to prepare for that game – a point which outraged their outspoken centre Eliota Fuimaono-Sapolu. They had just three days, and he pulled no punches on his Twitter feed. Perhaps he had a point, but later comparisons with the Holocaust and slavery somewhat undermined his cause. Either way, it added a little spice to an encounter that needed none. Samoa were our bogey team, and we didn't need to be reminded of that. They had some very good players. Kahn Fotuali'i had just signed for the Ospreys, so I was interested to see how he'd go. Mo Schwalger, their hooker and captain, had played for the Scarlets. Anthony Perenise was an excellent player with a lot of Super XV and Aviva Premiership experience.

Whenever you play Samoa, you know exactly what's coming. Massive, thunderous, bone-jarring tackles. From one to fifteen, they are brutal, uncompromising defenders. You cannot allow yourself to be bullied. Robin McBryde had emphasised the need for what we call 'T-boning'. It's a technical term for running straight. Common sense would tell you that the best place to run when faced with an angry Samoan tackler would be to the side of him. But our game plan was to run straight at them, to seek contact. It sounds foolhardy, but we had big men too, and were determined to take them on at their own game.

Early on, Jamie came at an angle and 'T-boned' their prize centre, Seilala Mapusua. He absolutely smashed him. Shortly after, George North did a similar thing to his opposite number. It sent a powerful message to them that bullying us was not going to work. We were as big and as mean as they were. But despite our refusal to buckle in the physicality stakes, we didn't turn in a vintage performance. Once again, we relied on Shane to conjure a bit of magic. After his try, we had to endure a long, nervy period of Samoan pressure as they laid siege to our line. And ultimately, we had to resort to the dark arts to relieve the pressure.

We had a defensive scrum, close to our line, and it was time for me to delve into my bag of tricks – not as deep and interesting as Shane's, but sometimes as effective. I knew we had to win this scrum, come what may. Like a bowler switching his delivery, I made a slight change to my technique in an attempt to hoodwink the referee. It was subtle but it worked. I scrummaged marginally higher than usual, which allowed me to hit higher against their loose-head, and put some extra weight on the back of his head rather than his shoulder. This forced him to 'hinge' by bending at his waist. Simple physics, but it appears to an untrained eye – and sometimes to a referee's eye – as though he's deliberately collapsed the scrum. I won a penalty, and quite a few arse-taps from my grateful teammates. Technically speaking, I should have been pulled up for scrummaging down, rather than straight, and the ref should have reset the scrum. But like a good openside at the breakdown, you play on the edge of the law, and see what you can get away with. Any prop should have a variety of escape plans at his disposal for situations like this. I learned all mine during my apprenticeship at Neath.

I'm equally wise to the cheating tactics of the opposition. As a tight-head, it's always my intention to drive as hard as possible at the gap between the hooker and the loose-head, to 'shear the loose-head off', and dilute the front row's overall power. The bigger the gap for me to stick my head into, the easier it is to do. So opposition packs who realise they're up against a destructive tight-head will do whatever they can to keep that gap as narrow as possible. One illegal way to do that is for the left-hand lock to bind on both the loose-head and the hooker, helping to clamp them together tightly. It's illegal. When we played Australia in 2010, Nathan Sharpe did this, and the first scrum collapsed. I knew we were better than them in this department, so I observed exactly what was going on in the second. I spotted the illegal bind, and brought it to the attention of the referee. He was watched like a hawk after that, and we ended up destroying them because I was able to shear their loose-head off at will. Being a canny prop is as much about spotting opposition cheats, as using your own wiles. Stop me if I'm boring you, because I could talk about this stuff all day long.

I sat out the third game, against Namibia, which – with the greatest of respect – was a guaranteed win. Myself, Paul James and Mike Phillips formed the core of the dirt-trackers, and we went for a night out in New Plymouth to let our hair down. We had a good few beers that night, but we didn't go dwarf-throwing. It meant we had to remove our names from the now famous 'dry chart' on the team-room wall. There was a section on it called 'World Cup Winners' reserved for those who hadn't touched a drop of alcohol since Spała. Sam Warburton, George North, Dan Lydiate, Leigh Halfpenny . . . and Gethin Jenkins. For those who know the boys in the squad, there's a clear odd one out there. Melon enjoys a beer as much as the next man. And if the next man is me, then he enjoys at least a couple. Far be it for me to cast aspersions on one of the world's greatest props, but there were more than a few raised eyebrows within the squad at that particular claim.

After New Plymouth we drove up to Taupo and indulged in a proper Maori banquet. There were about 250 people there, and we were split into pairs and assigned to a table filled with locals. I was paired with Stephen Jones, which was convenient because he likes a glass of red wine as much as I do. It flowed that night. And fortunately so, because we needed a bit of Dutch courage to tackle the evening's main course. It was fermented mutton bird. We were assured it was a local delicacy. But to my untrained eye, it looked and smelled like a rotting seagull. (I'm not sure Stephen Jones will be putting that on the menu at his swanky new restaurant in Llanelli.) That aside, it was a fantastic night. The older I was becoming, the more I began to appreciate these cultural events on tour, seeing them as a privilege rather than a chore.

I met Colin Meads, and insisted on having my photo taken with him so I could send it to my old man. Once an All Black fan, always an All Black fan. I'm sure Richie McCaw would want his photo taken with Gareth Edwards, if he ever met him in Wales.

The media was keen to raise the spectre of 2007 when we faced Fiji in our final pool game. But there was no danger of a repeat performance. We had a much better side this time, and our opponents were in total disarray. We knew that if we played as well as we were able to, we'd win. It was far more comfortable than we could have imagined, as we romped to a 66–0 victory.

● ● ●

We were to face Ireland in the quarter-finals. Their surprise victory over Australia had essentially flipped the draw and given us a potentially easier path to the final. Because of the way the pool results had panned out, the draw was now split into a Southern Hemisphere half and a Northern Hemisphere half. That suited us perfectly, as we had no reason to fear anyone from the Northern Hemisphere. We really fancied our chances against Ireland, despite their status as favourites.

That week we trained in the Lower Hutt suburb of Wellington and were given another reminder of how good the New Zealand production line is. A couple of local kids asked if they could join in our touch rugby session, and we agreed, thinking we could teach them a thing or two. One of them – a nuggety little scrum-half – was outstanding. He was comfortably the best player on the park, and was making some of our seasoned internationals look decidedly average. And I'm not just talking about the fat props like me – some of our best three-quarters were struggling to keep up with the little bastard. I asked him what his name was, and he told me, 'T. J. Perenara.' Within two years, he'd been capped by the All Blacks.

Being shown up by a teenager didn't dent our confidence going into the Ireland game. Maybe TJ inspired Mike Phillips, because he was brilliant that day. He was at his brash, arrogant best, and he was a real handful for the Irish. His try in the second half was superb. He sniffed the opportunity and pounced over the line, finishing brilliantly. If the Irish were still angry about his 'illegal try' from the Six Nations, there was no argument about this one. Sam Warburton was imperious at the breakdown, and the scrum and line-out were solid all afternoon. I felt I had the measure of Cian Healy in the front row, and I managed to manipulate him into giving away a few penalties. Our defence – led by Dan Lydiate and Luke Charteris – was virtually impenetrable. Jonathan Davies's try, when he did a number on Healy, was priceless.

Those sorts of things steal the headlines, but one of my most memorable moments was seeing Jamie run hard at Donncha O'Callaghan within the first few minutes. It can do untold psychological damage to witness one of your locks being sent flying into next week by a centre. It was a harbinger of things to come for Ireland as they struggled to contain our rampant physicality. That simple act persuaded me that this was going to be our day.

As the match progressed, we felt stronger and stronger – a legacy of our Spała training camps – and the Irish seemed to wane, defeated in their minds as much as on the scoreboard. Oh, and I should mention that Shane scored. Obviously.

Perhaps the Irish were overconfident, but we dominated them that day, and it ranks as one of my favourite victories in a Wales shirt.

All the boys wanted to go out and celebrate, but Warby and Gats made the call not to. We were welcome to toast the win in the hotel bar, but we weren't allowed to hit the town. Warren mentioned this in the next press conference, which led to another series of newspaper articles about how the virtuous Welsh were showing the 'shambolic' English how to behave. He's a pretty canny operator, and not averse to a mind game or two. It may have sounded like a casual anecdote, but he knew exactly what he was doing.

England's World Cup came to a miserable end with defeat to France in the quarter-finals. It meant we'd be facing Les Bleus in the semis – a team we hadn't beaten for three years. Alun Wyn and I went to Eden Park to watch the All Blacks take on Argentina in the fourth quarter-final. It was a nice opportunity to experience the World Cup through the fans' eyes, and it was apparent sitting among the home crowd just how desperate they were for a home victory. New Zealand hadn't won the World Cup since the first tournament, in 1987. The current squad would probably be forced into exile en masse if they didn't win the trophy this time. But we were beginning to think the unthinkable. Could Wales be the ones to spoil the party this time? We were feeling increasingly self-assured, and looking at the four teams who'd made it through to the semi-finals – ourselves, New Zealand, Australia and France – we felt capable of beating them all.

Training was light that week. We felt ready, and the coaches didn't see the need to run us into the ground. The night before the game, I was heading out to the cinema when I was summoned back to my room by an urgent-sounding text from Nicole. When I opened the door she handed me her phone and said, 'Boris Johnson is going to ring you now.' I thought she was taking the piss. Her friend from the *Telegraph* had passed on our number, and Boris was apparently keen for a chat.

I was literally sweating in anticipation, inexplicably nervous. I'd played rugby in 80,000-seater stadiums, in front of TV audiences of millions, but the prospect of speaking to some floppy-haired Tory politician had sent me into a blind panic. Nicole was just as bad, pacing around the room, unable to relax. Eventually, the phone rang, and I answered nervously. The unmistakable clipped vowels of Boris Johnson came thundering through the receiver. He sounded as though he'd known me all my life and told me he felt some kind of kinship with me, because he'd played prop at school. I can safely say that's the only thing we had in common. Me, a working-class Welsh boy from the Swansea Valley. Him, a privileged member of the upper classes. I called him 'butt' and he called me 'old boy'. But for ten minutes over the phone on the night before the biggest game of my career, our worlds collided and the class divide dissolved. It was a surreal but welcome encounter. I can't explain why I felt so nervous. In my mind he was famous, rich and powerful, and that had some weird effect on my brain.

I couldn't wait to get back downstairs and tell the boys. But as you can imagine, my enthusiasm fell on deaf ears. When I announced that I'd just been chewing the fat with Boris Johnson, Paul James screwed his face up in confusion and said, 'Who?'

●　●　●

The day of reckoning dawned, and we were reminded of the enormity of the occasion when Alan Phillips told us that 60,000 Welsh fans were heading to the Millennium Stadium to watch the match on the big screen. Sixty thousand. To watch a game that was taking place on the other side of the world. That was more people than would be in the *actual* stadium in Auckland. Crazy scenes. There isn't another nation on earth that could rally that level of support in such circumstances. This was a very big deal. Wales had only reached a semi-final once before, and that was way back in 1987 when the World Cup was a long way from the global showpiece it's become. This wasn't just the biggest game I'd ever played in, but the biggest game any Welshman had ever played in.

But it seems that the hand of fate has developed a habit of plucking me prematurely from such occasions. During the last scrum of the Ireland game, I'd felt a slight twinge in my calf, but thought nothing of it. Training had gone smoothly in the build-up to France, but during the second scrum at Eden Park I felt a strange thud in my lower leg. That's the only way I can describe it. Once the ball was out of the back of the scrum, I tried to run and found I couldn't. My calf was torn. Carcass came on and strapped it up, but I knew it was gone. As Carcass was doing his bit, I looked up at the stadium clock and saw that only seven minutes had elapsed. World Cup quarter-final against England 2003. Lions second test against South Africa in 2009. World Cup semi-final against France in 2011. Three times now, I'd psyched myself up for a game of monumental proportions. Three times, I'd had it taken away from me.

As you've probably deduced by now, I'm a bit of an emotional bloke, and I'm not afraid to shed a tear. This was another of those occasions. I limped off towards the bench, covered my head with my coat, and had a little cry. I couldn't bear to watch for a while, so I sat there with my head in my hands and my mind in a blur. A few moments later, I felt someone sitting down next to me. I emerged from my cocoon to see our captain, Sam Warburton, alongside me.

'What the fuck are you doing here?' I inquired politely.

'I've just been sent off,' came the solemn reply.

I didn't believe him. Sam Warburton. Our paragon of virtue. One of the most decent players in the game. Sent off?

He pointed up to the big screen, where endless replays of his tip tackle on Vincent Clerc were being shown on a loop. Sam was shell-shocked. Others would have been cursing, swearing, punching, kicking and throwing things around in a rage. He just sat there in a silent trance. Like me, this was the biggest game of his career, and he was aiming to be the first Welshman ever to lead his side to the promised land of a World Cup final. Instead, he'd been given his marching orders with an hour still to play.

While he had my utmost sympathy, a selfish thought flashed unexpectedly through my head: 'He's stolen my thunder here! If we end up losing, this is all anyone will be talking about!' I'd been trending on Twitter for that short period between me limping off and Sam being shown the red card. I told him I was pissed off with him for that, but I don't think he found it particularly funny. It was too early for jokes.

I can barely remember anything else about the occasion. I can just about picture Mike running around Pascal Papé for the game's only try. And I can vaguely recall some of the missed kicks, but I couldn't tell you who missed them or at what point in the game. It all went by in a blur. It was a miracle we were still in it as full time approached, given how critical

Sam had been to us. Not many sides could cope with the loss of their openside, but we hung on until the bitter end, and had a number of chances to win.

If I do remember anything, it was the fact that France seemed to play like *they* were the team with a man down. Instead of spinning it wide, and trying to exploit their numerical advantage, they shut up shop and tried to wind the clock down. These were odd tactics, but they'd been beaten twice in the pool stages and clearly lacked the confidence to cut loose – that and the fact they were in disarray off the field. Rumours had persisted throughout the tournament that their coach, Marc Lièvremont, had lost the dressing room, and they were on the verge of open mutiny.

When the dust had settled and my emotions had levelled out, I could accept that according to the letter of the law, Sam's tackle had warranted a red card. But when someone of Clerc's size runs into someone that big and that powerful, and jumps into the tackle, the outcome is inevitable. Sam is not a malicious player. If he was guilty of anything, it was of being a tad overzealous. But who wouldn't be when they're captaining their country on the biggest stage of them all?

There was an astonishing outpouring of hate directed towards referee Alain Rolland in the aftermath, with most Welsh fans laying the blame for the defeat squarely on his shoulders. I understand that emotions were raw, but the level of vitriol was ridiculous, disproportionate and plain wrong. International referees are brave and committed professionals, and their integrity should be respected. Earlier in the tournament, Alain had bumped into Nicole and Ryan Jones in Hamilton. He ended up hanging out with them, and having a cwtch with Isla. He has kids of his own, and told Nic how much he'd been missing them. I knew nothing of this until the Samoa game, when he came into the changing rooms to check our studs and ended up telling me how beautiful my daughter was. He's clearly a decent, likeable bloke, and he did not deserve to be dehumanised in such a way. Whether the Warburton decision was the right one or not, I personally don't hold it against him.

You don't need me to tell you that the changing room after the game was a sad place. Our incredible journey had come to a devastating end, in the worst possible circumstances. I was injured, and we'd lost by a single point to France, having played the majority of the game without our skipper. It was a horrible, empty feeling.

The rest of the boys had to rouse themselves for the third-place play-off against Australia, but it's a game nobody wants to play in. The dream of glory is over, and it's a meaningless contest. I went for a scan a couple of days after the semi-final defeat and discovered that my calf tear was a substantial one – thirteen centimetres, to be precise. Perversely that made me feel better, because it confirmed that my early exit from the field was down to a bona fide injury. I'd have found it harder to take if it had been a broken toenail, or something embarrassing and insignificant.

The last week for me was an opportunity to go 'off tour'. I had a nice few days sightseeing with my parents, and Nicole and Isla, and we had some lovely meals out. Adam Beard was on my case, asking if I wanted to do some weights sessions, but he had no chance of getting me in the gym. I just wanted to relax and try to enjoy myself.

We flew home on the day of the final, so saw nothing of it. But judging from how it unfolded, I think we'd have given New Zealand a good go if we'd been there instead of France. That French team had lost to Tonga in the pool stages, and they should have lost the semi-final to us. Truthfully speaking, they had no business being there, let alone coming within a point of lifting the trophy. I watched the highlights when I got home, and couldn't shake the idea that we should have been there. I could be sitting here now with a World Cup winner's medal. All the stars had seemed aligned before those two fateful moments in the semi-final. Ultimately, though, there were too many what-ifs, and I don't lie awake at night contemplating what might have been. Perhaps I would, if we'd made it to the final – and if it was there that I'd suffered the injury and Sam had been sent off.

Sport can be a cruel mistress. I hoped I would have one more shot at World Cup glory, but it looks as though that was it. Close, but no cigar.

CHAPTER 17

History Maker

IF we thought Spała was a gruelling experience, Gdańsk was on another level entirely. The bleak windswept town on the shores of the Baltic Sea was the location of choice for our 2012 Six Nations training camp. That tournament offered us a chance of redemption following the World Cup. We travelled there in the depths of winter, and it was brutally cold. The pitches were either frozen or covered in snow, forcing us indoors for hour upon hour of fitness work. When we did venture out, it was horrendous.

One beach session remains lodged in my mind as a particularly unwelcome memory. When I say beach, don't be imagining some beautiful cove with golden sands being lapped by gently breaking waves. Picture instead a gnarly stretch of windswept gravel twisted by the bitter Baltic winds, blowing like a blanket of ice over the frozen ocean. We were forced to do a brutal succession of military-style drills, most of which involved crawling around on our stomachs. Exhausted doesn't come close to describing how I felt. As the session neared its end, we all had heaving lungs, blinding headaches and empty stomachs. Then, the masochist Adam Beard ordered us to strip down to our pants and walk into the sea up to our necks. Muscle recovery time. Nobody took him up on it – nobody apart from Robin McBryde, and he hadn't even done the session. There's something different in his DNA. He's made of sterner stuff than your average man.

We had cryotherapy chambers in Gdańsk too. But it was so cold out there, they barely made a difference. For the entire week, I felt as though I couldn't feel my extremities. My hands and feet were like blocks of ice for the duration. Training-wise, I got nothing out of that trip. The weather was so extreme that it severely limited what we were able to do. What it did do was sharpen our mental resolve. We journeyed to some dark places, and had to push ourselves beyond the limits of our endurance. We weren't to know it then, but those trials would come in useful during the Six Nations at times when the chips were down, and our will would be tested to its limit.

● ● ●

Ireland were first, in Dublin, and they were clearly miffed about what had happened in the World Cup. Because of that, the bookies had installed us as favourites – not just to win at Lansdowne Road, but to win the entire tournament. But the odds were considerably shortened by a glut of injuries we suffered in the run-up. Melon, Smiler, Dan Lydiate, Alun Wyn and Luke Charteris were all out, meaning we travelled with some new combinations up front. Ireland, though, were missing a certain Brian O'Driscoll, and it always helps when he's not playing. As much as rugby's a team game, one player can make an enormous psychological difference. Drico was one of those players.

We started brilliantly, working a five–two overlap on the blind-side, and Rhys Priestland delayed his pass beautifully to suck in two defenders and put Foxy in at the corner. But they hit back through Rory Best and were 10–5 ahead at half-time. It was an odd game for me, because there were only about two scrums in the entire match. It meant I was busier elsewhere – cleaning out rucks and making tackles – but given that scrummaging is what I'm there for, it's difficult not to feel redundant in those anomalous games where it takes a back seat. Every player wants to put a marker down against their opposite number, and my chance to do that comes in the scrum. I'd had a good day against Cian Healy in the World Cup, and had been hoping to dish out some more punishment.

As it was, we didn't need a destructive scrum, because we had George North careering through the Irish defence like a runaway freight train. He'd already excelled in the World Cup, but in Shane's absence he seized the vacant match-winner role. His power and dexterity were both in evidence for our second try, as he smashed through Fergus McFadden's attempted tackle before delivering a delicate offload to Foxy, who steam-rollered his way to the line. It was an outstanding display of pace and power. And after Tommy Bowe had sneaked past him for Ireland's second try, George got his revenge by bulldozing Bowe, and a number of other Irish defenders, en route to a try of his own. The pendulum had swung back in our favour.

But as seems to be the way with games against the Irish, the eventual outcome hinged on a couple of controversial incidents. Donnacha Ryan cleaned me out of a ruck with a similar hit to the one Bakkies Botha put on me in 2009. I went flying, and Bradley Davies took umbrage. His retaliation was none too subtle as he scooped Ryan up, tipped him, and dumped him on his shoulders. The only decision the referee had to make was whether it was a yellow or a red card. He got away with yellow, but Ireland nudged themselves back ahead with the penalty.

The final act came two minutes from time. Stephen Ferris was adjudged to have spear-tackled Ian Evans. I'm sure Ianto's Oscar-worthy performance helped persuade the referee that it deserved a yellow, but crucially it gave us a penalty in front of the posts. Leigh Halfpenny knocked it over, and gave us the victory by 23 points to 21. It was the fifth time the lead had changed hands, and it was the end of an epic, breathtaking test match. I was delighted for Leigh – he's his own worst critic and had allowed himself to be haunted by a penalty he'd missed in the World Cup semi-final. That match-winner in Dublin allowed him to lay that particular ghost to rest.

The Irish boys were devastated. We'd knocked them out of the World Cup, and now we'd had the audacity to turn them over on their own soil. In fairness, they were gracious in defeat, and we shared a beer or three at the post-match function. I've always enjoyed the company of the Irish. They can be pretty much divided into two camps. On the one hand you've got the Leinster boys – middle class, sophisticated and stylish. On the other you've got the country boys, largely from Munster. They're much more down-to-earth farmer types. As a valley boy, I'd gravitate towards the latter, but they were all, to a man, good guys who were willing to leave any rancour out on the pitch and sink a few ales in the spirit of rugby.

It's part of the unique psychology of our sport. When we line up in the tunnel pre-game alongside the opposition, there's not even a flicker of recognition. You're so deep in the zone at that point, you wouldn't dream of glancing across and acknowledging a Lions teammate – or, in the case of Tommy Bowe, a clubmate. It just doesn't happen. By that stage a switch has been flicked, and you've transformed from a regular human being into a gladiatorial warrior. I love Tommy to bits, and consider him a close friend, but when Wales are playing Ireland that goes out of the window for eighty minutes. If I found him lying on the wrong side of a ruck, I would do whatever it took to get him out of the way. If that meant stamping all over him, then so be it. And I'd have no issue if he, or anyone else, did the same to me. It's part of the game. You've got to be willing to go out there and inflict pain.

I remember watching Audley Harrison fight, not long after he turned professional, and Marvin Hagler was commentating. He was outraged when Harrison touched gloves with his opponent, arguing that he was showing him too much respect. It was his take that when you step in the ring, you're looking to batter your opponent and that touching gloves, as is the custom in boxing, undermines that. It's the same principle in rugby. You can't show any affection to your opponent before the game. That's not to say I condone dirty play, because I don't. There's a line you shouldn't cross. But you need to be as hard and uncompromising as you can be within the confines of the law.

It's the polar opposite of modern football in that respect, where diving and play-acting at the highest level are seriously undermining its image. It's been said that rugby players spend the entire game pretending they're not hurt, whereas football players spend the entire game pretending they are. It's something you hear in rugby clubs across Wales, and some diehard rugby fans have no time for football for precisely that reason. They think the game's been hijacked by foreign investors and ruined by prima donnas who set a bad example on the pitch.

Personally, I've always enjoyed football, and I watch it whenever I can. Sharing a stadium with Swansea City allowed me to become mates with a few Welsh internationals. I even introduced Joe Allen to his wife. She's an Abercrave girl, and I used to play rugby with her uncle. We ended up going to their wedding last year.

I've also become quite friendly with Aaron Ramsey after a chance encounter on a night out in Cardiff. Someone asked me if I'd mind if Aaron came over for a chat. Now, as much as rugby is the national sport in Wales, and we players get our fair share of attention, boys like Aaron who play in the Premier League enjoy an entirely different level of fame. I found it bizarre that someone that famous was asking for permission to come and talk to me. We both initially claimed to be starstruck in each other's presence. But after a few minutes, it was just two Welsh boys chatting about sport in a bar. He asked for a selfie, and tweeted it a few days later with the hashtag #legend. My Twitter account has never seen so much action. For days, I was receiving tweets from all over the world asking who on earth was this big, fat-curly-haired guy that Aaron Ramsey considered to be a legend?

• • •

Scotland were next, in Cardiff, and we had some adjustments to make in the pack. Bradley's little indiscretion had earned him a seven-week ban, so Ryan was pressed into emergency second row cover. He was then elevated to captain when Warby pulled out on the day with a dead leg. That meant Jug Head equalled Ieuan Evans's record for captaining Wales the most times. It also meant Aaron Shingler made his test debut as an openside flanker – a position he'd never played before at any level.

I was up against Allan 'Chunk' Jacobsen who is, hands down, one of my favourite ever opponents. In this modern professional world where even prop forwards can look like athletes, Jacobsen was even more of a throwback than me. He looked for all the world like an amateur playing for a village club, with his rotund belly, pudgy face and double chin. But here he was – like me – playing on the biggest stage at the highest level.

He's the very epitome of an 'old school' prop. What he lacked in raw talent he more than made up for in tricks of the trade. He was a master of knocking you off balance just before the hit. He'd reach over and pull your arm down, or pull you into him to force a collapse. He was a strong little fella, and a clever one too. I'd always make a point of having a pint with him after the game, even though I could barely understand a word he said.

Despite the disruptions we were too good for Scotland, winning 27–13. Leigh Halfpenny and Alex Cuthbert scored all our points between them, before we let Greig Laidlaw in for a soft try towards the end. It was to be the last try we'd concede that tournament – a stat that fills Shaun Edwards with glee to this day.

Stuart Hogg came on for his debut in that game and announced his talent to the world. A pasty little Scottish fella with a dangerous turn of pace, and an enormous chip on his shoulder. He was denied a try that should have been given, but it would have made little difference to the outcome.

● ● ●

The win against Scotland meant our third game was for the Triple Crown, and it was England who stood in our way. After laying the twenty-year hoodoo to rest in 2008, Twickenham no longer held any fear for us. This team was probably the only one since the seventies to travel to Twickenham with genuine confidence. Visits there during the eighties and nineties were almost always about damage limitation, but this time, we were going there to win. In recent years, the pre-match etiquette has changed, and the buses are forced to park at the back of Twickenham car park. Instead of sneaking into enemy territory unnoticed, we're forced to weave our way on foot through the hundreds of Hooray Henrys nibbling prawn sandwiches and quaffing Pimm's. It's a psychological trick Stuart Lancaster has employed to try to unnerve us. But when you've run the gauntlet at Loftus Versfeld past a group of Afrikaners who want to tear you limb from limb, a couple of hundred poshos clustered around their Range Rovers amid a sea of open hampers is easy enough to handle.

England had a good side, full of dangerous players. Manu Tuilagi was a match winner, and Chris Ashton had developed a habit of scoring spectacular tries. His 'swallow dive' had become a talking point in the media, with many pundits and ex-players decrying it as crass and unsportsmanlike, but I had no problem with it. There's room for a bit of showboating in rugby. I'd probably do it if I ever scored any tries. I'd be a hypocrite if I slagged him off for it, because Shane – one of my best mates and favourite players – used to do similar things all the time. He had a bigger repertoire too, including the mistimed one against Italy where he nearly broke his arm. So if Shane's allowed, I guess Ashton is too. Just as long as it's not against Wales.

The player who made the biggest impression on me in that game was Owen Farrell. He was really young, and finding his way at test level, but he had the attitude and courage of a senior international. Rhys Priestland got sin-binned five minutes into the second half, and we decided to tighten things up and play a pick-and-go game to run the clock down. Ordinarily, the first two or three defenders on the edge of a ruck would be forwards, because it's inevitably a forward who'll be picking and carrying. But Farrell kept positioning himself tight into the rucks and acting as one of England's primary defenders.

I'll never forget one carry when Alun Wyn picked up from the base and charged forward. Farrell stood there shouting at him. 'Come on, then! Fucking run at me, you c**t!' Language aside, I couldn't help but be impressed. It was his first appearance at Twickenham, and he was deliberately provoking a Lions colossus who was twice his size. He backed it up too, smashing into Alun Wyn with all his might – not knocking him backwards exactly, but certainly stopping him in his tracks. Can you ever imagine a seventies fly-half doing that? Standing at first or second guard at a ruck, and making tackle after tackle? It's why I get furious when I hear people like Jonathan Davies say 'run down the fly-half's channel' as though that's a sure-fire way of breaching the defence. It may have been in his day, because fly-halves didn't tackle, but things have changed.

And while we're on the subject, I'd like to get another thing off my chest. People who make constant references to the Welsh teams of the seventies are living in the past. Yes, it was a wonderful era, but to suggest that they were superior to any Welsh team that's followed is ridiculous. All they had to do back then was pass the ball to Gerald or JJ, and they'd score. You simply cannot compare generations, because the game has changed beyond all recognition. The scrums are different, the line-outs are different, the rucks are different, the kicking is different, and the players are different. Back then the biggest players weighed in at around seventeen stone. Nowadays, there are four players in our backline heavier than that. Granted, I've played in this current 'golden generation' so I don't look back on the seventies with the same misty-eyed romanticism that many do. But if you ask me whether the game is better today, I'd say unequivocally, *yes*.

Looking back at the old footage is like watching sixteen ants swarming around a brown ball, while fourteen backs stand around in immaculate kit with their hands on their hips. Or line-outs where the ball is launched down the middle between two rows of flailing, flapping arms. The modern line-out by comparison is a masterwork of skill and precision. The game is a lot more skilful now. A lot more. Don't believe anyone who tells you otherwise.

Anyway, rant over. Back to 2012, and the England game. It was Owen Farrell's performance that prompted that rant, and I was so impressed that I made a point of seeking out his dad, after the game, and telling him what an outstanding player his son was. He played a big part in England's attempt to deny us the Triple Crown. Under Stuart Lancaster, they looked a far cry from the ragged bunch that had limped out of the World Cup. Tuilagi was wreaking havoc in the midfield, and were it not for a heroic tackle by Sam Warburton on the half-hour mark (which earned him a broken nose), England would have been further ahead than 9–6 at half-time.

They had a chance to extend their lead early in the second half, when Mouritz Botha charged down Rhys Priestland's clearance kick. The bounce was unkind, but their heads were up, and 'Swing Low, Sweet Chariot' was being sung with a little more gusto. This was a game destined to turn on one incident.

I was engaged in a personal duel with Alex Corbisiero, the New-York-born English loose-head whose reputation was becoming more fearsome by the day. We knew he was good, and had spent hours poring over video clips of him to try to pinpoint a weakness. He had to be neutralised if we were to have a platform. There are two things that I can reveal about Corbisiero. One, he has a long back, which means he's more prone to 'hinging' and collapsing the scrum. Two, and crucially for an attacking tight-head like me, he leaves a wide gap between himself and his hooker on the bind. That's the gap that I ram my head into. If a loose-head and a hooker bind really tightly together, there's less space for me to shove my head into, and less chance of me splitting them apart (which is my primary aim). If you split them, then the loose-head becomes ineffective, and the front row battle becomes a three-on-two.

My chance to split Corbisiero off was dependent on these two factors. Firstly, if I aimed slightly down, forcing his long back to bend towards his knee, I'd neutralise his natural strength. To compensate he'd 'kick his arse out' and try to shove in sideways. Once he'd done that, I knew he was out of the equation, and I could shift my weight inwards towards Dylan Hartley, the hooker. And if I timed it to perfection, I could get right underneath Hartley and force him to stand up. See? Scrummaging is an art form. It's not just a load of fat, hairy blokes grunting and groaning. There's an awful lot more going on than just shoving. It's about preparation, research and execution. Melon and I had spent a lot of time during the week studying our opponents' habits, and it won us a few penalties on the day. In games as tight as this one, penalties mean the difference between victory and defeat.

You wouldn't have read about that in any match report, because our work goes largely unseen, taking place in the dark, forbidding depths of the front row. The pretty boys in the back are the ones who do the outrageous things that garner all the attention, and what Scott Williams did that day was worthy of a movie script. There were eight minutes left, and the score was locked at 12-all. England had the ball on halfway, and shipped it out to their enforcer, Courtney Lawes – a man who prides himself on his reckless physicality. Looking up and seeing a centre in his way, he dropped his shoulder and went on the charge. But Scott is a Newcastle Emlyn boy, from farming stock in West Wales. He doesn't take a backwards step for anyone, reputations be damned. Not only did he stop Lawes in his tracks, he ripped the ball from his grasp, and booted it downfield. England appeared to have an ample number of defenders scrambling back, but Scott accelerated smoothly, like a Porsche going through the gears, and outstripped them all. The bounce was a thing of beauty, landing squarely in his chest before he dived over for one of the most dramatic tries Twickenham will ever witness.

Most of our backs had set off in hot pursuit, and were now leaping with joy in the in-goal area, in front of a packed stand of miserable-looking England supporters. Our forwards had all hung back, and my most vivid memory is of a forlorn-looking Courtney Lawes being verbally abused by Ianto. He loves to get a dig in, and he couldn't resist. 'How does it feel to be schooled by a back?' was the gist of it – embroidered with a generous flurry of swear words. It wasn't the kind of sledging that a cricketer would be proud of, but Ianto was enjoying himself.

It was the first time we'd been ahead, but it wasn't the final act. That fell to their winger, David Strettle. With the clock in the red, he ended a period of relentless English pressure by squeezing over at the corner. The crowd were in raptures, thinking he'd scored, but I'd seen Leigh Halfpenny's last-ditch tackle up close. I thought he may well have held him up.

There followed an agonising wait as Steve Walsh referred the decision to the TMO. The incident was played over and over on the big screen. Someone appeared behind me and asked whether I thought it was a try. Not recognising the accent, I was surprised to turn round and see England's replacement fly-half, Toby Flood. He was hanging around to take the conversion. My response was a little harsh: 'If it is, butt, the pressure's all on you!' The conversion would have drawn the scores level, but Flood didn't get the chance. 'No try' was the decision from the TMO.

The Triple Crown was ours. And it was the first time we'd won it on English soil. You can't get more satisfying than that.

● ● ●

You'd think the tension would have slackened following the win against England, given we had Italy in Cardiff next. But if anything we tightened up. We had our eyes on the prize, and it was difficult not to think ahead to the French game in the final round. Italy should have been a speed bump along the way, but we'd underestimated them before. Collectively, we seemed worried. Fretful. Passes were being dropped. The ball was being lost. And we couldn't establish any forward momentum. Italians are known for their style and sartorial flair. But there's nothing fancy about their rugby side. They're hard and obstinate, and you can't even think about cutting loose until you've won the battle of attrition.

Our pack had a hard time of it that day, and I had my usual arm wrestle with their wily old Sicilian warhorse, Andrea Lo Cicero. After nearly an hour of battering down the door, the gaps eventually appeared, and we capitalised on two of them with tries for Jamie Roberts and Alex Cuthbert. The win in the end was comfortable, but the atmosphere in the changing room was curiously flat. Deep down we'd been hoping for a wave of tries that would carry us buoyantly into the title decider against France. That hadn't happened, but we had successfully negotiated stage four of our Grand Slam journey. We could say the words now. We were just a win away.

For many of the boys this was a step into the unknown. The exuberance of youth had got us this far. The George Norths, the Alex Cuthberts, the Rhys Priestlands. They hadn't suffered hurt and humiliation in the Welsh shirt like some of us; they hadn't been inhibited by the burden of expectation. They'd just gone out and played, and played bloody well for the most part. Now they were about to step through a portal into a different world. The Six Nations trophy was within their grasp. It's a prize that has monumental significance in Wales. Our performance in the Six Nations sets the barometer for the nation's mood in those cold, crisp first months of the year, as winter turns to spring. What had been a distant dream at the start of February was now morphing into reality, and these youngsters were getting nervous. Training in the build-up to the France game was edgy and uncontrolled. Teetering on chaos. I've never considered myself a leader, but that week I took it upon myself to instil some focus. Only Melon, Jug Head and I remained from the 2005 Grand Slam-winning team. We'd been through this twice. We knew what to expect.

During a particularly slapdash session, I called a halt, summoning the boys together into a huddle. For the first and only time in my Wales career, I delivered a motivational talk. The essence of my message was, 'Chill out. The only pressure we're feeling is the pressure we're applying to ourselves. We've done this dozens of times before. The pattern hasn't changed, the moves are the same as they've been throughout the championship. Just breathe, think, concentrate, and go through your routines.' I basically delivered Isla's Christmas Eve speech with a few tweaks. '...I know you're excited, I know Santa's coming tomorrow, but you just have to train normally and stay calm.'

I was looking into their eyes, hoping to see something akin to respect – if not awe. Most of them just appeared surprised that I was speaking at all. The collective expression, if it said anything, said, 'What the fuck is Bomb piping up for? He's normally mute!'

Talk of revenge in rugby is often misplaced, but there was no doubt we owed France one. They'd robbed us of a place in the World Cup final. Sam and I had missed out that day, and this was our chance to set the record straight. I was more nervous before that game than I'd been before either of my other two Grand Slam deciders. If the titles in 2005 and 2008 had been unexpected, this one was predestined. If we had nothing to lose then, we had everything to lose now. Our trajectory was travelling on a steep upward curve, and to fall at the final hurdle would be catastrophic. I was very excited. Don't think for a second that the sheen of excitement wears off once you've done something already. I wasn't bouncing around like a ball of nervous energy, as some of the youngsters were, but my heart was pumping hard, and the adrenaline was coursing through my veins.

It's impossible to shield yourself entirely from the media, and we were all too aware of the hysteria that was swelling at the prospect of another Grand Slam. It's an immense privilege to play for Wales. Every single man, woman and child across the country was desperate for victory that day. But there were only fifteen of us who could wear the jersey. We were representing everyone. Our parents, our brothers and sisters, our sons and daughters, our neighbours, our friends, our village, our town, our city, our country. And also, fittingly, Merv the Swerve – the totemic Welsh Number 8 from the seventies – who died on the eve of the game.

Emotion needs to be cooled ahead of these big games. While we all felt the passion, it was the coaches' job to keep us calm. Fire in the belly, ice in the brain. There was a pack of marauding Frenchmen out there, desperate to derail the celebrations. They'd already proved themselves party-poopers by insisting the roof was kept open for the rain to flood in. The pitch was soggy, and the ball was slippery. An early kicking duel was the order of the day. We prodded and probed in the opening quarter, but France defended stubbornly. They'd been patchy throughout the championship, but seemed to have saved their best until last. The deadlock was broken in spectacular fashion twenty minutes in when Alun Wyn stole the ball on the floor. We worked it down the blindside, and Cuthy shredded the French defence. He had little room to manoeuvre, but his footwork was outstanding – and when he pins his ears back, it's good night, Cardiff. It was a truly world-class finish. There wasn't a better finisher in the game at that point. His predatory instinct was sharper than anyone's.

The French refused to drop their heads. They kept coming, blowing an absolute gilt-edged chance to score. Their big Number 8, Imanol Harinordoquy, went on a dangerous bullocking run before being smothered by a trademark Ianto tackle. As much as Cuthy's try generated the headlines, that tackle was equally important to the Grand Slam.

Nobody personified the defensive effort more than the player of the tournament, Dan Lydiate. The Mid Walian farmer's son terrorised the French runners, launching himself at their ankles all day long. His technique was so effective, those watching the game from the high seats would have been forgiven for thinking his victims had been shot. Only a few years earlier, he'd broken his neck playing for the Dragons. To come back bigger, stronger and more determined, as he did, tells you all you need to know about the man. He's willing to chuck his head anywhere and do the dirty work that goes unseen. He was our most destructive defensive weapon during that campaign, and he deserved all the praise that came his way — although Jug Head did do his best to steal some of the limelight.

Lyds put in a big tackle on Louis Picamoles in our 22, and forced a knock-on. Next thing I knew, Ryan was flying through the air like some Hollywood superhero. His face contorted into a dramatic Sly Stallone-esque expression as he flew through the air and landed on the ball. You'd swear it was a ticking bomb, and he was about to sacrifice himself to save the lives of everyone in the stadium. It didn't go unnoticed. I made a personal note to myself not to allow him to get away with that. I swear he looked around when the ball was cleared to see if any cameras had picked up on it. He was suitably chastised by myself and Jon Fox later that evening, don't you worry about that.

The last five minutes were knackering. Whether it was the enormity of the occasion, or the cumulative effect of a long, hard tournament, I'm not sure, but I felt drained. Most of those last few minutes were spent on the floor. Making a tackle, getting up, making another, hitting a ruck, and willing the clock to wind down. Eventually it did. Rhys Priestland booted the ball high into the stand, and we'd done it again. Grand Slam champions. Our third Slam in eight seasons. *My* third Slam in eight seasons.

All the backroom staff piled on to the field, and Shaun Edwards made a beeline for me. 'Bomb, Bomb! That's your third. Do this for the camera!' He held three fingers up to signify my three Grand Slams, and I duly copied him. I'll do anything Shaun Edwards tells me to. The camera bulbs were flashing and popping all over the place, and I was combing the crowd for Nicole and my parents. My only regret was that Isla wasn't there to see her daddy. I felt a twinge of jealousy when Ryan brought his son, Jacob, out on to the field. We'd decided the occasion would be too big, and too loud, for her. But I'd have given anything to have her in my arms for that precious moment.

After the trophy presentation, I swiped a bottle of champagne and we set off on a lap of honour. The crowd was going insane. Somebody threw me a daffodil hat and, against my better judgement, I put it on. As a result, I look like a clown in many of those celebratory shots – although Jamie's pink cowboy hat was clearly the biggest sartorial error. Mark Jones's dignity deserted him for a moment when he scooped up the corner flag and played along to Status Quo's 'Rockin' All Over The World' as though it was a guitar. I think he might have even attempted a Chuck Berry-style duck walk as well. Risky. Ryan and I enjoyed that moment together. As much as I love to take the piss out of him, he's one of my best mates, and it's a privilege to represent your country alongside your closest friends. We'd suffered in a Wales shirt many times together, yet here we were celebrating our third Grand Slam. If you told me that would be happening when I was being subbed off after half an hour during the 2003 World Cup, I'd have thought you were a madman.

Laps of honour should be reserved for occasions like this. Too often, teams feel the need to do one after a routine victory. That shouldn't be the case. You need to feel like you've earned it, and we had that day. It gives you a chance to look into the faces of the loyal fans, and to witness the joy and happiness victory brings. There is no other feeling like it, and I've been lucky enough to experience it three times, all in my home stadium, in front of our home fans. It's impossible to compare the three, but I think 2012 might just have been my favourite – if only for the fact I was still on the pitch when the final whistle blew. That and the fact that the foundations felt strong this time. I didn't feel as though we might slip back into a trough of mediocrity, like we did in 2005 and 2008. We were too good for that.

Or so I thought. By the time our title defence came around the following February, we'd played seven and lost seven. We were hurtling towards a crisis.

Statistics can be damning. Three of those defeats were on our summer tour to Australia, and we could – perhaps should – have won all three. Then came the autumn internationals. We lost, unforgivably, to Argentina and Samoa. And, more predictably, to New Zealand and Australia. Australia had become our arch nemesis. That particular defeat, by 14 points to 12, was the worst of the lot. Kurtley Beale scored a breakaway try in the eightieth minute, and Leigh Halfpenny got knocked clean out trying to tackle him.

Rob Howley was in sole charge of Wales during this run of defeats while Warren was on Lions duty. The knives were being sharpened behind his back. Without Warren, it seemed Wales couldn't win.

CHAPTER 18

Trampling the Red Rose

WE entered the 2013 Six Nations Championship on the back foot and feeling the heat. After a miserable run against Southern Hemisphere opponents, you might have thought our old friends Ireland would have provided some cold comfort. Not likely. Angered by their recent run of defeats against us, they saw their visit to Cardiff as a chance to plunge the knife into the twitching corpse of Welsh rugby. Simon Zebo was the one wielding the blade. He scored a brilliant try within the first ten minutes, before displaying some Maradona-esque footballing skills in the build-up to their second. Dan Biggar had been charged down by a marauding Rory Best, who gathered the ball on the run. Jamie Heaslip's pass was behind the onrushing Zebo but, in one of the most audacious moves I've seen on a rugby pitch, he flipped it up with his left leg, caught it in one fluid movement, and carried on running. A few phases later, Cian Healy was barging over for their second try.

It was 23–3 at half-time, and we were desperate to get into the dressing room to regroup. There was nothing complicated about the team talk: get the ball, hold on to it, and bloody score.

Ireland must have been eavesdropping because, within minutes of the whistle blowing for the second half, Brian O'Driscoll had barrelled his way over. It was 30–3, and we were fast becoming victims of a massacre. Only Wales knows feast and famine on this scale. From Grand Slam champions to this within less than a year. So much for my theory about solid foundations.

But then, something strange happened. From the depths of despair, we glimpsed a flickering light of redemption. A residual sense of pride – which had been lost amid all the defeats – returned to the surface, and we began to play again. Alex Cuthbert reignited those Grand Slam memories with another brilliant finish, and Leigh Halfpenny helped create an overlap before dabbing down in the corner. Five minutes from time, my replacement, Craig Mitchell, took route one to the try line.

It was 30–22 when the final whistle blew. But had that game gone on any longer, we'd have won. The shift in momentum couldn't have been more pronounced. If that hoary old cliché 'it was a game of two halves' ever applied, it did so here.

It's not often you take comfort from a defeat, but we did so that day. Until we saw the papers. There was plenty of stirring stuff about our heroic comeback, but a whole lot of criticism too. The axe was hovering over some of our heads, and there were many voices calling for wholesale changes. Melon and I had been two of the first names on the team sheet for many a long year. But this losing sequence had harmed our reputations. We were two more defeats away from equalling our worst run of all time. Gethin and I had to go, screamed some of the less sympathetic headlines.

We were past our sell-by dates. The scrum hadn't gone badly in the Ireland game, but I'd given away a few penalties, and the consensus seemed to be that my powers were on the wane. Criticism in the press is normally like water off a duck's back. But because this was a Lions year, I was extra sensitive.

● ● ●

We played France in Paris next. Nobody gave us a prayer. But our stubbornness prevailed, and we ground out the ugliest of victories. It was a win based on suffocating defence, pinpoint kicking, and a moment of magic from George North. His dad was so pleased he ran on to the pitch for a hug, and was intercepted by a phalanx of stewards. A lot of fuss was made about George ignoring his old man, but he genuinely didn't know it was him. It wasn't until our analyst, Rhys Long, showed him the photos on his laptop at the end of the game that we all realised. It didn't surprise me in the slightest. George's parents and mine had become good friends during the World Cup, and I'd got to know 'Papa' North well. It's fair to say he's one of life's eccentrics. A one-man pitch invasion is exactly the kind of behaviour I'd expect from him – and good on him! Some hectoring fans and po-faced journalists condemned his behaviour as irresponsible, but they need to chill out. It was a great advert for our sport and the kind of passion it stirs.

It was an enormous relief to have ended the losing run, but I was feeling pretty low on a personal level. The scrums, again, were poor. Yannick Forestier had the better of me during the first half, and his replacement, Vincent Debaty, came on to compound my misery. He's big, heavy and awkward to shift, and I couldn't exert any kind of influence. The pitch was awful, and I tried to persuade myself that that was the issue.

Deep down I knew it was a cop-out. I was starting to think that people had figured me out. I'd lost my mojo, and my confidence was seeping away. Had I been resting on my laurels, or was old Father Time just catching up with me? Was my seniority – so long an advantage in the murky world of scrummaging – becoming my weakness?

It happens to every sportsman at some point in their career. You hear about golfers remodelling their swing, cricketers changing their batting technique, or snooker players tweaking their cueing action. Sometimes you need a fresh approach to reinvigorate your game. Rugby changes and evolves, and you have to evolve with it. In the fortnight between the France and Italy games, I did a bit of soul searching, and a lot of training. I spent a good deal of time on my own working on the mechanics of my game, and doing one-on-one sessions with my old pal Paul James.

Robin McBryde and I sat down together like pupil and teacher, and started to strip things down. My strength had always been my ability to win 'the hit'. Now, for whatever reason, I was losing that element of dominance. My confidence was beginning to plummet. For so long, I had felt like I was in charge at the scrum. *I* was the Daddy, and the opposition would have to try and beat *me*. I would set out the rules of engagement and invite my opposite number to do his best. My ability to win the hit meant I always went in hard and fast. I'd noticed against France, part-icularly against Debaty, that I was being far more passive – standing still, and allowing him to come to me. That's the first battle lost. Props are like sharks in open water. They can smell doubt and fear, and don't need a second invitation to go in for the kill. My mentality against France had become one of survival rather than dominance. I was trying to dig in and get through it. Adam Jones, the predator, had become Adam Jones, the prey. I'd never, ever been afraid of an opposition prop. But if there was fear in my mind at this point, it was fear of whether I was still good enough.

Because of my size and weight, if I time the engagement well, and connect at the right angle, physics take over and I become an irresistible force. We looked at all the mechanics of my game in precise detail to determine what might have changed. Were my feet in the right position? Was I bending my knees low enough? Were my legs too straight? Was I pushing my chest through flat enough? Were my hips bent enough? Was my head low enough? Was my neck at the right angle?

People don't realise how technical scrummaging is. It's a lot more than just head down, arse up, ball out. The slightest change in angle or emphasis can change all the stresses and pressure points. The problem with developing a reputation, as I had, is that people want to take you down. You become more of a target than before. People spend more time analysing your technique, and figuring out ways to counteract it. It's equally flattering and infuriating. But that's rugby for you. It's a game of brute force and collisions. But it's also a game of strategy and guile. Chess with life-size pieces.

An easy way to try to counteract my 'hit and chase' is for the opposition to narrow the gap between the loose-head and the hooker's shoulders. The smaller the space for me to ram my head into, the harder it is for me to drive through and force a fault line. A lot of teams had cottoned on to this, and were being coached to bind more tightly in order to make me work harder.

● ● ●

Suffice to say, I felt under a good deal of pressure going into the Italy game. They're a side who pride themselves on their scrummaging ability, and I considered this a big test of my credentials. How would I respond when the chips were down?

Alun Wyn Jones was making his return from injury with a place on the bench, which meant I'd have Andrew Coombs and Ian Evans in the second row behind me to start with. This worried me. Coombsy had come in to solve the second row crisis we'd had at the start of the campaign and had played brilliantly. In fact, he'd probably been our best forward in those first two games. But he was a converted flanker, and not the biggest of blokes. That meant Ianto was shifted to the right-hand side of the scrum, directly behind me. With the greatest of respect, having Ianto behind you is like having a wasp up your arse. There's no weight there whatsoever. He's a big fella, but he's rangy and doesn't have the power of an Alun Wyn Jones. When Al's behind you and you win the hit, there's only one direction the opposition scrum is going in. He loves scrummaging as much as I do. Ianto would tell you he's got better things to do – like running around the field, and pretending to be a back.

All the hard work paid off, because we took Italy's scrum to pieces. Our dominance set the platform for victory, and we destroyed their pride. Things nearly kicked off on a few occasions, so incensed were they at being shoved around at will. I was driving hard and square at Lo Cicero, forcing him to shear off and manoeuvre around me. It's like driving a nail into a piece of wood. If you hammer it in hard enough, the wood will splinter into pieces. We did it every time, and it worked like a dream. Lo Cicero was getting more and more wound up, and I knew I had him on the ropes. Early in the second half, Paul James and Alun Wyn came on to replace Melon and Coombsy. Those substitutions made our scrum stronger still, and Italy lost the plot. Their venerable lord of the scrum, and captain for the day, Martin Castrogiovanni was sent to the sin bin. I don't remember any of the tries, or who scored. I just remember the scrums. My pride had been hurt badly against France, and it was fully restored during those eighty minutes. My mojo had returned, in the grandiose surrounds of the Stadio Olimpico. What better place to reassert your status as a rugby gladiator?

After the game, I needed five minutes to myself. The pressure had got to me more than I'd realised. I went for a lie-down on one of the physio beds, away from the mayhem of the dressing room. Mark 'Boycey' Jones – who was backs coach at the time, and a former teammate – approached me. I snapped at him: 'Butt, can you just fuck off and leave me alone!' I immediately felt terrible, because he hadn't deserved it in the slightest. But I needed that time alone. I'd internalised a lot of the pressure, and it felt as though I'd opened a valve with that performance. Those five minutes allowed it all to flow out. I lay there for a while with a towel over my head, only vaguely aware of the muffled celebrations coming from next door. If you're reading this, Boycey, I didn't mean it.

● ● ●

The win against Italy was our fourth successive away win in the championship – the first time it had been achieved since the late seventies. Those eight consecutive defeats were beginning to recede in the memory. Make it five in a row against Scotland, and we might even be talking about the title. Not many would have thought that possible at half-time against Ireland.

Craig Joubert was referee for the Scotland match, and he'd been good to us in the past. McBryde had some issues with the way Ryan Grant had been scrummaging, and he made sure that he filled Joubert in the night before the game. That happens all the time, by the way. A while ago, there was an outpouring of rage on social media when the England forwards coach Graham Rowntree was photographed having a coffee with Steve Walsh before a game. (The implication being that some form of bribery was taking place.) It's entirely standard practice. In the modern game, where interpretation of the scrum laws can easily mean the difference between winning and losing, you'd be negligent as a coach if you *didn't* bend the ref's ear. Let's call it the planting of a seed.

There were two issues ahead of the Scotland game. Ryan Grant was a purveyor of the 'pull-wheel', a tactic used by props who are under pressure, to make it look as though a wheeled scrum is the opposition's fault. We wanted to raise that, and to address accusations from the Scottish camp that I was getting away with murder at the hit. The mind games were well underway.

As you can imagine, the forward battle in that match had a little extra spice. Early on, we started an 'old school' rolling maul, drove them backwards at a rate of knots, and trampled all over their pack. My old Lions colleague Euan Murray found himself at the bottom of the pile of bodies, and I gave him an extra few digs with my studs for good measure. Nice to renew your acquaintance, Euan. One–nil. Moments later, we packed down for the first scrum, drove hard, and marched them towards their own line. Two–nil. Accusations of cheating in the build-up negate the need for a team talk. Scotland had done the job for us. That doesn't mean I don't cheat in the scrum, mind. Everyone does. I just don't like being called out in the press about it!

There was only one try in that game, and it came from an unexpected source. If you'd had him in a sweepstake for first try-scorer, you'd have been gutted. But Richard Hibbard delivered the goods. Like a human missile weighing 120kg, he battered his way to the line. As much as he's a flamboyant figure, with his flowing locks and full-body tattoos, he's actually a pretty modest sort of bloke. He declined to celebrate his try – which he may come to regret, because there might not be many others!

Despite the victory, we doubted we'd still be in the hunt for the championship. England had Italy at Twickenham the following day, and the consensus was that they would rack up the points and open up an unassailable lead at the top. Instead, they laboured to an 18–11 victory, putting an entirely different complexion on the championship.

If we beat England by eight points in Cardiff, the title was ours. It was an incredible turnaround in fortunes from the opening weekend.

●　●　●

We had assumed our only motivation in the game against England would be to stop them winning a Grand Slam. Now, we had a shot at glory ourselves.

I've never heard a coach publicly say they're going to go all out to win by the required margin. The stock line is always, 'Victory first! Worry about the points difference later.' But eight points is not thirty points. An eight-point margin, especially at home, was achievable. We were going for it from the off. The last thing any of us wanted was to deny England the Slam and end up coming second. Of all the games I'd played for Wales, the motivation had never been so strong. The obvious elements were there – England coming to Cardiff, on the hunt for a Grand Slam – but it was the other stuff that stoked the fires within me. There was my previous drop in form, and the run of defeats beforehand. I didn't need any pep talks that week. I was ready to rumble.

The pre-match warm-up was more intense than usual. There were fewer laughs and more scowling faces. The Millennium Stadium was shrouded in darkness, and the atmosphere was uneasy. Gethin Jenkins was captain, and he gave us a brief but focused talk. He's a surprisingly good speaker. There was no shouting. No Phil Bennett-esque call to arms. No borderline xenophobic rant. Just a strict laying down of the law. No backwards steps. No lapses in concentration. Win all the one-percenters. Win every scrum, win every line-out. Win every collision.

I looked at each and every one of my teammates, and the confidence began to surge. Justin Tipuric looked back at me. The openside flanker had been handed a rare start because of Dan Lydiate's injury. He'd been picked on the openside, and Sam Warburton had been switched to the blindside. This pleased me. I knew how good Tips was. Had he been any nationality but Welsh, he'd have had more than fifty test starts by now. I'd played with him for a while at the Ospreys, and his talent was jaw-dropping. He was one of the best footballers in the squad, and had handling skills that most backs could only dream of.

As we walked down the tunnel we could literally *feel* the noise. The stadium was rumbling. We all know that rugby is more than just a sport in Wales. The national side is supported with a religious fervour that borders on the fanatical. That day the Millennium Stadium felt like a sanctified cathedral packed with hysterical worshippers being whipped into a frenzy. The flames were scorching, and the noise was deafening.

The English anthem impressed me. It was loud and passionate – a far cry from the tuneless dirge it often is. They were bang up for this. And at that point, it wasn't obvious who the home side were. Their supporters had poured over the border in anticipation of a first Grand Slam for a decade, and they were backing their white-shirted heroes to deliver.

I knew that our anthem had to be special. This was our home, our crowd, our people. As we approached the chorus, the musical accompaniment faded out. An a capella version of 'Hen Wlad Fy Nhadau' by a male-voice choir sounds impressive. An a capella version by more than 70,000 people is enough to reduce you to tears. And in the case of Leigh Halfpenny, it did. It was a truly spine-tingling moment, and I knew then that we were going to win. You hear people say that glibly after the event, but that is genuinely what I thought. It's what I knew. I looked over at the English players and thought, 'You haven't got a chance, boys.'

The first half was tense and cagey, but we were winning the small battles, and our scrum was on top. Steve Walsh, the referee, had no patience with England, and was penalising them for everything. I have to admit, there were a number of 50/50 calls that day, and they all seemed to go against England. I wasn't complaining, but I felt we had luck on our side on more than a few occasions. So much in the scrum comes down to perception, and impressions can be formed early. On our first ball, we had a strong, steady platform, good forward momentum, and the ball came out cleanly. On their first ball, Melon did a good job on Dan Cole, forcing him to turn in. Both front rows popped up, but the perception in Walsh's mind was that England couldn't control the ball on their own put-in. An early seed of doubt had been planted.

Scoring opportunities were few and far between. A counter-attack saw George North set off on a trademark explosive run, but a despairing tap tackle from Mike Brown brought it to an end. Their most dangerous back, Manu Tuilagi, was being kept quiet by Jamie Roberts, who had him in his pocket for most of the night.

We were 9–3 ahead at half-time, thanks to the unerring accuracy of Leigh Halfpenny's boot. It was short of the eight-point margin required, but we had forty minutes left. The changing room was a calm place. 'Just keep building the lead,' was the message.

I'm not sure if there's such a thing as the perfect half of rugby, but that second half came pretty damn close. Another penalty after a long period of pressure took us to 12–3. And then the game – and the stadium – erupted. Ken Owens forced a turnover near halfway, and we launched a counter-attack. The ball moved swiftly through the hands to Alex

Cuthbert on the right wing. England's full-back, Mike Brown, appeared to have the angle on him as he sprinted across to cover. But Cuthbert swatted him away and accelerated off for another spectacular finish. The roar from the crowd was like nothing I'd ever heard: 17–3.

The second try was even better. Our back row was dominating at the tackle area, and Toby showed off his dancing feet to evade a number of flailing tackles before going to ground. The English didn't send anyone into the ruck, so Warby scooped up the ball and set off on a barnstorming run, covering forty metres before anyone laid a hand on him. It was Owen Farrell who eventually hauled him down, but Phillsy was there to recycle the ball. Biggar to Halfpenny. Halfpenny to Roberts. Roberts to Tips – who'd popped up in the midfield – and the rest was poetry in motion. Tips straightened up and made Mike Brown look like an amateur. He sold him the perfect dummy before cutting back inside, creating a two-on-one, and then waited for Brown to make a tackle. Once Brown committed himself, Cuthbert was free on the right and Tips delivered a perfectly weighted offload. A masterclass of three-quarter play. From a forward. He could probably have gone all the way, and would have been given the keys to the city. But the fact that he didn't tells you all you need to know about Tips. He's the most humble bloke I know.

The tries were both tremendous. It was fitting that such a game, with so much riding on it, should be crowned with scores that were as beautifully crafted as those. But for me, the defining moment was Dan Biggar's drop goal to put us 20–3 up. That was what killed the game off. Dan has had his critics for not conforming to the Welsh ideal of a jinking, darting fly-half. But his game management is unrivalled. The first try meant the door was closing on an England victory. Dan slammed it shut and bolted it.

When the final whistle blew, we'd recorded our biggest ever win over England: 30–3. There can be no better way for a Welshman to win a Six

Nations Championship. All the players who had been subbed off piled back on to the field to savour the victory, which in many ways was sweeter than the Grand Slam the year before. We were beside ourselves with joy. The English players were devastated, and amid the euphoria I felt a pang of sympathy for them. I made a point of jogging over to Dan Cole and Joe Marler, both of whom looked like their worlds had ended. I told them I thought they'd been unlucky in the scrums and that some of the 50/50 decisions that went against them were harsh. It was cold comfort for them, but I hope they appreciated the gesture.

England's forwards coach, Graham Rowntree aka 'Wig', was a little less cordial when I saw him at the post-match function. 'Adam Jones, you're a fucking prick,' was his opening gambit, as I approached him for a chinwag. Compliments don't get much better than that from Wig. We had a hug, and I told him I'd see him on the Lions tour. Hopefully.

Mike Cuddy had arranged a victory party for the Ospreys boys that night at a restaurant in the Pontcanna suburb of Cardiff. We were driven there in a fleet of Porsche jeeps that he'd laid on. As you can imagine, a fair amount of alcohol was imbibed in a fairly short period, and when we arrived at the Hilton for the official do, my head was a bit fuzzy. The rest of the evening passed in a drunken, celebratory haze. Rob Howley told us how proud he was of us all, and we toasted the title in a flood of beer and red wine. Apart from Warby, that is. Being the ultimate professional, he didn't touch a drop. I offered to buy him a drink back at the hotel bar, but he wasn't interested. He'd had his protein shake, and he was ready for some rest.

He was the obvious choice for all the press interviews the following morning. None of the rest of us surfaced until at least midday.

CHAPTER 19

Lions Rampant

YOU'VE heard the phrase 'I feel like a million dollars'. For a brief moment in April of 2013, I knew exactly what it meant. Actually, I felt like a million pounds, which is technically even better. I'd been selected for the British and Irish Lions tour to Australia, and was sat before the insurers. Two earnest men in suits told me I'd be entitled to a million-pound payout if I suffered a career-ending injury on tour. I was then interrogated as to my medical condition, and asked to reveal any ongoing niggles. I confessed that I had a minor knee injury – a meniscus tear, fairly common among props. They're not serious and usually clear up without too much fuss. As soon as I mentioned it, my value dropped to £800,000. I was worth nearly a quarter of a million less because of some poxy knee injury. It was at that point I banished any ideas about faking a serious injury and becoming a millionaire overnight. I think Phillsy gave the idea some considerable thought.

The squad contained a record-equalling number of Welshmen. There were 15 of us in the 37-man squad, along with 10 English, 9 Irish and 3

Scots. Warren Gatland was head coach, and openly admitted that our 30–3 victory over the English had had a profound effect on his final selection. A number of players who'd been outside bets had secured their places, while a number of 'shoe-ins' had fallen out of contention. The biggest casualty was England's captain, Chris Robshaw. He'd been the bookies' favourite to lead the squad, and if they'd beaten us, it would have been hard to overlook a Grand Slam-winning captain. But he failed to make the cut, and the honour of leading the Lions went to our skipper, Sam Warburton.

Justin Tipuric would have been in the selectors' minds anyway, but his performance against England meant he was absolutely nailed on. They probably booked his flight within minutes of Cuthy's second try being scored. And there's no doubt that Ianto's barnstorming performance saw him leap up the pecking order too, as did Richard Hibbard. His hit on Joe Marler alone probably got him on the plane. They're all good mates of mine, and I was as delighted for those three as I was for myself when I saw our names appear on the TV screen at the end of my bed in Merthyr Tydfil. I wasn't in training this time, so was nervously anticipating the announcement. I was having a cup of tea and a leisurely lie-in with Nicole. She was over the moon when my name was read out by the tour manager, Andy Irvine, and my huge noggin appeared in the plasma screen behind him. She gave me a big hug and a kiss.

My phone went into overdrive. Texts, tweets and calls from all my friends and family flooded in. It was a very proud moment. Amid the celebrations, I spared a thought for Dan Biggar – the only member of the Welsh starting XV from the England game who had failed to get selected. His opposite number that day, Owen Farrell, had squeezed in ahead of him. I'd have said he'd be the next cab off the rank, but that was of no consolation to him at the time.

I sent some texts of my own – to Ianto and Richard Hibbard, offering my congratulations. I know how much it would have meant to Hibs. He'd been a mainstay of the Ospreys side for the best part of four years, but his international career had been stop-start because of a series of badly timed injuries. And he'd got a lot of shit the previous year for giving away a penalty on the Australia tour that cost us one of the tests. He's a tough, hard bloke, but he's got a sensitive side, and that kind of thing can get him down. To be picked for the Lions would have meant the world to him. Validation that he's one of the best players in these isles. I also had a natural empathy with Hibs because, like me, he's had to bat away constant accusations that he's too fat and too unfit to play at the highest level. With some justification in his case, obviously.

The organisation that goes into a Lions tour is mind-boggling. We spent a day at Syon Park in West London meeting up with our fellow squad members and getting measured up and fitted for our tour ward-robes. We spent all day trying on chinos, formal shirts, polo shirts, blazers, dinner jackets, velvet jackets, brogues, and all kinds of other accoutrements. We even had bespoke compression socks made for each of us, to aid our recovery after training. Each of us had our foot scanned and measured so the sock would be a perfect fit. The science was explained to us in detail, but all I can remember was the claim that they squeezed your legs a bit tighter.

When we weren't being measured up, we were mingling with our new teammates. Welsh boys have a reputation for being a bit shy, so the fact we made up the majority didn't make for the most social of gatherings. Toby Faletau and Justin Tipuric helped reinforce that stereotype by retreating to the corner of the room and remaining mute for most of the day. It was left to the brash and gregarious Irishmen like Jamie Heaslip to hold court, and get the conversation flowing. In the afternoon, we were divided into groups to go and perform various activities with the sponsors. I was sent, incongruously, to do a Maximuscle photo shoot with Geoff Parling and Dylan Hartley from England. I think they might have mixed me up with Warby for that one – I spent the entire shoot holding my gut in.

Dylan Hartley may have a Welsh name, and a Kiwi accent, but he's as English as they come, and a convenient figure of hate for Welsh fans because of his chopsy attitude and tendency toward ill-discipline on the field. Which is a polite way of saying he gets sent off a lot. I take people as I find them, and that day I saw him as a polite, quiet bloke who wasn't remotely like the caricature imagined by Welsh fans and certain sections of the press. Unfortunately for him, history would repeat itself, and he'd never make it to Australia. He was sent off during the Premiership final a few weeks later for swearing at the referee, and banned from playing for eleven weeks.

We spent the first week of Lions training at Wales HQ in the Vale of Glamorgan. It was good to be at home and in familiar surroundings, but I think some members of the backroom staff were worried that we'd be giving away some of our secrets. Gatland relished it, though. In terms of facilities, we were streets ahead of the other home nations, and he knew it. There was definitely an element of showing off what we had, and Gats was rightly proud of it. Our indoor barn is the envy of the other nations, and our gym and our outdoor pitches are far better than those at Pennyhill Park in England or Carlton House in Ireland.

We had a few sessions against the Welsh squad, who were preparing for their tour to Japan. It made me laugh at the time because Robin McBryde told the press that they'd given the Lions forwards a run for their money. I remember thinking, 'Come on, Muckers! Half of us couldn't be arsed to do anything!' He was obviously bigging up his squad but it raised an eyebrow or two among the Lions boys, who'd essentially just volunteered to be sparring partners. One of my personal highlights from those early training sessions was hearing Andy Farrell call me Bomb. He'd been selected as defence coach ahead of Shaun Edwards, and was another Rugby League legend. I'd grown up watching him play for Wigan, and was as in awe of him as I had been of Shaun. During a defence session, he shouted, 'Good work, Bomb!' from the touchline. I felt an enormous surge of pride because the 'man of steel' knew my nickname. I'm still just a big kid at times.

Another highlight was out in Ireland when Gats offered to cancel a particularly gruelling fitness session if Owen Farrell landed a penalty kick from the halfway line. I think he felt more pressure then than he would have at a packed Twickenham. There was a whole bunch of grizzled Lions forwards staring at him, willing him to get it over. He went and nailed it, and was enveloped by us all in the mother of all pile-ons – probably a worse fate for him than the fitness session he'd just put an end to.

The back of the bus in rugby is a sacred place. You have to earn your right to sit there, and that usually comes with seniority. I wasn't allowed anywhere near the back when I started with Neath, and you'd have to deal with the glowering stare of Gareth Llewellyn if you ever did stray too far beyond your station. When the 2013 Lions squad boarded the bus to take us to Heathrow, I decided that I was at a point in my career where I'd earned the right, and boldly made my way to the back. I was joined by some of the more rambunctious Irish boys like Cian Healy and Rob Kearney, neither of whom lack for confidence. As we were settling in, Richard Hibbard came to join us, and took up the last remaining seat at the back.

'Oooohhh, Drico's not going to be happy!' exclaimed Kearney, taking the piss but meaning it deep down. It was Brian O'Driscoll's fourth Lions tour, and he was one of the world's best, if not the best player in the world. If anyone had a divine right to sit at the back of the bus, it was him. He should probably have had a throne to go with it.

Hibs played it cool, claiming that he sat at the back of the bus for Wales, and wasn't moving for anyone. If Brian wanted to sit at the back, he'd have to cwtch up with everyone else. Hibs was talking a good fight, and sat there stubbornly with his arms folded. Then Saint O'Driscoll appeared at the front of the bus, and began making his way down the aisle. It was like a scene from a film, happening in slow motion. If it had been a movie, the soundtrack would have been dark and foreboding at this point, signifying that some sort of conflict was imminent. Kearney was grinning, his eyes flicking back and forth between Drico and Hibs, relishing the situation. Hibs was feigning nonchalance, but his heart was racing. He'd put himself in this position, and was now facing a big test of his manhood. Drico was getting closer.

As he neared the back, ever the gentleman, he headed towards another seat. But Kearney, eager to follow this through, shouted, 'All right, Bri? Aren't you going to sit at the back?'

Hibs's arse fell out. He leapt to his feet nervously and started muttering, 'Sorry, Bri. Sorry, Bri. I didn't realise, sorry!' like he'd breached some kind of royal etiquette and was about to be hanged.

He scuttled like a nervous schoolboy into the seat in front of me, and Drico calmly moved into the vacant seat at the back. The natural order had been restored, and Hibs had made an almighty fool of himself.

● ● ●

Twelve hours after taking off at Heathrow, we landed at the hottest place I've ever been to. Hong Kong. It was insanely hot. Mind-numbingly hot. And for a sweater like me, dangerously hot. I was desperate to escape to the air-conditioned sanctuary of my hotel room, where I'd discovered my roommate would be Cian Healy, the Irish loose-head I'd propped against many times. I knew he was talkative and never shuts up on the pitch, but what I didn't know was quite how hyperactive he was off it. During that week he never slept for more than three hours in one night. He was a fast-talking, childlike bundle of raw energy, bouncing around the place like a bottle of pop. Many was the occasion when I'd be dropping off to sleep, and I'd be startled awake by his iPad powering up as he prepared to watch yet another of the hundreds of movies he'd downloaded for the trip. He was almost entirely nocturnal. I blame the coffee. He drinks gallons of the stuff. He probably had more coffee in his veins than blood on that trip. And for a man who prides himself on his fitness, he's not averse to the occasional fag. I'd often wake in the middle of the night to discover he'd sneaked out with Rala, the baggage man, and they were working their way through a pack of Marlboros on the balcony.

And Rala fed his caffeine habit too. At training sessions, he'd set up a trestle table with coffee urns on it, along with jugs of milk and sachets of sugar for the players to get an energy hit. Cian would drink at least half of it. There'd always be plates of biscuits there as well – which I'm sure weren't approved by the nutritionists – but the boys loved him for it. I don't know where he got all his stuff from, but I do know that you'll want for nothing when Rala's around. After every game, he'd have set up a table in the changing room with every little luxury you could possibly need. Shoe polish, shampoo, brushes, razors, shoe laces, spare cufflinks, pants, socks, hair gel, moisturiser, aftershave, deodorant. Literally anything you could want or need. I'd never seen anything like it before.

Cian Healy's coffee habit seemed even more extreme when you consider the conditions we were forced to train and play in. Humidity was hovering around the 98% mark, and the temperature rarely dropped below

35° Celsius, so dehydration was a real fear. We were all losing a lot of weight. Some of the bigger boys were losing as much as 6kg in an hour. Even the smaller boys were shedding three or four. There were industrial-sized fans lined up at the side of the pitch, but because the air temperature was so warm, they offered little in the way of relief. And despite the amount of fluids we were taking in, we felt constantly parched. There was little in the way of contact because that may well have killed us! If we were smashing into anything, it was pads and tackle bags. It struck me that things might be getting a bit dangerous when Hibs nearly passed out. He was preparing to throw the ball into a line-out towards the end of a session, with a soaking wet towel over his head, and sweat pouring off him. As he raised his arms, his eyes lolled back, and he started swaying from side to side. Wig was shouting at him to chuck it in, but he was off in his own world. Us front rowers weren't built to train in those conditions.

It caused us to question what on earth we were doing there. The Lions will tell you it was part of their mission to spread the gospel, but it felt more like a sop to the sponsors to me. The Barbarians had a local guy from Hong Kong in their squad, but they declined to pick him for the match. If the two organisations were serious about spreading the gospel, they should have selected him. I certainly didn't feel like I was doing it for the love of the game.

My old pals Paul James, Duncan Jones and James Hook were in the Barbarians squad, and the day before the game, we met up for a coffee. Contrary to what their coach, Dai Young, had been saying in the press, they'd been on the piss for about ten days straight, and they were looking rough. Excessive drinking in that climate was a recipe for disaster, and I knew then they wouldn't be in a position to put up much of a fight come match day. Dai had underestimated the power of social media. While he was making his claims to the press that they'd imposed an alcohol ban, photos were popping up all over Twitter of the boys lounging on yachts, surrounded by empty bottles and glasses.

Despite our long acquaintance, I'd never played against Assey at a professional level before, so it was a unique opportunity. I'd witnessed at first hand how he'd intimidated his opponents over the years, and wondered if he would extend the same treatment to me. For so long, he'd been one of my bodyguards on the pitch. Now he was my opposite number. As it happened, he was too knackered to impose himself. It was insanely hot out there. Easily the most draining conditions I've played in. It felt like running around in a sauna. My head was pounding, my mouth was constantly dry, and the sweat was cascading off me. Everything felt slippery and soggy. The scrums were the worst. You'd get up off the floor, and your legs would be gone. Trembling and turned to jelly. The slightest thing seemed to use untold amounts of energy. Defending a driving maul for about five seconds would leave you panting and gasping for air. I lasted for fifty-five minutes, and they felt like the longest fifty-five minutes of my career.

But I could comfort myself with the fact that, if I felt bad, the Barbarians felt a whole lot worse. They were clearly struggling. Drinking is a big part of the Baa-Baas tradition. But ordinarily, the presence of a core of world-class players allows them to play above themselves – to play through their hangovers. That wasn't the case in Hong Kong. After twenty minutes, it was obvious they were spent, and we taught them a lesson, scoring eight tries in a 59–8 rout. Seven of them were scored by Welshmen, and when Hooky came on for the Baa-Baas, he became only the second player in the professional era to play for and against the Lions. I love my trivia. I'll be saving those nuggets up for my next appearance on *Question of Sport*. What was also pleasing for me was that our scrum dominated – despite the jelly legs – and I got a couple of penalties out of Assey.

He hated that. That aside, I'm not sure we learned anything from the game. It was an exotic pit stop en route to the real business in Australia, but I did take comfort from the fact I'd started the first game on tour, as I'd done in 2009. I always remember Geech's words about how being in the first Lions team on tour was special, and it had now happened to me twice.

● ● ●

I wasn't selected for the second match against Western Force in Perth, so I donned my number ones for the game. I was still rooming with Cian Healy, and he pointed out that I was missing a button on my blazer. I shrugged that I didn't really care, and he chastised me for being sloppy. He insisted I hand it to him, and with the skill and dexterity of a seamstress he sewed me on a new one. Talk about incongruous. This massive meathead of a bloke with enormous fat fingers, delicately sewing on a new button with the precision of a concert pianist. He really was full of surprises. Unfortunately, that turned out to be one of his last acts on tour, because he got injured during the match, and had to fly home soon afterwards. It was a big loss.

There was a lot of fuss in the press about Western Force selecting a weak side. Robbie Deans, the Wallabies coach, had apparently insisted that internationals were rested. This, according to many scribes covering the tour, undermined not just the game but the very concept of the Lions. It also denied players a unique opportunity to play their part in a chapter of rugby history. The Lions only visit Australia once every twelve years, making it, in all reality, a once-in-a-lifetime opportunity. I totally agreed with the pundits. If the shoe had been on the other foot, I'd have been desperate to play. But that's what professionalism does for you.

Lions tours are big business these days, and winning the test series is the primary objective. The tour games are a mere sideshow, as far as the head coach is concerned. Their second-string team barely put up a fight, and we won 69–17.

The Queensland Reds had won the Super XV title in 2011 and were dangerous opponents, coached by Ewen McKenzie – the favourite to succeed Robbie Deans as Australia coach. They also had a certain Quade Cooper in their ranks – a mercurial fly-half whose unpredictable style thrilled the loyal crowds at Suncorp Stadium. Depending on who you believed, he was either a rampant, un-coachable egotist or a free-spirited maverick whose genius could win you games. Robbie Deans clearly subscribed to the former view, as he'd left him out of the Wallabies squad – a decision that had left Reds fans up in arms. This game was being seen as Quade's big chance to impress, and to force Deans to change his mind.

I was glad they didn't pick him for the Wallabies, because I'd witnessed at first hand what he was capable of. He's been the scourge of Wales on many an occasion, and when he's on song he's virtually unplayable. From my experience, he was far more likely to turn on the razzle-dazzle and win a game than he was to mess things up and lose one. Cooper aside, the Reds were shorn of their superstars, just as Western Force had been. There was no James Horwill, no James Slipper, no Rob Simmons, and no Will Genia, so we didn't consider them the banana skin they might have been. Perhaps we should have. They were outstanding, and for long periods they looked as though they might pull off an upset. They went ahead early through a stunning try from their winger, Luke Morahan, and their scrum was giving ours plenty to think about. The breakdown was ultra competitive too. Warby was playing his first game on tour, and the young, rampaging Beau Robinson was keeping him honest.

Dan Cole and I were subbed on after an hour, to try to shore up the creaking scrum, and we clung on to victory in front of their raucous home crowd. After the first two romps, this had been a real test of resolve. A defeat at this stage would have been an enormous setback. It was a bruising encounter as well, and there were a few casualties – most notably Tommy Bowe, who appeared to have broken his hand. Everyone thought he'd be following Cian Healy back to Ireland. But as we were to discover, the medical team could work miracles when they needed to.

Strangely, their loose-head prop, Albert Anae, came looking for Coley and I afterwards to ask if he could have a photo with us. I was bleeding and sweating, and he'd spent the last twenty minutes trying to shove my head up my arse, but here he was, all sweet and seemingly starstruck, asking for a photo. The mystique of the Lions, eh?

Prior to that Reds game, we'd been joined on tour by two new loose-heads following the departure of Cian Healy and Gethin Jenkins. Alex Corbisiero and Ryan Grant were the new boys, and were subjected to the ritual humiliation of singing a song on the team bus. Ryan mumbled his way through some saccharine pop song which no one else recognised, before Corbs strode confidently forwards to accept the mic. Sean O'Brien announced him with a series of embarrassing facts about his New York roots, and the fact he'd had a pizza named after him because of his wheat intolerance. Corbs was on the back foot, but what followed was the most eloquent and poetic putdown I've ever heard. He launched into an improvised rap in which he tore Seany to pieces. It was all off the cuff and spontaneous, and Seany was lost for words. I think he was 'free-styling', to use the rapping vernacular. We knew Corbs was a bright boy, but we all learned a lesson there – don't take him on in a battle of wits, because there'll be only one winner.

He became a good mate on tour, which pleased me because, if I'd had my way, he wouldn't have been there. Melon and Cian's injuries amounted to a prop crisis. With due respect to Mako Vunipola, those two were the first- and second-choice loose-heads, and the coaches summoned me to a selection meeting to ask for my advice on potential replacements. Assey should come, I blurted a little overenthusiastically. They immediately saw through my bias. My second choice was Andrew Sheridan – my old roomie from the 2009 tour, and a man I knew the Aussies were terrified of. He'd been keeping Melon out of the Toulon side, but Gats argued that he wouldn't last two minutes. He said he'd been in France too long, and was out of shape. So Corbs and Grant got the calls. And in Corbs's case, in particular, things all worked out rather well.

● ● ●

The fourth game was against a Combined Country XV in Newcastle, north of Sydney. Rugby League country. On paper, it was the easiest game. More than two-thirds of the side was semi-professional. There were carpenters, plumbers and electricians among their ranks, and for most of them this game represented the pinnacle of their rugby careers. They showed an admirable degree of commitment, but we barely had to shift out of the low gears to cruise to a 64–0 win.

I wasn't involved, so my highlight of the trip to Newcastle was returning from a weights session on the team bus and spying Matt Stevens tucking into a massive piece of cake in a cafe. Paul Stridgeon insisted the driver stop outside the cafe, and beeped the horn continuously until Matt had finished. He thought it was the funniest thing in the world. I'm not sure the other customers agreed with him. Matt didn't care in the slightest. He just carried on eating and grinning away to himself.

He was just happy to be on tour. He knew his chances of making the test side were slim, so he embraced the role of head of entertainment. He's a tidy guitar player, and a surprisingly good singer, so the journey between Newcastle and Sydney was an excuse for him to get out the guitar. He dished out lyric sheets to all the boys, and insisted we all join in. I was happy to add some fairly muted harmonies from the back of the bus, but some were singled out for solo performances. Owen Farrell bellowed out a spirited, if largely tuneless rendition of 'Rock 'n' Roll Star' by Oasis. He was a little put out that no one joined in.

Sydney is quite simply a stunning city. Visually it's beyond compare. The harbour is breathtakingly beautiful, and a bunch of us got to see it from a unique perspective when HSBC took us out on a yacht. It wasn't quite the casual boat trip I was expecting, mind. Upon boarding we were told we were part of the crew, and would need to muck in. Myself, Mako Vunipola, Tom Youngs, Dan Lydiate and Rob Kearney were given our roles. Being a working-class boy from the Swansea Valley, it's fair to say I hadn't had much experience of sailing before, and felt a little out of my depth. I had no idea how knackering it was – just winching the sail up puts a hell of a strain on the old arms. It was a good laugh, but the experience was eclipsed by what happened on the way back to the hotel.

We were wandering through Circular Quay, when I bumped into the former Everton midfielder and Australian international, Tim Cahill. I was beside myself with excitement, and fear I may have embarrassed myself a little bit. (I was a huge Everton fan, growing up. At the time, there were no Welsh teams playing in the top flight, but Everton had a Welsh captain in Kevin Ratcliffe, so I picked them as my team. The fact they were going through a pretty successful period probably influenced my decision too.) Before I knew it, I'd gripped him in an awkward bear hug, and started gushing about how much I admired him. Had I not been wearing official Lions clobber, he'd probably have shouted for the nearest policeman. The sports fan within me is never far from the surface, and encounters like this turn me into a giddy schoolchild. It's ironic, because I never really under-stand why someone would want my autograph, but I'm like a starstruck fool in the presence of international footballers. I get excited when I see guys like Joe Allen, Ben Davies, Aaron Ramsey, and I know them! I've met rugby superstars like Jonah Lomu and David Campese, and been quite relaxed in their presence, but footballers send me weak at the knees. I'd probably pass out if I ever met David Beckham. I've got a massive man-crush on him.

Back at the hotel, a few hours later, my phone buzzed. It was a direct message from Tim Cahill via Twitter. He'd started following me. I was absolutely landed! He'd obviously Googled me to reassure himself I wasn't a demented stalker. And now he was suggesting we meet up and swap jerseys. He may have Samoan heritage, but he's a little on the slight side. I can't imagine he's ever actually worn my shirt, and I'll never be able to get into his, but it remains one of my most prized possessions.

Only one other celebrity encounter comes close, and that was when I met Tom Jones in Vegas, during a holiday after the 2009 Lions tour. Nic and I had done a road trip through California, which ended with four days in Vegas where she'd bought me tickets to see Tom Jones at the MGM Grand. On our way to the gig, I had a phone call from my agent who knew Tom Jones's PA. He said he'd arranged for us to meet backstage once the concert had finished. The instructions were to report to a black door by the side of the stage and knock twice. A burly security guard opened the door and looked us up and down.

'All right, butt?' I said nervously. 'I'm Adam Jones.'

'Ah, come on in, Adam. Sir Tom's expecting you.'

We strolled into the empty green room, where we were surrounded by free booze. We made ourselves comfortable, and sank a quick beer to calm the nerves. Ten minutes later, the big man appeared. I say big man, but he was actually a lot smaller than I'd imagined him to be. It was all very formal. He asked if we'd enjoyed the show, and what we were doing out there. I told him I played rugby, but modesty prevented me from revealing I played for Wales. He didn't have the faintest idea who I was. I wish he had, but I'd have felt like a right knob if I'd told him I'd just returned from a Lions tour. He seemed to have a vague interest in rugby, and told me he used to play when he was growing up in Pontypridd. He also mentioned that he'd sung 'Delilah' at Wembley before the famous Wales v England game in 1999 – as though I didn't already know.

● ● ●

I was selected for the game against the New South Wales Waratahs in Sydney. As with the game against the Sharks on the 2009 Lions tour, I considered this a dress rehearsal for the first test. It was my first start since the Barbarians game. I probably didn't prepare for it in the best way possible – with a night out in Kings Cross with some old pals from Abercrave. We laid off the booze, but my meal choice of a massive rack of ribs followed by a steak didn't fit strictly within the Lions nutritional guidelines. That's what I like about the Lions, though. There's no mollycoddling. They trust you to do the right thing, and treat you like adults. A far cry from Steve Hansen's Wales regime in which you got dropped if you dared leave the hotel without permission. That fate once befell Dafydd James when he sneaked home for a night with his family. He got back to the Vale at the crack of dawn, but Steve caught him in the act, feeling his car bonnet to see if it was still warm. Busted, Daf. Never try to outsmart an ex-copper.

The protein overload the night before didn't affect my performance. Things went well for me personally, apart from the moment I took a swing at someone who was tugging my jersey. It was out of character for me to lash out, and I got a firm ticking-off from the coaches. Do that in a test match and make contact, and you'd be off. Graham Rowntree was to blame, though. He'd delivered a rabble-rousing speech before kick-off that ended with the line, 'We're not here to be nice tourists. Let's go into their house, and smash it up.' I was just following orders.

The front row was taken off en masse after sixty minutes, which I took as another clue that I was in line to start the first test. The damage was done by then – the Waratahs had been comprehensively beaten. Leigh Halfpenny underlined his status as the outstanding full-back on tour. By the end of this game, he'd landed 22 of his 23 shots on goal. That's one hell of a strike rate. Jonathan Davies also turned in a really classy performance. He scored one try, and had a hand in virtually every other as we romped to an impressive 47–17 victory over a team that would win the Super XV title the following year.

I was sat next to Brian O'Driscoll on the bus ride back, and he was waxing lyrical about Jonathan Davies. He was very generous in his praise, which is Drico's way. Little did he know that his battle with Foxy for the 13 shirt would come to be one of the defining stories of the tour. Once he'd finished praising Foxy's sublime performance, he got out his laptop to play me 'Blurred Lines' by Robin Thicke. It was riding high in the charts at the time, and had come in for a bit of stick for its apparent sexism, but Drico was fascinated by the songwriting process. He played it over and over again on the journey back, repeatedly asking me, 'How do they do this, Bomb? I don't get it. How do you even begin to write a song like this? Where do you get the imagination to come up with this sort of stuff?' I was in no position to shed any light.

• • •

Nobody has had as many last hurrahs as Shane Williams. He had a big farewell at the Liberty Stadium, when he scored a try in the final play of his final game in an Ospreys shirt. He had an even bigger farewell at the Millennium Stadium, when he scored a try in the final play of his final game in a Wales shirt. And then, just when you thought you'd seen the last of him, he pops up on the Lions tour, and waltzes straight into the team.

We were down to the bare bones in the backs. George North, Jamie Roberts and Tommy Bowe were all crocked, and I knew we'd sent for reinforcements in the form of Brad Barritt, Billy Twelvetrees and Christian Wade. But there was to be another, according to our analyst, Rhys Long. He challenged me to guess who. I must have named every winger playing professional rugby in the British Isles. I even started to speculate about Aussie wingers who might be claiming British or Irish parentage. I never would have guessed it. Shane? Seriously? Another finale to his glittering career? He was to become the oldest back ever to wear a Lions jersey at the grand old age of thirty-six.

But there was to be no fairly-tale ending for him this time. He was thrust into a patched-up team to face the Brumbies in Canberra, and we suffered our first defeat of the tour. The build-up had been poor. Canberra is one of the least inspiring cities to visit, and the Australian Institute of Sport, where we trained, was like a relic from the past. It was full of primitive weights machines and medieval-looking equipment, which was a far cry from what we'd become used to with Wales. There was a harness above the swimming pool that ran lengthways along an overhead rail. It was meant to make you 'over-swim' but it nearly made me drown.

I'm not sure whether it was the experimental nature of the side, or the lethargy in the build-up, but we were poor against the Brumbies. I didn't play, but there appeared to be a lack of urgency from the sidelines, and our core skills let us down. Poor old Rory Best had one of those nights where hardly any of his line-out throws seemed to find the target, and we were turned over with alarming ease at the contact area. It was an ill omen ahead of the first test, because we knew how good the Wallabies were on the floor. It was the first time the Lions had lost a provincial match since 1997, and it didn't feel good.

Geoff Parling seized the initiative in the changing room, and implored the boys to stay positive. He gave a very good, measured speech about how positive the culture had been so far, and how we were more than capable of dealing with this setback. I was impressed by his attitude, and the clarity of his message. The same couldn't be said for Ianto, who'd made way for Parling during the second half. 'Look at him piping up,' he said to me, a little too loudly. 'I bet this little speech of his gets him a place on the bloody bench on Saturday.' I really liked Geoff Parling, and knew he was being genuine. But Ianto being Ianto convinced himself he was putting on a performance to impress the coaches. I think that's what people mean when they refer to Welsh insularity. Instead of piping up himself, Ianto was content to hide in the shadows and sulk. I love him to bits, but the cynical old goat was wrong on that occasion.

I felt sorry for Ianto on that tour. I thought he was offering more than Richie Gray and Geoff Parling in the build-up to the tests, but he seemed to be slipping down the pecking order. And starting in a losing cause against the Brumbies didn't help his case. One thing Ianto is, he's a really good rugby player. One thing he's not, is keen. When he's warming up, you'd swear he's about seventy. When it comes to the sprints, he's never going to win – even if he was actually the fastest. He's a great line-out forward, but he doesn't study them like an Alun Wyn or a Paul O'Connell.

He's an athlete, but not a scholar. His apparent lack of enthusiasm on tour may have been what cost him a test place.

It's ironic, because away from the training paddock, he's one of the biggest characters in the squad. He has this languid way of speaking that belies a sharp wit, and it took some of the other boys a while to get used to him. Once they'd figured him out, they loved him. He made it his personal mission to torture Paul O'Connell every day. He'd sit next to him on the bus and bombard him with inane questions. Who's your favourite player, Paulie? Who's the best player you've played against, Paulie? Tell me three things about yourself, Paulie. Who's your favourite singer, Paulie? A less patient man would have crumbled, but Paulie loved him.

Ianto's prediction was right – Geoff Parling was rewarded with a place on the bench for the first test. But in more important news from my point of view, I was starting in the front row alongside Tom Youngs and Alex Corbisiero. Tom Youngs had been a centre a few years earlier, but you'd never have guessed. He was the perfect build for a hooker – as wide as he is tall, and a real pocket dynamo. He'd picked up a lot of tips from Mefin Davies, who'd had a spell at Leicester, so we'd both learned from the West Walian scrum guru. Even though the indications had been promising, you can never take anything for granted on a Lions tour, particularly when Gats – who's been known to throw a curveball or two – is in charge. To be fair to Dan Cole, he came over straight away to shake my hand, as I'd done with Vicks four years ago. I was disappointed for Hibs, who had to settle for a place on the bench, but I thought our pack looked strong, and I fancied our chances against the Wallabies eight. Paul O'Connell and Alun Wyn were in the second row, and Warby, Crofty and Heaslip were in the back row.

Wig clearly thought Corbs was a better technical scrummager than Mako, and told him to get stuck into their tight-head, Ben Alexander.

We spent a lot of time on the scrum in those few days before the test because it was an area we knew we could target them. Training had been intense throughout the tour, but there was a real edge to things that week. The looming presence of a test match galvanises the mind, and sharpens the senses. And the atmosphere in Brisbane was reaching fever pitch. Since our arrival on Australian shores, the travelling support had been gradually swelling in size, and now it was huge. Red-shirted fans were swarming everywhere like some kind of invading tribe.

'Mr Lions' Ian McGeechan was brought in for the jersey presentation the night before, and gave us one of his trademark, spine-tingling speeches. I celebrated my selection by going out for a coffee with Alun Wyn and our wives, who'd now arrived on tour. Matt Stevens came along too, and spent most of the time hanging out with Isla who seemed to love him. Halfway through my latte, Nicole received a phone call and passed it over to me. It was my old mate Boris again. Boris Johnson. Johnno. The John-meister. It was becoming a standard part of the big-game ritual. An eve-of-the-match pep talk from the Mayor of London.

Everyone else then retired to the hotel, but Hibs and I fancied a trip to the cinema, and headed out to watch *Fast and Furious 6*. Hibs's choice. It was around eleven o'clock when we emerged on to the street, and found it thronged with pissed-up Lions fans. Being the least inconspicuous members of the squad, with our long hair and sizeable physiques, we were predictably mobbed. A hundred-odd selfies later, we decided the only way we could escape was to literally run away. So that's what we did. With midnight approaching, we found ourselves legging it down Queen Street being chased by groupies like two fat members of the Beatles.

● ● ●

Running out at the Suncorp Stadium – one of the world's great rugby stadiums – in front of tens of thousands of fans to start for the Lions was a phenomenal experience. This was it. My chance to right the wrongs of four years ago in South Africa. Much had been made in the press about our apparent loss of physicality in the backline following the withdrawal of Jamie Roberts, but Foxy put that concern to bed within the first minute by knocking Christian Leali'ifano out. He ran straight and hard at him, and Leali'ifano got his head in the wrong position trying to make the tackle. No one likes to see a head injury, but it set the tone for what was to be a physical encounter. With one crunching hit, he'd altered the balance of the entire Wallaby backline. We reinforced our superior strength at the first scrum by squeezing them hard, and driving them back ten metres.

It was the Wallabies who took the initiative, though, sniffing an opportunity from nothing as they so often do. We were attacking in their 22, going through the phases with the referee playing advantage. But the ball slipped carelessly out of the back of a ruck, and they pounced for the turnover. Will Genia – never one to take the conservative option – decided to run the ball out of his own 22. His weaving run kept our scramble defence guessing, and neither Phillsy nor North were able to commit to the tackle. Before we knew it, he was up to our 22 with support runners inside and outside him. He opted for the outside and found Israel Folau, who cantered over for a try on his debut. It was an outstanding piece of counter-attacking rugby, and they were 7–0 to the good.

If the fans thought that was impressive, George North's response was off the scale. Fielding a high ball deep in our half, he set off on a mesmerising run, weaving his way through the flailing tackles of a disorganised Aussie defence. It had it all. Vision, composure, a subtle sidestep, scorching pace, and even a cheeky finger-wagging taunt to Will Genia as he crossed the line.

Folau was clearly thinking, 'Anything you can do, I can do better,' because he then produced a scintillating piece of individual skill to finish off his second try. Again, it was Genia with the scoring pass, but Folau was left with an awful lot to do. He hypnotised the three Lions defenders in front of him. Johnny Sexton was frozen to the spot as Folau feinted one way, went the other, and turned on the afterburners to score.

They were three of the best tries you're ever likely to see. And they all happened within half an hour of each other.

During the second half, Alex Cuthbert decided he wanted a piece of the action. By this point, the Wallabies had had three players stretchered off, and had been forced to move their openside flanker, Michael Hooper, into the midfield. It was an obvious place for us to target, and Cuthbert is one of the deadliest finishers in international rugby. When the gap opened up, he didn't need a second invitation. It was another absolute beauty of a try. A real treat for the spectators. Australia 12 Lions 20. We had a bit of breathing space.

The tries were all memorable, and each of them has been burned into my consciousness, but one of my favourite moments was when Alun Wyn was subbed off in the second half. He was so outraged by the decision that he sprinted full-pelt from one touchline to the other to prove he still had plenty left in the tank. That is so typically Alun Wyn, and it underlined the level of desire that goes into wearing that Lions shirt. I'd already been subbed off, and as I went to shake his hand I could see the anger in his eyes. 'What the fuck have they taken me off for!? I'm fucking fresh, look at me!' Brilliant. It proved to be a questionable substitution, because we ended up losing an attacking scrum-five on our own ball moments later. Had we scored from that, we'd have buried the game.

We also suffered from a bit of naivety, particularly as the scrum battle evolved. We weren't getting quite as much change out of Messrs Robinson, Moore and Alexander as we'd hoped, but we continued to go for the 'double-shove'. A double-shove, to the layman, is when the Number 8 keeps the ball at his feet, and the pack attempts to march the opposition pack backwards to force a penalty. It's a very Northern Hemisphere tactic. Southern Hemisphere sides, who are more attack-minded, see the scrum more as a means to restart play. Get the ball in. Get it out. Play. We're more primal about our attitude to the scrum, and if we can use it to milk penalties, we will. We did it with the Ospreys for years. But you have to know when these things are working, and when they aren't. If you mistime a double-shove, or execute it badly, it can lead to a collapsed scrum, for which you can get penalised. That's exactly what happened during the last play of the game when we were clinging on to a slender two-point lead. We should have secured clean ball from the scrum, and cleared our lines. Instead, we opted for the double-shove, screwed it up, and gave Kurtley Beale a chance to win the match.

You probably all know what happened next. Beale lined up the kick. The stadium fell silent. The Lions fans turned away in unison. The tension on the bench was unbearable. For want of a better expression, my arse was gone. To have lost that game would have been a real blow to the solar plexus. A blow from which we mightn't have recovered. Watching him line up that kick, I felt physically sick. I didn't see him slip, but I remember following the flight of the ball, and noticing immediately how wobbly and uncertain it looked. When it fell short, we all felt a massive, massive rush of relief. The Wallabies flocked around Beale to comfort him, because he looked a broken man, but I just thought, 'Unlucky, butt. See you next week.' Justice had been done, as far as I was concerned. We were the better side, and had deserved to win. I celebrated with a McDonald's at two o'clock in the morning.

Brian O'Driscoll was on his fourth Lions tour, and had yet to win one. So when I suggested we all buy ourselves a nice Cuban cigar ahead of what we hoped would be a celebratory night next Saturday, he vetoed it. 'Come on now, Bomb. We can't count our chickens. Let's not tempt fate.' And he was right. I wasn't even sure I'd done enough to retain my place. Things had gone reasonably well for me, but you never knew with Gats. And as much as I loved Wig, he was a Leicester boy, and my main rival for the shirt was also a Leicester boy.

● ● ●

The pressure was on that week. We had a chance to put the series to bed; to claim a first Lions series win for sixteen years. But as with Grand Slams, there was no talk of that to the media. It was taboo.

The injuries were continuing to mount. We lost Corbs that week, and Paul O'Connell had been ruled out of the rest of the tour. That was tough on him. He was an absolute talisman, and a truly inspirational bloke. He wasn't afraid to show his emotions, but he rarely showed any vulnerability. I remember asking him how he was feeling during the build-up to that second test, and he just replied, 'Not good, Bomb.' The big man started to well up. I leaned in to give him a hug, because I could see how much he was hurting, but he didn't meet me halfway. A bit awkward. I tried to turn it into a more manly arm-around-the-shoulder type of affair, but I could tell he was thinking, 'All right, Bomb, chill out.'

The second test was a very different game. Our scrum was far less dominant. Mako Vunipola struggled, and found himself on the wrong end of the referee's whistle. The Wallabies had done their homework and were back to their 'clever' best. They had figured that Mako wasn't a world-class scrummager, and were ganging up on him. Their tight-head and hooker were combining to give him a hard time, which meant I wasn't getting much attention on the right-hand side. You're only as good as your weakest link, and I was concerned that I was being judged on what was a meek scrummaging performance. It descended into a lottery with penalties seemingly being awarded at random. Eventually, Coley and Hibs came on to replace Youngy and me, and the scrum improved vastly. I put it down to Coley being fresh, but the demons started to creep into my mind. The game was slipping away from us, and it was looking as though the series would go to a decider in Sydney.

North and Folau may not have scored any tries like they did in the first test, but they still combined to provide the moment of the match. The two titans were about to collide. George was carrying the ball at pace; Folau was steeling himself for the tackle. But it was George who ended up making the tackle. Instead of trying to sidestep, he scooped Folau up in a fireman's lift and continued his forward charge, with his hapless opponent wriggling on his shoulders. Israel Folau is not a small man. It was a jaw-dropping display of strength and power, and the crowd absolutely loved it.

That aside, there were few highlights for us. We played shit, if we're honest. The Aussies, in contrast, played their best rugby for some time, and should have won by more than a point. The try from Adam Ashley-Cooper five minutes from time proved the difference, but they left a lot more points out there on the park. For the second week running, the result hinged on a last-minute kick – this time awarded to us. Leigh Halfpenny's was much further out than Beale's and he just didn't have the distance. It was a horribly tight and nervy game to have played in, and their narrow victory meant our hope of a series victory was hanging delicately in the balance.

● ● ●

The Aussie media went into hyperbolic overdrive after the Lions' defeat in the second test. They'd been measured up until then, even going so far as to install us as favourites. But the Wallabies' victory flicked a switch in their minds. If you believed the papers, momentum had swung irresistibly in their favour, and the Lions were on an inexorable downward slide. Sam Warburton had torn his hamstring off the bone in the second half, so we had lost our captain as well as our mojo. With his predecessor, Paul O'Connell, also out, the experience was fast draining out of our side.

The day after the test, Adam Beard organised an open ocean recovery session in the sea at St Kilda Beach. Within minutes of us entering the water, a gaggle of bikini-clad girls ran in and started splashing around. My suspicions were immediately aroused, as the assembled press photographers began eagerly snapping photos of the Lions supposedly flirting with them. We thought it was a bit of classic Australian subterfuge – how to unsettle the Lions during the week of the crucial third test. The married boys nervously kept their distance, fearing an unholy backlash from their spouses. Tommy Bowe wasn't so savvy, and was his usual loquacious self with the ladies. His missus wasn't happy, let me tell you. Alun Wyn, never the charmer, ignored them all. It turned out that they were the Victoria Maidens American Football team, and that they actually *play* in bikinis. And far from being there in a mischievous capacity, they'd turned up at the request of Adam Beard who'd invited them down as part of his ceaseless quest to glean knowledge from other sports. What he thought we'd learn from a bikini-clad female American Football team while frolicking in the sea, I have absolutely no idea. Thankfully, I'd stayed inside in the salt pools with Geoff Parling, so we didn't have to suffer the same awkward conversations with our wives that many of the other boys did.

The management took a calculated decision to take it easy in the week between the second and third tests. We decamped to Noosa on the sunshine coast for a few days of rest and recuperation. Within an hour of our arrival, we'd met in the hotel bar where the drinking games began in earnest before continuing late into the night. It was a welcome blowout after the intensity of the tour, and did us the power of good. After a good old-fashioned swill on the Sunday, we were given the Monday off. Some of the boys went surfing, others went kayaking or walking. I just hung out on the beach, soaking up the rays and swimming in the sea. I considered it a management masterstroke – an opportunity to freshen ourselves up mentally and recalibrate ahead of the final hurdle.

Not everyone saw it that way. A number of journalists thought it was a terrible idea, and one that would end in catastrophe. None other than Clive Woodward spoke out publicly, decrying the side trip as a disaster, claiming it would blunt our focus ahead of the biggest game of our lives. A little rich, considering the Lions tour he presided over in 2005 was one of the least successful in history. The idea that it was some kind of jolly was way wide of the mark. There were some boys who knew they were out of the running for a test place, who could relax and drink a bit more, but no one went 'off tour'. They all fronted up to training on the Tuesday, and nobody took a backward step.

If the trip itself caused a few ripples among the press, what followed amounted to a tsunami. Years later, the aftershocks are still being felt over what some regarded as the most controversial team selection of all time. Headline one: Brian O'Driscoll has been dropped from the starting fifteen. Headline two: Brian O'Driscoll isn't even in the match-day squad. Headline three: there are ten Welshmen in the starting fifteen. *Ten!* It was a Lions record, and sent the English and Irish scribes into an almighty tailspin. Outrage doesn't even come close. Some of the Irish journos and pundits were cataclysmic with rage. Snubbing Brian O'Driscoll in such a manner was akin to desecrating a saint. How dare Warren Gatland treat him with such disdain! Brian O'Driscoll is undroppable, untouchable, who on God's green earth do you think you are?

The Welsh were understandably more measured and, with hindsight, I challenge anybody to question the legitimacy of each and every one of those selections. Anyone who knows Warren Gatland knows that Jamie Roberts is his first name on the Welsh team sheet. He's absolutely central to Warren's game plan. 'Warrenball', if that's what you want to call it. Realistically, he was always going to be recalled when he returned to fitness. That meant the 13 jersey was a straight choice between Foxy and Drico. Foxy had arguably been the player of the tour, and he and Jamie had an almost telepathic understanding. Whether or not you thought Drico was past his prime – and a few people did – Foxy's case for inclusion was compelling. Three into two don't go. Rugby doesn't have much room for sentimentality – and, as I was to find out myself a little further down the line, neither does Warren Gatland.

The furore over the dropping of O'Driscoll rather overshadowed the fact that my best mate, Alun Wyn Jones, had been awarded the captaincy. He was born to captain the Lions, and nobody deserved it more than him. He did a good job of restoring harmony after the chaos around the team selection. I heard a lot of grumblings from the outside about certain people getting the hump for being dropped, and being intent on destabilising the group. From the inside, I witnessed nothing of the kind. We were united as a squad, and our one goal was to beat the Wallabies in Sydney.

I sat next to Drico on the bus to training after the team had been announced. He was utterly crestfallen. His family were all in Sydney, and he was desperate to be with them. They'd flown over to watch him play for the Lions one last time, and now it wasn't going to happen.

I didn't know what to say. 'Sorry, butt,' was about all I could muster.

'Ah, it's grand,' came the reply. But he couldn't hide his devastation. His eyes were glassy, and his look was vacant.

It was a cruel way to finish. Alun Wyn played it cool at that first training session after being named captain. There were no histrionics, no emotional call to arms. He addressed us all briefly, told us to knuckle down, and not to panic.

But there was an element of panic beneath the surface. The climax was fast approaching, and what happened in Sydney would determine whether the entire tour was a roaring success or an abject failure. Sport can send you on the most brutal emotional journeys, and we were nearing the end of ours. Tensions were beginning to boil over in training.

Johnny Sexton is an absolute perfectionist, and expects everybody to operate on the same plane. During one session, Hibs messed up a couple of moves and Sexton unleased a tirade of abuse at him. It takes a brave man to do that, because Hibs has a short fuse and could easily have knocked him out. I could see his eyes narrowing into a death stare, which is a sure-fire sign that the red mist is descending. Thankfully, he wound himself back in, and realised that planting one on the star fly-half probably wasn't the right course of action. Johnny, for his part, realised that he was poking an angry bear, and backed down.

● ● ●

I'm a fan of night kick-offs, but on the day of the third test I was as nervous as I've ever been before a rugby match. We'd decamped to a hotel near the ground, where Hibs and I were sharing a room. We tried to chill out and watch TV, but every time we looked out of the window, the crowd had swelled further, and it was impossible to think about anything but the game. You'd swear you were playing at home, so numerous were the red jerseys. The Lions' travelling support is a sight to behold. In among the thousands of replica Lions shirts thronging Sydney's Olympic Park, I counted about six green and gold ones. It was simultaneously humbling and baffling. Around 40,000 British and Irish fans had made the trip.

The clock in the room was ticking inexorably towards game time. With a few hours to spare, we were summoned outside for a walk through the line-outs. There was a big wide plateau outside the hotel, and we were surrounded by a ring of security guards as we went through our moves, committing the calls to memory one final time. We knew exactly what we were doing at this point. Accuracy and execution were the buzzwords.

The bus was deathly quiet. There was none of the usual banter or jibber-jabber. Silence reigned. On the one hand, I was trying to savour the enormity of the occasion. On the other, I was trying to keep the demons at bay. It was a short journey of half a mile, but not a word was spoken.

The dressing room offered a last chance of private sanctuary before we emerged through the tunnel for our public trial. It's difficult trying to calm your nerves when everyone around you is tightly wound. People were restless, unable to sit still. Gestures become amplified in that space. A nod, a tap, a squeeze or a wink can be more powerful, more meaningful than words in that environment. A tiny part of you doesn't want to cross that threshold on to the pitch, because you're aware of how exposed you'll feel. More than 100,000 spectators filling the stands. A hundred thousand pairs of eyes scrutinising every move. Millions more watching on TV screens around the world. My home village seemed a long way away. People in Abercrave I'd known all my life were stirring about now. Wandering into their living rooms with a cup of tea and a bacon butty. I thought about them. About my coaches. About kicking the ball around on the field behind my childhood home in the Brecon Beacons with my dad and my grandmother. Then I was at the bottom of the mountain – figuratively and literally. Now I was at the summit.

As if he could hear my thoughts, Warren Gatland came over to speak to me. He leaned in, with his hand on my shoulder, and told me that this was the last time I'd wear this jersey. 'Make sure you go out there and do it proud. Make sure that the legacy lives on.'

It's easy to become overwhelmed by emotion in situations like this, and a good captain will be able to subtly adjust the pressure barometer in the room. Alun Wyn is the most aggressive player you're likely to meet, but he's capable of instilling a zen-like calm in the eye of the storm. He was the last to speak as we formed a final huddle in the centre of the dressing room. Everything was in place. We'd worked incredibly hard. We knew exactly what was required. Alun Wyn's speech was brief, focused and reassuring. He barely raised his voice above speaking level. Dominate them up front. Don't take any risks in our own half. Starve their back three of ball. Kick accurately. Take the points whenever they're on offer.

We were all proud. There was no need for him to deliver some grandiose, Shakespearian speech about the significance of the day; no need to incite hatred of the opposition. It was a rugby match, and one we could win. It was time to bring sixteen years of hurt to an end.

I'm not a great believer in omens, but when Will Genia – the world's best scrum-half at the time – dropped the ball off the kick-off, I wondered if the stars were aligned in our favour. Less than a minute later, Corbs went crashing over the line for the first try of the game. It had been our intention to bully the Aussies up front, and we allowed them no let-up after that. Hibs was playing like a man possessed, smashing everything that got in his way. The Wallabies had recalled their veteran flanker, George Smith, and within minutes he'd been forced to leave the field after a sickening clash of heads with Hibs. Our new-look pack was destroying theirs. The scrum was yielding penalty after penalty, and Benn Robinson was sent to the sin bin for one collapse too many before the half-time whistle had been blown. He never returned. Leigh Halfpenny was worth his weight in gold, knocking over every penalty that came his way. With half-time approaching, we were 19–3 to the good, and comfortable.

But the Wallabies never know when they're beaten, and they refused to let their heads drop. Their policy of turning down kicks at goal eventually paid off when they found themselves deep in our territory, and James O'Connor skipped his way through on the stroke of half-time. We were furious with ourselves. 19–10 was a world away from 19–3. They were right back in it.

'Keep your foot on their throat, and don't let them back up off the canvas. Keep doing what we're doing, and the tries will come. And stop giving needless penalties away.' These were the half-time messages from the coaches, all of whom were calm despite the injury-time defensive lapse. As instructions go, they were pretty easy to follow, and we re-entered the arena with the intent to play, and not to just sit on our lead.

I often like to look back and persuade myself that I played a bigger part in turning games than was actually the case. I'll retrospectively view certain scrums as turning points, as momentum swingers. It's the prerogative of a front row forward who's only scored two tries in an international career lasting more than a decade. No matter which way you dress things up, I was unable to do that with the third test. The harsh truth is this: I was subbed off for Dan Cole, and within minutes of me leaving the pitch, the Lions transformed into an unstoppable, irresistible force that crushed the life out of the dying Wallaby corpse. It was a quite astonishing period, and I could only watch in awe as we tore them to pieces. Three tries in ten minutes. All of them beauties. Sexton, North and Roberts. Leigh Halfpenny was instrumental in the first two, and if his name hadn't already been carved on to the man-of-the-series trophy, it could safely be now.

After the two nail-biters that preceded it, the closing minutes of the third test allowed us the rare luxury of being able to celebrate long before the final whistle had blown. There would be no heart-stopping last-minute penalties, no killer blow in injury time. The lead was unassailable: 41–16 at the final whistle. We'd won. And we'd done so in scintillating fashion. The coaches slung down their walkie-talkies and came down to join us pitch-side with five minutes to go. Their work was done. Everybody was hugging each other, slapping each other's backs, and dishing out high-fives. The fans were beside themselves with joy, the anthems were reverberating around the Olympic Stadium. It was, without a shadow of a doubt, the best feeling I'd ever experienced in rugby. I'd been held spellbound by the Lions' mystique since I was a young boy in Abercrave watching grainy videos of the 1971 and 1974 tours, and now here I was carving my own name into that long and illustrious history. I'd become part of a small and unique tribe that can say they've won a Lions series. That's why it felt more special than a Welsh Grand Slam. It was the uniqueness of it, the special bond that develops when you travel to the other side of the world with a motley crew of individuals who become friends for life. That night in Sydney banished for good any doubts that the Lions would survive in the professional era.

Our lap of honour was the longest I'd ever experienced, but I didn't want it to end. Scott Quinnell was working for the media, and he ambushed Corbs and me for a TV interview. He'd been part of the squad that had lost to Australia in 2001, and was as excited as any of us wearing the jersey. He is a very excitable man. No matter how hard I strained my eyes, I couldn't find Nicole, Isla and my mam and dad in the crowd. I was very jealous when Drico brought his little one out on to the field. I was desperate to have Isla with me at that point. Memories don't come more precious than that. Drico's reaction tells you why he's the ultimate Lion. He may not have played in that final test, but he contributed massively to the series victory. Of course he'd have preferred to be saluting the crowd in his Lions strip rather than a blazer and slacks. But if he was disappointed then, he didn't show it. The lap of honour was evidence, if anyone needed it, that this was a squad effort. Everyone was a Lion. There were no barriers. No hierarchy. We were all winners. I was just one of the lucky ones who'd started every test.

The changing room was a sea of foaming champagne. Foaming champagne and Daniel Craig. The James Bond actor had found his way into the inner sanctum, and everyone wanted a piece of him. He's in every post-match photo, looking sharp in his suit, while each of us had our picture taken with him, drenched in sweat and caked in mud, blood and beer. Nobody wanted to leave. It felt as though the minute we left the spell would be broken. I felt a strange kind of exhaustion. We were all physically and mentally drained, but there would be no rest. A first series win for sixteen years calls for the mother of all celebrations, and we were going to do our best to drink Sydney dry.

It was one o'clock before we reached the official post-match function and finally caught up with our close friends and family. The period between that and the flight home has become a hazy, drunken blur, punctuated with the occasional memorable incident: Simon Zebo falling fully clothed into a nightclub swimming pool; Leigh Halfpenny running out of the hotel in his pants to flag down the bus to Bondi beach; me putting a comatose Alun Wyn Jones to bed. And most memorably of all, Hibs losing credit-card roulette at a Darling Harbour steakhouse.

That was on the Monday night after two days of solid drinking, and we were starting to feel the burn. The Welsh clique of myself, Shane, Alun

Wyn, Ianto and Hibs met up for some much-needed sustenance. The bill came to around $750, and we all put our credit cards in the middle of the table and invited the waiter to select one at random. He plucked out Hibs's, meaning he had to foot the entire bill himself. To add insult to injury, he'd had a modestly priced cod and chips, and a single glass of Coke. For a man who's tighter than cramp, it was a painful experience. His entreaties to split the bill fell on deaf ears. At the end of it all, nothing had changed. We were still just a bunch of mates taking the piss out of each other. We could have been in a cafe in Port Talbot. Hibs probably wished we still were. You could buy five breakfasts there, and still have change from a twenty-pound note.

CHAPTER 20

Feeling Blue

RARELY has a fall from grace been as dramatic as the one I suffered after the Lions tour. To quote Jim Telfer, the legendary Scottish and Lions coach, it had been my Everest. I'd scaled many peaks in my career but that had eclipsed everything. I suppose when you've breathed the rarefied air at the top of Everest, there's only way to go. But instead of taking the scenic route down, I fell over the edge.

I'd missed three of the four autumn internationals that year after suffering another calf injury in the opener against South Africa. But my rapid descent began with the unravelling of my relationship at the Ospreys. My contract was up at the end of the 2013/2014 season, and while I'd had offers from elsewhere, my preference was to re-sign. The Ospreys, together with the other three regions, were engaged in an ugly dispute with the WRU, which was threatening to reduce Welsh rugby to rubble. The Union's CEO, Roger Lewis, had issued an ominous threat via the media, saying the regions would 'cease to exist' unless they signed a new participation agreement. The regions were refusing, saying it was tantamount to signing their own suicide note. The saga dragged on like a depressing soap opera, infecting the whole of Welsh rugby with its negativity. Crowds began to slip away, enthusiasm began to dwindle.

I became an unwitting pawn between the two warring factions. The Ospreys said they couldn't offer me a new deal until an agreement had been signed. Because until then, they couldn't calculate their budget. Good business sense, you might say, but it didn't stop them re-signing more than a dozen other players during that period. Granted, those players weren't as senior as me, and weren't on as high a wage, but it was the principle I felt was being breached. If you don't know what your budget is going to be, then don't sign anyone. The longer it went on, the more I suspected they were using my profile as a stick to beat the WRU with. They were trying to curry favour with the public by saying, 'Look, we want to sign Adam, but we can't, and it's the union's fault.' It made me feel used and undermined.

I also felt that they wanted to keep hold of me because of my 'celebrity' status, rather than my rugby ability. Because of my image, my international career and associated fame, I was a more marketable commodity than most. My presence would help them shift more season tickets and sell more jerseys. They were trying to make inroads into the Italian market at the time, and knew that potential sponsors would recognise me or Alun Wyn Jones – maybe Duncan Jones at a push – but that would be about it. I wanted to be re-signed on merit, not so they could stick my face on a poster, or send me out to schmooze with their corporate partners.

I'm not suggesting I was blameless for the breakdown in relations. I returned from Wales duty in March, having been dropped from the last Six Nations game against Scotland. I was bitter about it, and my attitude when I returned was poor. By the end of the season, I'd been relegated to second choice, behind Aaron Jarvis, and was barely playing. I'd become lazy and disinterested, and it was noted. Steve Tandy invited me for a coffee and had it out with me. He told me I wasn't working hard enough, and it was time to pull my finger out. I agreed with him. It was the kick up the arse I needed, and the catalyst for what I hoped would be a fresh start.

The season limped to an end before anything had been resolved, and after the Wales summer tour to South Africa I found myself in the bizarre scenario of having no club. The Ospreys charitably offered me a month's pay, but decided it would be 'disruptive' if I reported to pre-season training. That summer was the loneliest of my career. After more than a decade of being beasted in pre-season by a succession of crazy fitness coaches, I found myself isolated and on my own. Camaraderie is what gets you through those torturous, lung-busting sessions. A little joke here, a wry smile there, and the knowledge that you're all in it together is enough to push you through the pain barrier. Running up Merthyr Mawr sand dunes on your own in the stifling July sunshine, with your legs the consistency of jelly, and your lungs screaming for air, is no fun. Training is a journey, and match day the destination. With no destination, it becomes one long, depressing, energy-sapping ordeal.

I documented the period in a video diary for the BBC, which was just a sequence of pieces-to-camera with me looking increasingly sweaty, miserable and forlorn. My wife and family were amazingly supportive, but solace was hard to find. The support of those who knew me was undermined by those who didn't. An army of keyboard warriors took to social media to cast judgement on me. I was either greedy, selfish and self-obsessed, or I was spent and over the hill.

Perhaps I was naive in hanging on and hoping for a favourable outcome. Sentiment was clouding my vision. I loved the Ospreys, and I loved playing for them. It was my home region and I was incredibly proud to have been involved with them from the start. Ultimately, though, my livelihood was at stake, so I had to start casting around for other options. Steve Diamond at Sale wanted to sign me but needed to iron out the finer details with his chairman. My agent and I met with Steve Tandy and Andrew Hore to explain that I'd had enough of the brinkmanship, and was leaving. The meeting was an emotional one. Tandy is one of my best mates, and it was a wrench to tell him I was off. I even felt as though Horey and I were finally seeing eye to eye after twelve months of backstabbing and mistrust.

I had a phone call the following morning saying Sale had pulled out. I immediately re-entered negotiations with the Ospreys, but they now had me over a barrel. The pendulum of power had swung back their way, and there was significantly less money on the table. I was loath to buckle to their demands. Time was running out and I needed to know where the next pay cheque was coming from. I spoke to Lyon and Grenoble out in France. Both were second-tier sides. The last French side to have come sniffing around had been European champions Toulon. It was an illustration of how far my stock had fallen. There was even an option to go and play for the New Zealand side Waikato Chiefs, in the Super XV. Warren Gatland had called Horey to say they were on the lookout for a tight-head. I spoke to their coach, Tom Coventry, and he seemed pretty keen. The Ospreys were willing to give me a three-month contract to tide me over until the start of the Super XV season but it was on 'taking-the-piss' sort of money, and Nicole wasn't keen to move to the other side of the world.

● ● ●

It was a Sunday evening in the middle of August, with the new season fast approaching, when I received a call from my agent asking, 'What do you think about the Cardiff Blues?' I was taken aback, because I knew they'd signed Craig Mitchell, and already had Tau Filise and Scott Andrews on their books. All three were international tight-heads. But he insisted they were keen and arranged a meeting with their new coach, Mark Hammett, for the following day. I warmed to him immediately. He was sympathetic to my situation, and seemed genuinely astonished that a player of my pedigree had been thrown on the rubbish heap. He asked about my mindset, and whether the desire still burned inside. I assured him that it did, and that I was determined to get back to full fitness, and win back my Wales place.

On the Tuesday, the Blues chief executive, Richard Holland, called to say he had a contract drawn up and he wanted me to go in that day, sign it and pose in the Blues team photo. It was a cheeky publicity stunt on their part that caused more than a few waves on social media. Because it had all happened so quickly, nobody in the rugby world had had a sniff of it. The team photo appeared on Twitter, and within minutes there was a feeding frenzy. It didn't take long for journalists and the public to twig that there was a nineteen-stone long-haired fatty sat in the front row. I've never been, and never will be, the most inconspicuous member of a team. It was certainly a novel way of announcing it to the wider world. After months of uncertainty and wrangling with the Ospreys, I'd negotiated and signed a contract with the Blues within three days.

Shortly after the announcement was made, the Ospreys released a statement that filled me with rage. It was an attempt to cast me as the villain of the piece in a needless attempt to seize the moral high ground.

It amounted to an exercise in propaganda in which they laid the blame entirely on my shoulders. The insinuation seemed to be that I'd called their bluff, and lost the battle of nerves. It had been a game of brinkman-ship, and I had blinked first. They're entitled to their interpretation of events, but it was entirely inappropriate to air it publicly. I'd had ample opportunity during my forced exile to mouth off to the media, but had chosen to hold my counsel.

The press release added fuel to a fire that should have been extinguished with my signing of the Blues deal. And it encouraged a militant fringe of Ospreys supporters to rail against me on social media. Once again, the keyboard warriors took to Twitter to accuse me of being a mercenary, and of holding the Ospreys to ransom. I had complete strangers telling me it was my fault I'd been forced out, and that I'd got what I deserved. The truth was I was being offered significantly less money. Again, you could argue my powers were on the wane and that offering me a pay cut was good business sense. But is that really the way to treat one of your most loyal employees? I'd been with them for more than a decade, and during the contract negotiations, I'd effectively been a free agent. I hadn't gone behind anyone's back, or tried to stitch anyone up. As far as I was concerned, I'd behaved honourably throughout. What hurt the most was that no one thanked me or wished me well for the future. It was such an easy gesture to have made, but all they cared about was exonerating themselves of any blame. As if that really mattered. Who cared? All those years of loyal service. All the blood, sweat and tears I'd shed for the region, and their parting shot was some mealy-mouthed press release about whether I'd turned down a contract or not.

When the dust settled, Steve Tandy and I had a really good chat to clear the air. There was never any danger of the two of us falling out, and I don't hold Steve accountable in any way. He totally understood my reasons for leaving, and was as gutted as I was at the way things had turned out. He told me he'd had plans for me helping out on the coaching side, acting as a mentor to some of the younger props like Dmitri Arhip. It would have been nice if those sentiments had been expressed in the press release. I don't hold a grudge against Andrew Hore, but the whole episode has left a sour taste. When the Blues played the Ospreys that season, no one from the Ospreys hierarchy acknowledged me. I had a pint with Tandy and Andy Lloyd, and Alun Wyn presented me with a jersey, but the management team all blanked me – even Andrew Millward, who I played with for years and years. If my missus had her way I'd sever ties with them for the rest of my life, because she thinks they shafted me. But as long as my relationship with the coaching staff doesn't suffer – and it hasn't – I won't allow any resentment to fester.

I should have followed the money to France when my stock was at its highest. I was stupid not to. After the Lions tour in 2009, I could have named my price. My agent was pushing for a big-money move to Toulouse, but it was around the time Nicole was pregnant with Isla and we weren't keen to move lock, stock and barrel. If I'd had a crystal ball I'd have realised that within a few years, with the changes to the scrum laws, those offers wouldn't be quite so forthcoming. Hindsight is a wonderful thing.

The whole sorry saga hasn't affected my underlying affection for the Ospreys. I still look out for their results every week. Their captain is my best mate, and I discuss their games with him with the intensity and passion of a fan. My season at the Blues was a forgettable one. Mark Hammett left halfway through the league campaign, and morale plummeted as quickly as the team imploded. I spent the latter half of the season pining for the familiarity of the Ospreys, and missing the company of my closest friends.

• • •

I had no idea that my departure from the Ospreys would foreshadow the end of my Wales career. Prior to the South African summer tour of 2014, Warren Gatland had held a trial match – the first of its kind for nearly fifteen years. I'd recovered from my post-Six Nations sulk to finish the domestic season strongly, and had lost a bit of weight in the process. So much so that Martin Castrogiovanni told me he'd have to come up with a new nickname for me. 'Fatty' had always been his preferred, and rather unimaginative moniker. I was picked for the Probables against the Possibles, and we romped to victory, helping Melon and myself reassert our status as Wales' two best props.

The first test against South Africa was to be my one hundredth international. Ninety-five for Wales, and five for the Lions. It was also to be my last. And my long, proud tenure as Wales' first choice tight-head prop was to end in humiliation. With half an hour gone, I was summoned off. It was happening again. We were 21–6 behind, having conceded three tries. I was being made a scapegoat for the team's sub-par performance. My head began to spin. I was no longer the young, green international novice. I was a triple Grand Slam winner, and a Test Lion. The rush of indignation I'd last felt in 2003 – and had suppressed in my subconscious ever since – came flooding back. I was fuming; there was a sick symmetry to it all.

The substitution happened before a line-out in South Africa's 22 on the opposite side of the pitch to our replacements' bench. It meant I had to trudge diagonally across the entire field in full view of everyone. There were no medics to accompany me off, because I clearly wasn't injured. I felt as though every pair of eyes in the stadium was focused on me, laughing. The proud warrior, competing in the test arena for the hundredth time, had been reduced to a figure of fun. It felt cruel and vindictive. What had begun as a day of personal celebration had become a day of emotional devastation.

The young Scarlets full-back, Liam Williams, was the first to speak to me. 'What's up, Bomb? Are you hurt?'

All I could muster was a shake of the head.

The half-time changing room was a swirl of noise and emotion, but I felt detached from it all. No one spoke to me. Everyone was avoiding my gaze. When they trooped back out for the second half, I stayed behind. Hunched in my cubicle, alone in the cavernous chamber, a discarded has-been amid the match-day detritus. Mud, ripped bits of tape and empty bottles littered the floor. The only sound I could hear was my own muffled crying. I felt like I was sinking into the floor.

Nicole called me after the game, and we spoke for more than an hour. I was in floods of tears and would have given anything to be able to snap my fingers and be at home in Merthyr Tydfil. She calmed me down, and persuaded me to meet with the rest of the team for a few beers. They were my friends, after all. Much later in the evening, I had a tap on the shoulder from Robin McBryde, the forwards coach. He was the last person I wanted to speak to. I was drunk, my emotions were raw, and I felt victimised and betrayed. Nothing he could do or say would convince me otherwise. He claimed he knew how I felt; that he'd experienced the same when he was subbed off after forty-five minutes during a Lions match. It was of no comfort to me. That match wasn't a test, and forty-five minutes is not thirty. I'd put away ten pints by this point, and wasn't in the mood for his pep talk. I declared angrily, and a little too loudly, that I wasn't the only one to have played like shit. We agreed to discuss it some other time.

Predictably, I was dropped for the second test. That was inevitable, but I wanted an explanation for the early substitution. Gats told me I'd looked lethargic, and blamed me personally for two of the tries we'd conceded. For one of the first times in my career, I refused to take it, and argued back. I'd been the third man out in the defensive line when Duane Vermeulen scored. There were two other players closer to him than I was. How could it possibly have been my fault? He refused to budge. If I'd been hoping for reassurance, I'd come to the wrong guy. When I continued to protest, he dismissed me, telling me I was lucky I'd stayed on for as long as I did. That was the end of the conversation. It lasted less than two minutes.

If I'd been in possession of a shorter fuse, I might have blown up at that point. Some of my hotter-headed colleagues most definitely would have. But my anger is the kind that boils beneath the surface. And beneath Gatland's gruff, stubborn facade I did detect a shred of empathy. He knew I was better than the account I'd given of myself, and he thought this would nudge me back in the right direction. This was his version of tough love.

The second test was a proper roller coaster. Twice, we were ahead by two scores, and we should have won at a canter. Watching from the stand, I was as pumped up and delirious as any fan, desperate for a first ever victory on South African soil. A small voice in my mind was lamenting the fact that, if it did happen, I couldn't say I was involved. But any personal disappointment was far outweighed by the growing sense of euphoria. These players were my friends, and I was supporting them with all my heart. Rugby is a team game, and no one is bigger than the team.

But the curse of the Southern Hemisphere struck again, as South Africa scored in the final play of the game to snatch victory. Liam Williams put in what looked like a heroic covering tackle to deny Cornal Hendricks in the corner, but the referee deemed it an illegal challenge, and awarded a penalty try. Heartbreakingly, it meant the conversion – rather than being from the touchline – was bang in front of the posts. Had Liam allowed him to score, we could well have won the game. He apologised to the entire team afterwards, but there was no need. On a different day, with a different referee, he may have been the match winner. The hero who delivered Wales their first ever win on South African soil. The margins are dangerously thin in elite sport.

The changing room was a lonely place. As the boys were getting showered and changed, I was sweeping up the mess with a broom. I'd volunteered to do it, as I often did when I wasn't in the match-day squad, but I couldn't help but note the irony. I'd begun the tour as Wales' most decorated tight-head prop. I was ending it as the team janitor. I was already on the periphery. My seat had been taken by Samson Lee. I felt like a hologram fading from view. That's the brutality of professional sport. When your time is up, you're erased, and the team moves on without you.

No one is indispensable.

● ● ●

I wasn't ready for it to end, but circumstances conspired against me. My summer of discontent continued with the Ospreys debacle, and I entered the new season with the Cardiff Blues undercooked. The inevitable conclusion was that I was dropped from the Wales squad for the 2014 autumn internationals. That was easily the lowest point in my career. Being dropped for the second summer test was one thing, but being left out of the entire squad was a devastating blow. I felt like a boxer struggling to my feet, only to be smacked back down to the canvas. It left me speechless and an emotional wreck, sobbing in the front seat of my car and scribbling angry letters to Warren Gatland. For a month or more, I became a recluse, hiding away in my house, and only emerging to train with or play for the Blues.

Once I'd emerged from the emotional whirlpool, I made a promise to myself: I was going to work harder than I'd ever worked, train harder than I'd ever trained, and force my way back in for the 2015 Six Nations. If I was overlooked for a second time, I would retire from international rugby.

By Christmastime, I'd established myself as first choice at the Blues, usurping the claims of Craig Mitchell, Tau Filise and Scott Andrews – all of whom were good friends. My form prompted a phone call from Robin McBryde, who invited me to the Vale Hotel for a chat. He'd compiled a series of video clips of my Blues performances, and was keen to go through them in forensic detail. His feedback was largely positive, and made me think I was right back in the reckoning. That feeling was strengthened when the WRU contacted the Blues and asked them if I could have a week off to do some specific fitness work with Wales. The Blues were happy to oblige, and I spent that week being beasted by the likes of Ryan Harris, Huw Bennett and John Ashby. It was a savage week, but it paid dividends. My Christmas calories were incinerated, and the weight dropped off. By the end of the week, I was down to eighteen and a half stone, which was as lean and trim as I'd ever been.

On the day of the Six Nations squad announcement, I was quietly confident. Rhodri Jones, one of the youngsters competing for my shirt, had broken his arm playing for the Scarlets, meaning there were fewer tight-head props in the mix. All the indications were that I'd returned to the peak of my powers, and was ready for a recall. We were between sessions at the Blues when my mobile buzzed, and Robin McBryde's number came up. I knew immediately that something was wrong. If you're in, you find out by watching the TV; you don't get a call. I was consumed with a sickening sense of déjà vu.

Robin dispensed with the small talk: 'Bomb, we're not picking you. We don't think you're in the right place.'

In the jumble of words that followed, I heard mention of Samson Lee and Aaron Jarvis, leaving me scratching my head as to the identity of the third tight-head. 'Who else?' I asked.

'Scott Andrews,' came the answer.

Scott was my Blues teammate who hadn't started a PRO12 game all season. He'd been picked to play lock the previous weekend against Rovigo. It was beyond farce. I'm really fond of Scott, and rate him as a player, but it defied logic to pick someone who'd barely played at the top level all season. Why throw him into the test arena against the best sides in the world, when you have a snarling Lion in the wings, ready to unleash fury after an enforced absence?

I angrily expressed those sentiments to Robin. I was far from speechless on this occasion, and let him know exactly how I felt. It was an absolute joke. Mark Hammett, my club coach, was picking me to start every week. *He* clearly thought I was playing well. McBryde's response was that different coaches have different opinions. His was that I wasn't doing enough work 'around the park', and that my scrummaging prowess had declined since the laws had been changed the previous season. That cut deep. Deep down, I realised that my influence *had* waned slightly since the 'hit' had been removed, but I was still holding my end up. No one had got the better of me that season. And destructive tight-heads around the globe were having the same issues. What upset me most was his blunt manner. I'd played with and against Robin for most of my career, and he made me feel just like a number on a spreadsheet – one he could conveniently delete when the conversation was over.

'Fuck it, then,' came my less than eloquent reply, and I hung up on him for the second time in three months.

Once my thumb had hit the 'end call' button, I knew it was over. It was time to put my promise into action. I felt as though my reputation, which I'd built through more than a decade of graft and endeavour, was unravelling before my eyes. I wanted to have some form of control over my legacy, and this was the way to seize it. I called Nicole and my agent, Mark Spoors, to tell them of my decision. Nicole knew what my intentions had been and backed me up immediately. Mark advised me to sleep on it, but I was adamant. The sooner I announced it the better. The only other person I told was Alun Wyn Jones. He asked me if I was absolutely certain. I assured him I was.

It was over. I was done.

● ● ●

Nobody has a divine right to be picked in rugby. Standards can't be maintained for ever, and creaking bones eventually take their toll. I understand that, and I don't begrudge Warren Gatland for choosing to dispense with me. He picked me for more than fifty internationals, and I owe him my Lions shirts. I would never have made it to that level if it hadn't been for him. He arrived at a time when I needed a rocket up my arse, and he was more than happy to light it. So I didn't feel like I was owed anything. And I didn't feel betrayed, as I had done in South Africa. Coaches are paid the big bucks to make the big calls, and he'd decided that my face – or more specifically, my arse – didn't fit any longer. I didn't like it, and I sure as hell didn't agree with it. But I could accept it.

What I struggled to accept was the way I was treated. I still haven't had a call from Warren, and that really hurts. I'd thought there was enough mutual respect between us for him to pick up the phone and talk to me. We were close. I've shared many a pint with him over the years, listened to him explain endlessly how he was so much better than Sean Fitzpatrick, the man who kept him out of the All Blacks side. He'd always shown an interest in my family, and been sensitive to the emotional demands of being on the road and in camp for long periods of the year. And he used to harangue me constantly about getting my hair cut. We were mates. There was always a line between us, because he was my boss, but there was a relationship beyond that line. That's why it hurts.

The only person who did pick up the phone was Shaun Edwards. It wasn't at the behest of the WRU; he was doing it out of respect. He caught me off-guard, and said some lovely things – about how it had been an honour and a pleasure to have worked with me – and I filled up with tears as I listened. He was able to put aside petty differences and see the bigger picture. The gruff northerner who'd played on with a broken cheekbone and fractured eye socket was the only one able to talk about his feelings.

While I'd made peace with myself over my retirement, the daily reminders prevented the wound from healing quickly. Everywhere I went – the supermarket, the pub, the park, the petrol station – I'd get well-meaning fans wishing me good luck for the next game. I'd become such a part of the furniture that people expected me to be playing. To the fair-weather fan, I was the big hairy guy who always played for Wales, come what may. I was enjoying a meal in Cwmbran with Isla and Nicole on the eve of one international, when a random stranger had a go at me for tucking into my chips when I 'should have been in camp with Wales'. On one level, it was flattering, but on another, it was rubbing salt into the wound. It must have happened more than fifty times over the course of the championship, and each encounter was like a tiny dagger to my heart.

The law changes that McBryde mentioned *have* had a massive impact on me. My weapon has always been the hit. Removing it, as they've done, is like asking a swordsman to fight without his sword. The old scrummaging sequence was crouch, touch, pause, engage. The engagement was when

I launched myself across the gap between the two sets of front rows, using my weight, body angle and momentum to drive them backwards. The force of the hit allowed me to manipulate their loose-head into the position I needed him to be in. Think of it as two phases: the first is the hit, to get the opposition prop where you want him; the second is the chase, in which you drive them backwards.

Let's use my old French adversary Thomas Domingo as an example. He was a nuggety little bastard, about five foot five, and strong as an ox. If I scrummaged square against him, aiming my head directly at the gap between his shoulder and his hooker's shoulder, chances were he'd out-scrummage me. So I'd angle myself slightly towards him and down, pinning his head to his outside knee. The force of the hit would allow me to do that, and help to nullify his own scrummaging strengths. Nowadays the engagement sequence is crouch, bind, set. You're bound before you connect, meaning there is no hit; just a chase. It's effectively become a wrestling contest. Samson Lee is built perfectly for such a role. He's short, squat and phenomenally strong. His lack of height means his centre of gravity is low, and his strength means he can hold his position for as long as it takes for the scrum-half to put the ball in. He will be incredibly valuable to Wales in the years to come, and will undoubtedly be a Lion in the near future.

● ● ●

I have no regrets about retiring. I'd love to have played in four World Cups, and I'd love to have won a hundred caps for Wales. Taking Isla on to the pitch for my hundredth cap would have given me the ultimate rugby memory. She doesn't understand yet what playing for Wales means, and I hope when she grows up she'll realise that her daddy wasn't too bad at his job. For now, she just thinks Daddy's stopped playing for the reds, and he doesn't play in the same team as Uncle Alun Wyn any more.

Some have accused me of throwing my toys out of the pram, but it wasn't an impetuous decision. I'd made a promise to myself the previous autumn, and I kept it. Others – like Ryan Jones – have said they'll never retire; there'll just come a day when they're no longer wanted. I respect that as well. Each to their own. Barely a day has gone by when I haven't been asked if I'd change my mind if Wales came knocking. Only if I was the last fit tight-head prop in Wales would I consider it – and it would take that scenario to unfold before they'd consider approaching me.

I can't imagine a life without rugby. My time with the Blues was fleeting and, if I'm honest, I missed the Ospreys desperately. I'm very much looking forward to a new challenge in Harlequins – or the 'multicoloured team', as Isla calls them. A condition of my move was that I carry on playing, but my future lies in coaching. I'm not clever enough to go into banking or finance like some of my erstwhile colleagues have done. Rugby is in my blood, and nothing would give me more pleasure than being able to pass on what I've learned to a future generation. My obvious area of expertise is scrummaging, and that's where I plan to begin. The Welsh Rugby Union had earmarked me for such a role when they offered me a central contract. It was their wish for me to start as a scrummaging specialist and then expand my remit to the contact area and the line-out, before becoming a fully fledged forwards coach. I remain fascinated by the mechanics of the scrum. I referred earlier to line-out forwards as being nerds. I like to think of us scrummagers more as scholars! The end of my playing days will probably trigger a more rapid descent into nerdism. All of this isn't to say I'm going to Quins for the novelty, or to pick up a pay cheque. I'm going there to be first choice. I have a lot left to offer, and am in no way ready to hang my boots up.

Perhaps retirement from all forms of rugby will allow me to indulge myself with a bout of misty-eyed reminiscence. People always ask what it feels like to win a Grand Slam, or a Lions series, and I find it hard to articulate. Life as a professional sportsman doesn't allow much time for reflection. Once you've conquered one mountain, there's another on the horizon. And another after that. The minute you start revelling in your triumphs is the minute your standards begin to drop. I have a room in my house with all my rugby memorabilia neatly arranged on shelves. Grogg figurines, old jerseys, photo albums and treasured international caps. As well as a series of photos charting my development from a tubby, shiny-faced skinhead to the ripped, hirsute 'Hair Bear' of today. Maybe in years to come, I'll spend more time in that room, and the mementoes will become more alive with meaning. But the time for nostalgic reflection is not yet upon me.

My international career didn't end the way I'd have liked. Neither did my time at the Ospreys. A championship-winning final season with them, a Grand Slam to celebrate my hundredth cap for Wales and a World Cup triumph would have given this book a compelling final chapter. But life isn't a Hollywood movie; it's messy, and there are always loose ends. Some bridges may have become rickety, but they haven't been burned. Broken relationships can be mended. I hold no grudges. It's not in my nature. My job for almost two decades has been to destroy other men physically. To drive them backwards and downwards. To inflict humiliation and pain. But I'll always have a pint with them afterwards. When the bruises are still sore, and the wounds still fresh, we'll clink glasses, toast the battle and anticipate the next time. Rugby has given me everything, and the bad times dissolve into insignificance when compared to the good.

Many, many years ago, when my father and I were kicking a ball about in the field behind my home, as the sun set over the Cribarth mountain, he turned to me and said, 'You need a bit of hate inside you to make it to the top.'

I disagreed with him then, and I disagree with him now. There is no hate inside me. I have a wonderful family, a beautiful wife and a daughter I love with all my heart. And I've survived more than ten years at the coalface of international rugby in the hardest, most physically demanding position without ever giving way to hate and anger. Rugby has opened up a new life for me. Were it not for my ability to shove other men into the dirt, I'd still be in Abercrave now laying paving slabs. That's not to say I'll never return. My roots run deep.

Perhaps they'll be recruiting the season after next. I wonder if they're on the lookout for a fly-half?

INDEX